THE PARANOID CHRONOTOPE

THE PARANOID CHRONOTOPE

Power, Truth, Identity

FRIDA BECKMAN

STANFORD UNIVERSITY PRESS
Stanford, California

Stanford University Press
Stanford, California

© 2022 Frida Beckman. All rights reserved.

No part of this book may be reproduced or transmitted in any form or by any means, electronic or mechanical, including photocopying and recording, or in any information storage or retrieval system without the prior written permission of Stanford University Press.

Printed in the United States of America on acid-free, archival-quality paper

Library of Congress Cataloging-in-Publication Data

Names: Beckman, Frida, author.
Title: The paranoid chronotope : power, truth, identity / Frida Beckman.
Description: Stanford, California : Stanford University Press, 2022. | Includes bibliographical references and index.
Identifiers: LCCN 2021049983 (print) | LCCN 2021049984 (ebook) | ISBN 9781503630482 (cloth) | ISBN 9781503631601 (paperback) | ISBN 9781503631618 (epub)
Subjects: LCSH: Paranoia—Social aspects—United States. | Social psychology—United States. | Critical theory—United States. | Neoliberalism—United States. | American fiction—21st century—Themes, motives. | Paranoia in literature.
Classification: LCC HM1027.U6 B43 2022 (print) | LCC HM1027.U6 (ebook) | DDC 302.0973—dc23/eng/20211108
LC record available at https://lccn.loc.gov/2021049983
LC ebook record available at https://lccn.loc.gov/2021049984

Typeset by Newgen in Minion Pro 10/14

CONTENTS

	Introduction: The Paranoid Chronotope	1
1	The Public Sphere and Paranoia / The Paranoid Public Sphere	35
2	Power and Paranoia / Paranoid Powers	54
3	Truth and Paranoia / Paranoid Truths	102
4	Identity and Paranoia / Paranoid Identities	153
	Acknowledgments	223
	References	227
	Index	239

THE PARANOID CHRONOTOPE

INTRODUCTION:
THE PARANOID CHRONOTOPE

When Ed Fletcher, in Philip K. Dick's 1954 short story "Adjustment Team," turns up late to work, he steps into a "rolling haze," an "indistinct gray" of a reality under adjustment. As he reaches out to touch the office building that he thought he knew, the building starts to crumble. "It rained down, a torrent of particles. Like sand. Ed gaped foolishly. A cascade of gray debris, spilling around his feet. And where he had touched the building, a jagged cavity yawned—an ugly pit marring the concrete." Because of a mistake on behalf of a member of the Adjustment Team, he has unwittingly discovered their existence. This team, he learns, exists to "supplement" the "natural process," to correct and adjust events for certain ends, in this particular instance to help ease the tensions of the Cold War. They are, a member of the team assures him, "fully licensed to make such corrections." To make a long story short, Ed is shocked at first but ultimately adjusts his view of reality and its components and incorporates this element into his conceptualization of the world and his role within it. At the very end of the story, he recognizes that the team has made further adjustments in order to save him from having to answer his wife's questions about the whole mishap—after his discovery, he roams around the city in shock and his wife thinks he has been unfaithful. Gazing upward in the final lines of the story, he says softly, "Thanks.... I think we'll make it—after all. Thanks a lot."

Fast-forward 50 years to a post-truth and conspiracy theory–ridden twenty-first century in which our very conceptions of reality clash, violently, and in which a recurring trope is that someone or something is purposefully working to hide the true reality behind veils of deceit and deception. One of the most extreme examples is found in online communities that strive to "red pill": to wake up the countless people—mostly men, mostly white—who have been duped into accepting the fake reality we see around us. Like Ed, these men are persuaded that they walk around in what they believe is reality but, as explained to them, this reality is one co-opted by liberals, feminists, and elites who have brainwashed them to the point at which they no longer recognize their own oppression. Piercing the veil of deception and waking up to reality—reality as characterized by misandry, elitist manipulation, and the undermining of white Americans with the help of unregulated immigration and abortion—is vital if white men want to recuperate their agency, power, and identity. And they have been getting considerable help in this effort by men in very powerful positions. The jagged cavity is yawning and promises a revelation of the real: Thanks—"I think we'll make it—after all. Thanks a lot."

The sense or idea or conviction—personal or collective, pathological or political—that our everyday existence is not quite what it seems, that others are not quite what they seem, and, critically, that we ourselves are perhaps not quite what we seem is a specter haunting the modern West. More precisely, what seems to be on the increase is the sense or idea or conviction—personal or collective, pathological or political—that our everyday existence is not governed according to the logic we thought we knew, that others are not people just like us, and, critically, that we ourselves are perhaps not who we thought we were. We can go further, that what seems to be accumulating is the sense or idea or conviction—personal or collective, pathological or political—that our everyday existence is manipulated, that others constitute a threat to us, and, critically, that we ourselves are perhaps not in control of our own thoughts and actions. This sense or idea or conviction is, of course, the looming specter of paranoia.

Historical, philosophical, and political conditions help determine the severity of the specter of paranoia as a social phenomenon. Indeed, the notion that we can profoundly know reality, others, and ourselves in the first place is itself historically, philosophically, and politically coded. Therefore, the paranoid tendencies of any one time and place tell us something important about a society and its culture.

In this book, I note a dramatic realization and politicization of paranoia in the West in general and in the United States in particular in the new millennium. At the core of my study sits an attempt to understand the nature and resurgence of this paranoia and how it emerged during the second half of the twentieth century and the first decades of the twenty-first. Because what do they all have in common—the commanding presence of continuous surveillance, filter bubbles, algorithmic radicalization, climate change deniers, fake news, alternative facts, Macedonian troll factories, identification of a perverted elite, ethnic profiling of Muslims, caged immigrant children, Fox News fear mongering, presidential accusatory tweets, Infowars, proliferating conspiracy theories, incel hatred of women, burgeoning nationalism, growing alt-right movements? Most centrally, they have in common a sense that everyday existence is shadowed by something menacing, a more or less explicit identification of a more or less clearly outlined enemy, and a fear or conviction that this enemy is out to get them or at the very least poses a threat to their individual freedom and identity. In other words, what they have in common is a tendency toward, or outright actualization of, a paranoid mindset.

On the one hand, we are quite right in not knowing whom to trust, in struggling to identify where real power lies, in questioning the sources of facts and truths, in anxiously scrutinizing our own agency and identity in the age of control and surveillance. On the other hand, we live in an age in which fear—and in particular the fear of the other—has been institutionalized, commodified, and systematically and continually rebranded. Where are the boundaries between reasonable doubt and downright paranoia? How is the precarious negotiation of such boundaries affected by a paranoid political climate that methodically identifies evil enemy others and promotes conspiracy theories in America in the twenty-first century? To what extent can this balancing act be explained by the increasingly evident disjunctions between diehard conceptions of the autonomous subject and the implicit undermining of this subject in the neoliberal control society evolving during the latter parts of the twentieth century? And why is the progressively populist and nationalist paranoia emerging in recent decades so decidedly white and male, creating unholy bonds between lonely incels in basements and the country's highest office?

Definitions of paranoia, David Trotter notes, have remained relatively constant over time and the concept has seemed obvious, transparent, naturalized (2001, 16-7). In its current, basic, pathological sense, paranoia is essentially "a pattern of pervasive distrust and suspiciousness of others such that their motives are interpreted as malevolent" (American Psychiatric Association [APA] 2013). APA criteria include assumptions of exploitation and deception, secrecy, mistrust taking the shape of minute scrutiny of people's actions, reading hidden—often demeaning or threatening—meaning into comments or events, and long-held grudges for perceived hostility (2013). This basic and clinical definition can be recognized in many of the phenomena analyzed here. However, I am not primarily interested in paranoia as an individual and pathological phenomenon but examine it rather as a significant feature of American society and culture more broadly: as a style in American politics, as a theme in fiction, as a mode in theory, and as a method in literary and cultural interpretation.

As a style in politics, paranoia reaches back at least to the American religious persecutions of the eighteenth century; as a theme in literary fiction, it reaches back at least to Cervantes; as a mode in theory, it reaches back at least to Descartes; and as a method in literary and cultural interpretation, it reaches back at least to Rousseau. But something happens toward the end of the Second World War. Dick's short story speaks to a philosophical preoccupation reaching back to Plato's simulacrum and the idea of flawed copies, but as it was published alongside many other fictional texts with a similar theme in the 1950s, it can also be said to mark the early days of the specter of American paranoia in its current form. The rise of the Cold War, the second Red Scare and McCarthyism, changes in the economic logic, and an escalating complexity of information technologies and social communication networks over subsequent decades were some of the key components that encouraged and shaped paranoia from then on. Intensifying over the later parts of the twentieth century, we see how the new social movements contested and changed social power relations; how late capitalism unhinged the relation between production and value; how globalization, digitalization, and advanced communication systems challenged the subject's capacity to conceive of and interpret its relation to the world; and how decades of intensifying neoliberalism dislocated the political subject's position.

Twenty-first century paranoia has become progressively apparent in politics and political discourse in the polarization of views, in institutionalized suspicion of "elites," in accumulative nationalism and xenophobia, in an aggressive white masculinity, and in shifting relations to news, information, and facts in what has come to be called post-truth society. Focusing on these difficulties, I pay particular attention here to the significant role played by a changing public sphere. The conditions of this sphere have been quite radically transformed since the 1950s, and the ways in which people communicate with and imagine relationships with one another have altered drastically. The spaces in which experiences, thoughts, and knowledge are shared and negotiated have multiplied but have also, arguably, become more complex and obscure. In the seeming no-space of the digital world and in the ungraspable totality of globalized capitalism, the world has become bigger and smaller at the same time. This, I suggest, aggravates and partly explains our growing uncertainty about how to locate and identify power, where to find truth, who can provide facts, and, indeed, what social and political reality is and what the nature of individual agency and identity is within it.

Attempts to understand the relation between subject and power, between subject and truth, and between subject and identity, in literature as well as in society and politics more generally, has largely been the work of critique. Therefore, I also interrogate the disenchantment with, or even critique of, critique that has grown in recent decades as linked to literary, societal, and political developments. It has been argued that theoretical developments during the second half of the twentieth century contributed to the burgeoning paranoia in the period I study. John Farrell, for example, points to the overarching and inescapable dimensions of language, ideology, and power theorized during this period and a common trend of ascribing agency to discourse, to capital, and to power while displacing the freedom and intentionality of individuals to "an unfixable and unaccountable locus of control" (2006, 5). Whether we choose to see such theories as paranoid or not, we can see, with Farrell, how such approaches to understanding structures, systems, and power really do complicate the possibility of envisioning oneself as an autonomous individual. Indeed, this is not a failure—quite the contrary. The very aim of many of these theories has been to rethink the nature of the subject and of the humanist traditions underpinning our conceptions of it. Thus it is arguably not these theories themselves so much as the tension between them and liberal notions of subjectivity that create the paranoid response. The tension in how to negotiate agency in relation to structures, systems, and power has intensified in recent debates on postcritique. In fact, as we will see, postcritique echoes society's more general anxieties surrounding interpretation and critical thinking while failing to fully take into account the conditions of its own existence.

Centering on what I identify as three key dimensions—power, truth, and identity—in the contexts of society, literature, and critique, I try to explore and explain the increasing paranoia in our society that began in the second half of the twentieth century. This endeavor relies on and is enabled by the construction and subsequent employment of the central concept of the *paranoid chronotope*. I demonstrate that a paranoid chronotope emerges essentially as two spatiotemporal logics chafing against each other. One is typically recognized as a commonly accepted reality; the other is not directly visible but is rather sensed as an underlying and perhaps even hidden but ultimately truer reality. As we will see in the various analyses of society, literature, and critique, subjects seem to sense that dimensions such as society, politics, and economy affect them but they refuse to recognize the limits of liberal individual subjectivity. Nervous attempts to consolidate an awareness of social and political influence over the subject with a strong belief in the subject's freedom and agency result not in a renegotiation of the conception of the self in relation to the social but in the construction of clear enemies and hidden realities in relation to which this self can be reinforced.

Preliminary Definitions

"The trouble with paranoia," Trotter says, "is that we all think we know what it is" (2001, 16). Its definitions, as we have already established, have not changed that much over time. For example, the contemporary definition provided by the APA does not differ that much from earlier clinical diagnoses (even if the APA would likely have problems with earlier accounts of the causes of paranoia). The term *paranoia* appears already in Greek literature and philosophy—in Euripides, Aeschylus, Aristophanes, Aristotle, Plato—but is then often loosely employed as crazy or mad or "thinking amiss" or "going astray" (Lewis 1970, 2). It is also from the Greek that the term stems etymologically: being "beside" (*para*) the "mind" (*nous*).

Medical classification of paranoia began in the eighteenth century and continued through the nineteenth. With the German physician and psychiatrist Johann Christian August Heinroth, we see the germination of its modern conception. Heinroth identified four species of paranoia according to Aubrey Lewis: *ecnoia* ("a single false idea is responsible for gross distortion of a subject's relation with the outside world"), *paraphrosyne* ("delusions about the supernatural"), *moria* ("a sort of megalomania"), and *paranoia catholica* ("a general mixture of emotional, cognitive, and volitional aberrations") (1970, 3). Various and disparate engagements with the term continued during the nineteenth century. The closest they got to a consensus, Lewis suggests, is with Ludwig Snell in 1890, who saw paranoia as a chronic illness that centrally features delusions of influence, persecution, and, frequently, grandeur.

With the rush to science during the nineteenth century came numerous ways of understanding mental disorders, and various diagnoses and names were tested out: monomania, dementia praecox, paraphrenia. Paranoia as a concept started gaining ground toward the end of the century. An article from 1882, "Are you a Paranoiac? Or the Latest Nickname for Cranks," described how Henry S. Williams, a medical superintendent at a hospital came up with a new term, one the article believes, "will soon pass into the current coin of civilized intercourse." Paranoia was a "new kind of mental illness," "a modern form of insanity," and we recognize its symptoms already in this early description: "delusions of persecution, or hallucinations, or delusions of grandeur" (*Review of Reviews*, n.p.). However, Dr. Williams was either well informed or perceptive of the times, since at this point several psychiatric studies had been published.

The first extended approach to a clinical conception of paranoia can be found in J.E.D. Esquirol's pioneering work on insanity. In *Mental Maladies: A Treatise on Insanity* (1845), he described what he called "monomania," a condition that can beset the intellect, the emotions, and the will. In this he saw a disorder with a very strong focus, in which patients "seize upon a false principle, which they pursue without deviating from logical reasonings, and from which they deduce legitimate consequences, which modify their affections, and the acts of their will" (320). Noting the systematicity of this disorder, as well as its suspicion and grandeur, Esquirol's monomania clearly seems to be paranoia *avant la lettre*. Precursors of the concept of paranoia can also be found in James Cowles Pritchard's work, as Trotter points out, primarily in his *Treatise of Insanity* from 1835, which discussed the "moral insanity" of monomania, a conviction characterized by suspicion and grandeur and pertaining to one particular area and circumstance (2001, 24). Esquirol's and Pritchard's conceptions of the systematic and methodical nature of paranoia were echoed in Richard von Krafft-Ebing's *Textbook of Insanity* (1870).

With Krafft-Ebing, the interpretative dimensions of paranoia become clearly visible: "Accidental, harmless remarks by others; frequently meeting the same person; accidental departure of those that were present when he enters a room; the passers-by that avoid him or stop; clearing the throat or coughing"—these are all interpreted as signs that reinforce growing suspicions. This is the passive stage of the disease, in which the patient withdraws, brooding over the hostility of the world around him (1905, 382–3). A more active stage is reached, either gradually or suddenly, when suspicions intensify and turn into "terrible certainty" and delusionary systematicity. Previously generalized suspicion and scattered signs materialize and take shape as a starker situation and an identifiable enemy. Depending on the person's own position and convictions, this enemy may be an individual such as a companion or associate or a group such as Jesuits or socialists or the secret police (383). The situation now becomes much more acute and frightening. A third and final stage is reached when the paranoiac, previously in the dark about the reasons for his persecutions, searches for its rationalization and finds it in delusionary grandeur. He is really a very important person—a prince, a prophet, a messiah—and so it is no wonder that people are out to get him (386).

Many of these elements are also present in perhaps the most famous historical paranoiac of all: Judge Daniel Paul Schreber. Writing on his own disease in *Memoirs of a Nerve Patient* published in 1903, Schreber described how, having felt a desire to be penetrated as a woman, he was convinced that this desire was caused by experiments performed on him by doctors. He also accounted for periods in his life during which he was convinced that he was chosen by God. Schreber's case was made famous by Sigmund Freud's study of his memoirs, and although Freud had much more limited experience of real-life paranoiacs and their diagnoses and treatments than earlier psychiatrists, his work on Schreber has remained a key reference in the field (see Freud 2013). Freud's diagnosis—that Schreber's paranoia was caused by repressed homosexuality—also perpetuated and strengthened conceptions of paranoia and sexuality as linked.

In his thesis on paranoia, Jacques Lacan lifts paranoia from the sexual mires and sees it rather as an underlying dimension of all knowledge. This understanding emerges from his dynamic understanding of the three registers of subjectivity: the Imaginary, the Symbolic, and the Real. The Imaginary is constituted by our consciousness and awareness as it is constructed by our perception and conception of the world. This is a sensory realm in that it is based on our perceptions and conceptions of what exists beyond ourselves. But it is also necessarily an illusory realm; we do not have access to the Real but can only imagine it. Knowledge is reality as constructed in our fantasy and as such is fictional. Unfortunately, this is as good as it gets: imaginary knowledge is all we have. The Imaginary, in turn, is dependent on the Symbolic—on images, affects, interpersonal relations, and, most centrally, sociolinguistic constructions of the Real. This "symbolic order" is culturally specific, consisting of, for example, laws and norms and traditions, or, in short, collective conceptions and constructions of the real or, as Lacan calls it, the structure. The Imaginary with the help of the Symbolic produces the Real, but this is still necessarily a deluded conception. The Real is always and forever elusive. We think we have access to it, but because we can only reach out to it via the Imaginary and the Symbolic, we can never get to it.

The Imaginary, the Symbolic, and the Real coexist in tension, which Jon Mills describes as a "negative dialectic" without the possibility of a Hegelian synthesis. The dynamic is interdependent and conflictual, and while there may be momentary coalescence between them, they are essentially irresolvable (2019, 15). The subject emerging from this negative dialectic is fundamentally paranoid. Not only are we subject to our own Imaginary, which keeps us locked in conceptions of our surroundings that are only our own; this Imaginary is shaped by a Symbolic that is specifically not our own. Thus deluded by the I as well as by the Other, the Real is bound to haunt us. As we will see later, a concealed Real quite concretely haunts some subjects and groups today, often with the crucial difference that they believe it is actually accessible provided they adopt a gruesome enough tactic.

The idea of paranoia as an underlying element of life on a general level emerges even clearer with Melanie Klein, who also builds on Freud but deviates from him as well as Lacan centrally in terms of the temporality of paranoia. Rather than discussing stages, Klein identifies positions, suggesting that we do not put phases behind us so much as continue to vacillate between them through life. In response to anxiety, this vacillation can take shape on the one hand as a depressive position and on the other as a paranoid/schizoid one. The paranoid/schizoid position has its origins in the very early days of a child's life. Unable to experience and recognize complexity and wholeness, the child separates the world into good and bad, which in Klein's terms translates into the good breast (food, warmth, comfort) and the bad breast (pain, colic, intentional or unintentional cruelty by the parents). Around six months, however, and providing it has obtained enough sense of security, the child has developed enough to begin to recognize that the good and the bad breast belong to the same person, to see that good and bad coexist in the same individual. This brings on a depressive position, characterized my mourning and loss. Nothing will ever be all good or last forever. This is a stronger and more mature position in that it recognizes the vicissitudes and ambivalences that characterize reality. Both positions continue to coexist throughout adult life, but whereas a safe and loving upbringing will make the child better prepared to handle life's inconsistencies, a less fortunate start in life means that the child will likely handle anxiety by means of the strong separation, or splitting, as Klein calls it, between good and bad and thus in the projections of the paranoid/schizoid position.

That theories of paranoia materialize alongside the evolution of modernity is no coincidence. Developing alongside new types of knowledge and knowledge bearers is what Trotter calls a "paranoid modernity," in which the very status of knowledge is at stake. Trotter underlines the tension between knowledge and uncertainty for the new professional classes emerging in the late nineteenth and early twentieth centuries. With the authority bestowed on them arises what he calls the "psychopathy of expertise" (2001, 7). This is associated with the increasing dissemination of professional methods and ideals on all levels and in all activities of society in the nineteenth and early twentieth centuries. In this sense, and as Trotter puts it, paranoia becomes "meritocracy's illness" (82).

Paranoia also, like psychiatric diagnoses generally, is an example of how definitions and diagnoses evolve with, and function as, disciplinary power during this period. "Psychiatric power," as Michel Foucault has taught us, arose with the increase in and institutionalization of psychiatric knowledge in the nineteenth century, and establishes "that supplement of power by which the real is imposed on madness in the name of a truth possessed once and for all by this power in the name of medical science, of psychiatry" (2006, 133). In this way, psychiatric concepts not only help to produce the cases that fit their description, as David J. Harper notes, but also, as Nicholas Rose puts it "make new sectors of reality thinkable and practicable" (1994, 90; 1990, 105). Harper underlines that this means that influential historical accounts of paranoia, such as Lewis's, should themselves be subject to critical scrutiny. An example of the weakness in Lewis's historical account, Harper suggests, is the treatment of the struggle to classify paranoia as a problem isolated to psychiatry (Harper, 101) and thus the lack of contextualization when it comes to the philosophical and intellectual history of as well as the implications and interrelations between psychiatric diagnoses and power.

The weakness of the definition of paranoia that I rely on is the opposite of Lewis's. I am less interested in relying on or working toward a psychiatrically precise and finalized definition—an impossible task, as the brief history just provided intimates—and more interested in precisely the philosophical, intellectual, literary, and political contexts of paranoia and how they are related to certain conceptions of the subject. Paranoia is often associated with modernity, not only because of its burgeoning knowledge production and disciplinary power but also and quite centrally because of what is seen as nostalgia for a coherent subject. This nostalgia is commonly contrasted with what is seen as the affirmation of fragmentation, and thus of schizophrenia, in postmodernity.

Still, many theorists of paranoia as an American cultural and literary phenomenon recognize it as growing particularly strong after World War II, first as a result of Cold War tensions and McCarthyism—famously articulated by Richard Hofstadter's formulation of "the paranoid style in American politics"—and later as a response to anxieties related to radical progressions in globalization, communication, surveillance, and control systems during the latter part of the century. In particular, and of specific interest to me, are the recurring and frustrated struggles of identifying power structures thematized in postmodern literature. Indeed, the insistent paranoid tendencies in literary fiction during this period enforce a reconsideration of the common conception of the postmodern as a celebration of fragmentation, especially when it comes to the subject. At least in the paranoid genre, according to Timothy Melley, there is an easily discernable, deep anxiety triggered by a sense of loss of personal autonomy through postwar culture (2000, vii). In my treatment, the paranoid chronotope is a tool to help identify the similarities between such literary formulations of paranoia and paranoia's contemporary social, cultural, and critical expressions.

The Paranoid Chronotope

In this book, I pick up and build on a key element present in all foundational definitions of paranoia—its preoccupation with creating order, coherence, and meaning in an uncertain and unstable world—in order to identify and develop the concept of the paranoid chronotope. Early definitions of paranoia such as that by Krafft-Ebing emphasize how the paranoid reacts against mess and chance by constructing formal and systematized delusional structures. Referring to a study of Schreber's case, Melley identifies the paranoiac's propensity to locate coherence and motifs in what others interpret as chance or randomness, and how the psychoanalytic process itself seems to strive toward "a coherent system lying behind it all" (2000, 19). Trotter consults the Schreber case as well and notes that Schreber's paranoia "condemned him to meaning and value, to a universe devoid of accident" (2001, 4). Hofstadter sees that the paranoid mentality "is far more coherent than the real world" as it leaves "nothing unexplained" and comprehends "all of reality in one overreaching, consistent theory" (2008, 36). Fredric Jameson sees conspiratorial texts as perverted cognitive maps, as a means of creating order and overview in a global and essentially unoverviewable world. Melley recognizes in paranoia the means to protect notions of the coherent self and the autonomous individual against persistent and penetrating mechanisms of social regulation and control. As these definitions suggest, the characteristic features of paranoia include its inability to accept the randomness and messiness of the world and its concomitant difficulty in accepting and understanding diffused and noncentralized modes of power and control. While different, all of these definitions point to paranoia as a rejection of contingency and mess and as a consequent and enforced construction of order and meaning. The paranoid's view of the world is much more coherent than the world as it really is and so provides a crucial intimation of the dual and disjunctive doubling of realities of the paranoid chronotope.

The chronotope has proved to be a slippery concept, not least because Mikhail Bakhtin, who first transposed this concept from science to literature, offers such a broad definition. In the most basic sense, we see the chronotope as identifying the specificity of the intrinsic interconnectedness of space and time, especially, for Bakhtin, in literature. Bakhtin picks up on Immanuel Kant's emphasis on the significance of time and space to human perception and as key forms of cognition. But unlike Kant, he does not search for a universal or transcendent nature of these forms. Quite the contrary, he is particularly interested in examining their historical and formal conditions. In his classic study "Forms of Time and of the Chronotope in the Novel" (1981), Bakhtin shows how literatures from diverse periods and genres configure this interconnectedness differently. Separate and apart, time and space can be portrayed, for example, as more or less abstract, generalized, specific, extended, or condensed. Crucial to my study is the way in which such distinctive configurations have implications for how the relation between the individual and its surroundings is comprehended and portrayed. Thus, for example, Bakhtin shows how Greek romance literature positions its characters in abstract and interchangeable space—the places they visit are unspecified and vague—and in an "adventure-time" that exists beyond the characters. Space and time left no trace on them. As a result, individuals were portrayed as passive and as subjected to action rather than as agents with initiative.

Especially when compared with such spacetimes, or chronotopes, in later fiction, it becomes evident that the perception and depiction of space and time have profound implications for our understanding of the constitutive relationship between the individual and the world. By means of contrast to Greek romance literature, we can see, for example, how the chronotope in the renaissance novels of Rabelais was characterized by an externalization of characters—a "direct proportionality" existed between a character's actions and a purposefully humanist conception of its spatiotemporal conditions (Bakhtin 1981, 167), or how the provincial and petit-bourgeois setting of Flaubert's *Madame Bovary* (1856) and many novels of its kind yielded an everyday time characterized by cyclicality. In the case of the former, the chronotope is suggestive of a burgeoning belief in the human subject—"a new chronotope for a new, whole and harmonious man, and for new forms of human communication" (168)—while the chronotope in the latter indicates a realist entanglement of the individual with a trivial and uneventful existence of everyday life—"A day is just a day, a year is just a year—a life is just a life" (248). The figure of the chronotope, then, can help us better discern historical and philosophical conceptions of the subject based on how characters and individuals are positioned and quite crucially how they believe themselves to be positioned in relation to space and time in different genres and contexts.

For this reason, literary depictions from what we may call the usual suspects in American postwar paranoid fiction serve as an initial and brief but illuminating and instrumental key to my conceptualization of the paranoid chronotope both in and beyond literature during this period. Thus, for example, in the opening paragraph of Thomas Pynchon's *The Crying of Lot 49* (1966), Oedipa ponders "a sunrise over the library slope at Cornell University that nobody out on it had seen because the slope faces west" (1). Escaping the maze of the "irreal world," characters in Philip K. Dick's *Valis* (1981) insist, means getting away from time and space as "the binding, controlling conditions of the maze—its power" (210). The outlaw zones of Night City in Japan, where "computer cowboy" Case hangs out in William Gibson's *Neuromancer* (1984), he suspects might not be preserved for its inhabitants so much as for technology itself, a "historical park," an "unsupervised playground" (19). When Lauren Hardke, the body artist in Don DeLillo's novel *The Body Artist* (2001), tries to get a grip on her life after her husband's suicide, she takes to watching livestreaming video from a road in the city of Kotka, Finland: "It was the sense of organization, a place contained in an unyielding frame," it was "another world but she could see it in its realness, in its hours, minutes, and seconds" (38). The bunker that Paul Krovik builds in Patrick Flanery's *Fallen Land* (2013) is underneath the official house, which he built but no longer has the right to live in, and exists not only because he finds it "essential to plan" for attacks by foreign terrorists, hostile Americans, or "for an environmental, technological, or biochemical conclusion to the human era on this planet" (30), but also because the "house is the way he sees himself" so if he dies, it is the house that "should kill him" (82).

These brief examples suggest a commonality not just with each other but with numerous American novels from the 1950s to the present. This commonality consists of an unsettled and troubled relation between conceptions of the self and of the spacetime in which this self strives for agency and identity. Such unsettling and troubling relations are of course also a general feature of postmodern fiction. Classifying spatiotemporal configurations common across disciplines in postmodernity, including nonlinearity, decentering, deformation, deframing, and dedifferentiation (2000, 4), Paul Smethurst identifies a generalized "postmodern chronotope" and argues that it relies on peculiar spacetime arrangements that produce particular "ways of seeing and ways of responding to the contemporary world" (2000, 65). And it is no surprise that these ways, shaped as they are by preoccupations with problematizing conceptions of reality and agency typical of the period, tend toward paranoia.

The paranoid chronotope further specifies and elucidates the duality of such configurations while also lifting the discussion from an exclusively postmodern discourse and context. It points to a recurring sense in which the spatiotemporal conditions that characters negotiate on a daily basis are but a backdrop—a fake reality hiding a more real reality —or at least everyday spatiotemporal conditions that are not the most influential ones. In novels of this kind, then, characters frequently imagine another layer to the society in which they live: a level that exists beneath or above or beyond the everyday reality in which they and others perceive themselves as free independent subjects. Typically, it is only the paranoid protagonist who sees through this more or less malicious set-up and thus realizes that the free autonomous subject is at risk. In this way, these novels strive to maintain a sense of autonomous individuality by abstracting and repositioning institutions, communication, and critique as a distinctive and frequently malevolent layer of reality. Rather than conceding to a reality crisscrossed with more or less comprehensible social negotiations and power relations, and a subject position that emerges through and in relation to these relations, the paranoid chronotope separates and cleanses the spatiotemporal layers of such forces and constructs them instead as separate and separable spatiotemporal layers in which such forces are consolidated into one consistent and menacing layer. Somewhere beyond but always threatening to invade the individual freedom of the main characters, there is a coherent system, an ominous force, a true language, an all-encompassing technology, or a political structure that threatens to undo the subject position without which these mostly male, white American subjects, as well as the ideological underpinnings of a nation they see themselves as representing, are put at stake.

In other words, it is typically not a question of recognizing what some take as an experiential, existential, and political starting point: that the subject is inescapably entangled with and constantly influenced by forces of the social. Rather, the paranoid chronotope positions these forces as unitary, agential, and oppositional: an individual subject on one side and a system conspiring to undermine it on another. Crucially, and symptomatically, as we have begun to see, these systems, forces, and structures are typically perceived as a spacetime *other* than the one in which the subject spends its everyday life. This means that the social can be posited as against the subject rather than as an inextricable part of it. Thus a liberal conception of the subject (to be defined momentarily) can be maintained in the midst of radical misgivings about it during this period. The other spacetime is not always within reach, but, crucially, is projected as different from the everyday, thus allowing subjects to simultaneously worry about their own agency and protect it. As we will see in the literary analyses, this ambivalence frequently takes the shape of what Bakhtin calls the minor chronotope of the threshold: a spacetime in which historical forces and crises befall characters and force them away from the biographical and toward more momentous events and decisions. In our case, paranoid characters reluctantly recognize and at the same time resist such changes, an ambivalence that contributes to the building of the dual and disjunctive layers of the paranoid chronotope.

The paranoid chronotope clearly has similarities with the allegorical. Both figures exhibit a dual layering of representation and interpretation, which generates a transcendental category of cognition that shadows what is overtly given. On a fundamental level, allegory in this understanding is a "contrapuntal technique," as Northrop Frye once put it, that produces analogies between representation and world, between internal and external meaning (1957, 90). The sense is that the text or the object of study always means more than what is to be read or seen, which forces interpretation to expand beyond it. In its Benjaminian and De Manian orientations, these analogical relations are inescapably destabilized; no steady correspondence or stable meaning is possible. For Walter Benjamin, allegory emerges as the irreducibly impossible but nonetheless consistently critical attempt to tie together the fragments of totality and unity in modernity. Exiled from truth, unity, and transcendence, allegory ambivalently and vainly strives toward these even as it recognizes them as inexorably lost. Allegory, according to Benjamin, is inevitably left "empty-handed" (quoted in Lukács 2005, 411). In postmodernity, Jameson says, allegory regains force as a means of creating stability and overview in an otherwise fluid, global, and complex world. It seems to solve the problem of how to represent the relation between individuals and the social totality and collective processes that threaten to engulf them. This is where the allegorical approaches the conspiratorial, as it turns into "a degraded attempt," as Jameson famously puts it, to portray "that enormous and threatening, yet only dimly perceivable, other reality of economic and social institutions"—in other words "to think the impossible totality of the contemporary world system" (1991, 38).

A central difference between the allegorical and the paranoid chronotope is that the latter, unlike the former, is not left empty-handed. Indeed, where allegory looks to the transcendent level for fragments, the paranoid chronotope rewards us with a rather distinct and coherent layer. Indeed, this other layer, as we have begun to see, is much more consistent than the messiness of everyday reality. It is also much more distinctly agential, malevolent, and personal—it does not harbor the truth and unity toward which subjects aspire in abortive dreams of wholeness, but is constituted by malicious forces that are out to undermine this very subject. In this, the paranoid chronotope is similar to the conspiratorial mappings that Jameson sees in postmodern narrative. The aesthetic dimension is essential, and this becomes particularly apparent in literary expressions, as we will see, because the second layer of the chronotope needs to be peopled and filled with movement and action. This is why the spatiotemporal category of the chronotope becomes so useful: it captures and clarifies the way paranoia fleshes out and brings to life imagined threats and enemies. The hope is that the attention to specific spatiotemporal arrangements of paranoia that the paranoid chronotope illuminates will concretize how this duality functions in and across different paranoid discourses today.

Identifying the nature and conditions of the paranoid chronotope is not about excavating novel or alternative representations of paranoia but about actualizing and analyzing the links between dominant paranoid discourses in post-1950s American culture. As Bakhtin puts it, the "chronotope is an optic for reading texts as x-rays of the forces at work in the culture system from which they spring" (1981, 425). Many of the literary authors just mentioned were or have remained active during the several decades following the 1950s, and frequently it is not just individual novels but whole oeuvres that speak to paranoid preoccupations, as well as their developments, during this time. Dick's continuing obsession with parallel worlds stretched from the 1950s to the 1980s, Pynchon's incessant search for clues in old or new communication technologies started in the 1960s, DeLillo's recurring preoccupation with the relation between reality and fiction and between fiction and terrorism began in the 1970s, and Gibson's formative conceptualization of cyberspace and his continued attention to technologically configured realities has been with us since the 1980s. This makes them not just reflectors or representatives but also creators of an American paranoid imagination. The optic of the chronotope, as Smethurst emphasizes, is not suggestive of a direct correlation between art and culture but must be considered in light of the ways in which literature filters, refracts, and inverts the cultural forces and systems that it portrays (70). The paranoid chronotope allows us to see a changing chronotope across the historical period I am studying while also revealing the persistence of the form—the disjunctive duality—of the chronotope as such.

How time and space are connected in novels and the trace these configurations leave on characters tell us something about the genre at hand. A literary text may contain numerous minor, or local, chronotopes to fit specific motifs, Bakhtin's own most famous examples being those of the road and of the threshold, but larger—generic—chronotopes help us see how different genres are characterized by distinctive organizations of spacetime. Thus, for example, the adventure time of the Greek novel is controlled by chance and the individual is passive, unchanging, throughout his adventures (Bakhtin 1981, 94). In the Rabelaisian novel, in contrast, there is a direct relation—even a "special connection"—between a character and his actions (167), and Romantic literary texts are increasingly organized by contrasting the accumulative invasion of a large, abstract, and impersonal industrialism with a small, idyllic world. Central in all cases is the way the chronotope "as a formally constitutive category determines to a significant degree the image of man in literature as well," according to Bakhtin, clarifying famously that the "image of man is always intrinsically chronotopic" (85).

This suggests that the chronotope constructed in any one novel or genre tells us something vital about what kind of agency is envisioned for the characters emerging through and negotiating these conditions. As we have seen, for example, Bakhtin recognizes a proportionality between characters and their spatiotemporal conditions in Renaissance novels which provides fertile ground for an expansive humanist subject, while the realist novels he explores leave characters so entangled with the trivialities of everyday life that they risk becoming submerged by them. Along similar lines, Guido Mazzoni notes how the modern form of the novel takes shape via the laws and institutions of modern society. The fate of the characters is no longer governed by cosmic and impersonal forces of destiny but by more mundane, everyday, societal constraints (2017, 222). This, too, has clear chronotopic implications. It also inspires the question of societal constraints and their spatiotemporal arrangements in paranoid novels and how they shape the characters and their perception of themselves as agents.

This is not to suggest an authoritative and exclusive definition of the paranoid novel as such. While there is a decided recurrence of a fairly narrow set of authors in the scholarly writing on American paranoid literature, it is in fact rarely discussed as a coherent genre. Fiction of this kind tends to fall into various more commonplace and recognizable categories, such as science fiction, horror, suspense, noir, cli-fi, and, most prominently and decidedly most generally, postmodern fiction. Yet while we might want to avoid imposing a genre so broadly, and while noting the great amount of scholarly work on this literature that has already been carried out, identifying a set of common denominators allows us to accentuate some key features while approaching the specifics of the paranoid chronotope.

Language constitutes a key thematic in paranoid fiction. Whether a result of poststructuralist theories of language, as Melley argues, or a concomitant reaction alongside such contemporary preoccupations, as I am inclined to propose, this literature frequently positions discursive systems as direct and quite physical threats to the individual subject. Thus, for example, William Burroughs, frequently noted as one of the first influential authors in the paranoid tradition, obsessively returns to the notion of language as control throughout much of his oeuvre. This is not, or is no longer, language as a tool for communication but language as a mode of control that has, quite literally, eaten its way into the soft machines of our bodies. It is no longer, as Burroughs writes in *The Ticket That Exploded* (1962), a symbiotic relationship but a parasitic one. The word may once have been a healthy part of the organism—its "Other Half"—but it is now a virus invading and damaging the central nervous system. Modern man has lost control over the words and encounters in himself "a resisting organism that *forces you to talk*" (39).

Language is a recurring theme also in DeLillo's fiction, perhaps most overtly in *The Names* (1982), at the heart of which we find a mysterious cult that violently reinforces a correspondence between name and place by murdering people whose initials match those of the place they are in. These murders combine accident and deliberation: the victims are random insofar as their identity ultimately does not matter, but there is also highly deliberate planning as the initials of the victim and the place-name must coincide. The dream of language and reality coinciding is thus forcefully realized, but the dream turns out to be a nightmare not only because it leads to death but because it ultimately points to the utter insignificance of individuals. Compulsively circling around questions of language and identity are of course the writings of Paul Auster, most iconically *The New York Trilogy* (1987) and its central problem of what happens with our perception of identity and reality if deprived of language. A brutal awakening to the constructedness of language but also to our inability to be someone without it provokes the protagonist's identity crisis and existential dread. Agency—indeed, even existence itself—threatens to collapse and vanish. The man feels that "his words had been severed from him, that now they were part of the world at large, as real and specific as a stone, or a lake, or a flower. They no longer had anything to do with him" (131).

Related to questions of language are those of writing. Auster speaks to this preoccupation with writing itself as a struggle to construct some chronotopic stability in a world that has developed beyond comprehension and control. Losing control of narrative and identities, the three stories that make up his famous trilogy blur as do their identities, and how do you keep track when "anything can happen"? This, the trilogy suggests, is "when words begin to fail" (301). Perhaps we also fail to exist. "The last sentence of the red notebook reads: 'What will happen when there are no more pages in the red notebook?'" (132). Writing is a central theme throughout DeLillo's oeuvre, especially in *Mao II* (1992) in which the author withdraws from a world where terrorists have taken over the role of "shapers of sensibility and thought" (157). Society has become too blurry and messy; "there's too much everything, more things and messages and meanings than we can use in ten thousand lifetimes." In this context, according to the novel, the lives and ambitions of terrorists appear coherent because they stand outside of society and perform acts that acquire meaning (157). Terrorism is, of course, a theme in itself, especially in DeLillo's work, but it is worth noting the frequency with which it is associated precisely with the diminishing role and importance of art and literature in shaping reality. Here we see quite clearly a paranoid chronotope emerging from the realization that not only are our perceptions of reality shaped by others but the privilege of this shaping, one associated with being a white, male American writer, is on the wane: "Beckett is the last writer to shape the way we think and see" (157).

Not just writing but communication generally constitutes a central theme in paranoid literature. It is pivotal, for example, to Pynchon's novels and to what is seen as one of the most iconic paranoid novels of the period: *The Crying of Lot 49*. Here, communication is not only distinctly chronotopic but also conspicuously paranoid. Layers of communication are—potentially—splayed out across the city. As Oedipa Maas searches the city of San Narciso for a secret and subversive communication system known as W.A.S.T.E and its possible links to the eighteenth-century European postal system Tristero, both the reality and communication of supposed everyday life are progressively destabilized. The stamp collection at the heart of the narrative, Lot 49, which is supposed to carry revelatory power, is tellingly described as "thousands of little coloured windows into deep vistas of space and time" (29). While Oedipa perseveres in her efforts to locate that other, explanatory layer of communication that will yield the truth, even at the risk of madness, Richard Elster, the former war advisor to Iraq in DeLillo's *Point Omega* (2010), has given up on the idea of actually being able to access space and time in the world through cognition and mediation. Communication and information as the means to survey and comprehend the world is in question, and Elster is disillusioned because he is unable to make a difference in the world in terms of ever making meaning coincide with itself. He has given up aspiring to cognition beyond a mediation that only works to obscure it.

In addition to complications of language, writing, and communication, the snowballing amount and complexity of information generates paranoid chronotopes in novels such as Dick's *Time Out of Joint* (1959), Gibson's *Pattern Recognition* (2003), DeLillo's *Cosmopolis* (2003), and Pynchon's *Bleeding Edge* (2013). Albeit in different ways, the protagonists in these novels are all capable of detecting patterns in the world without having any real comprehension of that world or even which world is the "real" one. In other words, there is a perceived disjunction between their experience of everyday life and the world as a bigger picture in which the protagonists, in true paranoid fashion, play a crucial part. When Ragle Gumm in *Time Out of Joint* finds that what he assumed was reality has gradually been replaced by slips of paper: "soft-drink stand," "door," "factory building," this is the first step toward discovering that this reality is but a construction. Significantly, it is built especially around him, in proper grandeurish paranoid style, to enable clandestine employment of his talent for identifying the spatial and temporal coordinates of nuclear strikes in the real world— a world he does not know exists.

Ragle Gumm shares this ability of recognizing patterns in a world he does not comprehend not only with Pynchon's Oedipa Maas but also with Cayce Pollard, the protagonist in Gibson's novel. Cayce travels the world identifying patterns in fashion before anyone else recognizes them, pointing commodifiers at these patterns so they can be "productized. Turned into units. Marketed" (86). Cayce does not comprehend these patterns herself; rather, it is a physical allergy to corporate logos that generates her special gift. Eric Packer, the multi-billionaire who spends almost the entirety of DeLillo's *Cosmopolis* (2003) in a stretch limousine traversing a congested Manhattan, makes his fortune by trading currencies on the stock market. The very concrete and starkly demarcated spatiotemporal conditions of his physical location are consistently contrasted with the nano- or zepto- or yoktoseconds and global reach of this trading (79). As time and space are released from embodied experientiality, information becomes a governing but intangible dimension of the world. "The yen spree," as we learn, is "releasing Eric from the influence of his neocortex" (115).

The cumulative complexity of information is of course related to the development of technology. Here, Gibson's virtually iconic and anticipatory definition of cyberspace in *Neuromancer* as a "consensual hallucination experienced daily by billions of legitimate operators, in every nation, by children being taught mathematical concepts. . . . A graphic representation of data abstracted from the banks of every computer in the human system," (67) speaks to a disjunctive chronotope that has become part of everyday life in the twenty-first century. The paranoid vision appears largely in the novel's distinguishing between a neo-noir degenerated "meatspace" and the light, infinite but also highly controlled and increasingly corporate cyberspace. This attention to what one of Pynchon's characters identify as "bleeding edge technology" in his 2013 novel *Bleeding Edge* haunts Gibson's oeuvre up to and including his 2020 novel, *Agency*. Following the development of technology, these more recent novels, including Pynchon's, negotiate the inevitability and mounting complexity of disjunctive layers of reality in the contemporary world.

The very brief examples just described are intended to elucidate how various preoccupations of paranoid fiction recurrently build on the disjunctive and antagonistic layers of reality that I identify as the paranoid chronotope. In correspondence with the preliminary definitions of paranoia discussed previously, and compared with Bakhtin's outlining of earlier chronotopes, we can also begin to discern a set of spatiotemporal conditions that the paranoid chronotope disavows. For example, time is decidedly not governed by chance. As noted earlier, several central theorists of paranoia, including Krafft-Ebing and Schreber, Hofstadter, Trotter, and Melley, see as a key characteristic of paranoia its absolute averseness to chance. Indeed, the coherence of the paranoid universe is one of the features that reveal it as such; its coherence, as we saw via Hofstadter, outshines that of the real world (36). So while the adventure novel completely relies on chance, without which "there would be no plot at all" (Bakhtin 1981, 92), the paranoid novel creates its plot from the very lack of chance. Thus we see chance in DeLillo's *The Names* as the way in which whoever happens to be in a place that matches their own initials is at risks being recuperated into the larger system that is language; how "a beer can run over by a passing taxi" is "the source of the information and the help" in Dick's *Valis* (2001, 177), how it becomes increasingly irrelevant whom the protagonist follows on the streets of New York in Auster's trilogy; and how all encounters and events that make up Oedipa's adventures seem to be clues to the bigger picture that is or is not hidden in *Lot 49*.

A second spatiotemporal feature that the paranoid chronotope renounces is a congruous connection between a character and his actions. In this, it can be contrasted, for example, with the Rabelaisian chronotope in which, Bakhtin observes, space and time are both vast but they are so in a way that corresponds with character—it produces a world that adequately mirrors the spatiotemporal conditions of a whole and harmonious man (1981, 168). This is one of the grounds for laughter, the affirmation of connections, however crude and unmediated, that constitute life (170). Of course, the idea of a whole and harmonious man whose size and actions correspond to the spacetime in which he moves about is not typical of the paranoid novel. If anything, the paranoid novel displays the opposite—a fundamental disjunction between the size of the man and his actions and the spacetime he inhabits. This disjunction is twofold. On the one hand, there is a conspiracy much larger than the protagonist, who in this sense is revealed in his acute and devastating minuteness. On the other hand, there is a fantastical grandeur on behalf of the protagonist in that this larger framework is often constructed around him. Forces larger than the individual are geared specifically toward—or at—him. This makes for a disjunctive proportionality that constantly needs to be negotiated. We saw this in "Adjustment Team," described in the opening paragraph of this Introduction, and we see it in *Valis* in Horselover Fat's conviction that "the information fired at him and progressively crammed into his head in successive waves had a holy origin and hence should be regarded as a form of scripture" (23).

To the two dimensions at which we have negatively arrived—the lack of chance and the lack of congruous connection between character and action—we can also add a third and quite significant feature of the paranoid chronotope: the lack of a shared sense of reality between characters. Unlike other chronotopes, which tend to bring characters together precisely because they are positioned in a shared spacetime, the paranoid chronotope insulates characters and disables a sense of sociality among them. As answers are sought beyond the level of reality that paranoid protagonists see their fellow characters inhabiting, everyday reality ceases to be a common space. Even when the other layer is seen as a threat to everyone in a given space—like the body snatchers taking over the bodies of Americans in Mill Valley, California, in Jack Finney's *Invasion of the Body Snatchers* (1954) or the social media that have completely engulfed the lives and agency of a whole generation of Americans in Dave Eggers's *The Circle* (2013)—this threat is rarely perceived by many, if any, characters beyond the protagonists themselves. Largely prohibiting lateral engagement and dialogue, the individual subject position salvaged via the paranoid chronotope thus comes at the expense of mutuality and community. Agency is secured for the individual but prohibited as a collective effort.

Although I build the paranoid chronotope from literature, I am not concerned with the potential problem of the chronotope's applicability beyond it. Even so, I am aware that this has been a point of contention. On the one hand, Bakhtin positions the concept very clearly in relation to literature and narrative, but, on the other hand, he identifies "real-life chronotopes" as representational constructs that govern perceptions of space and time regardless of their ontological status. What is key is that meaning, even of the abstract cognitive kind, necessarily reaches us via our social, spatiotemporal, experience. It is a fact, he argues, that "Every entry into the sphere of meaning is accomplished only through the gates of the chronotope" (1981, 257). On this understanding, meaning is necessarily shaped by the spatiotemporal conditions of social experience. Essentially, the paranoid chronotope may be seen as a negotiation of exactly this crux. It positions the layers—or veils—of social experience that trouble our access to the world, to truth, to ourselves, not as co-constitutive but as antagonistic. The paranoid rejection of mess concretizes and stylizes this crux into the two related but disjunctive sides of a paranoid chronotope: one a messy, everyday spacetime that less observant people perceive as the real one; the other, an orderly, systematic spacetime that the paranoid subject or group perceives as the true reality. A preliminary reading of "Adjustment Team" within this framework will illustrate this mechanism.

On one level, Dick's story is suggestive of a realist everyday construction of time and space. Ed, the protagonist, lives in a small green stucco house in a neighborhood of lawns, sidewalks, and parked cars. When Ed takes the bus to town, we see a town described as a concrete space, with curbs and red lights, stores, and cafés. As the story opens, Ed and his wife Ruth are having breakfast. Ruth has to hurry to get to work on time but leaves work early to do the shopping, while Ed is in less of a hurry, at least until he gets waylaid by a life insurance salesman.

On another, parallel, level, the story constructs a completely different chronotope, where space is under constant construction and adjustment. This space is divided into numbered sectors. Ed's office is in section T 137, which on this day is scheduled for an adjustment. For the adjustment to work without fault, Ed needs to be there on time so that he will be "altered to coincide with the new adjustments." There are precise routines for making sure people are in the right place at the right time and team members to make this work. In this instance, a dog is due to bark at 8:15, setting off a string of events including "A Friend with a Car," leading to Ed being in the right sector at the right time. The dog is sleepy, however, and misses his cue, resulting in this whole chain being replaced by an unknown one—"There's no telling what will come instead," as one of the members of the Adjustment Team observes. What comes is a life insurance salesman who detains Ed, and what this results in we already know: an unsolicited collision of worlds. With this collision comes Ed's realization that the spatiotemporal construction he has hitherto perceived as reality—the "natural processes," the curbs and red lights, stores, and cafés, which he thought he was navigating by his own agency—are actually governed by a secret but extremely powerful layer of rules and logics.

Here, then, we have an exemplary instance of the paranoid chronotope. Such chronotopes look different in different contexts and periods but have as their defining feature precisely this kind of disjunctive doubling between two distinct spatiotemporal logics. A seemingly everyday reality in which individual subjects navigate the spatiotemporal logic of modern Western society is shadowed by a second reality that is more or less invisible and that threatens to unravel the logic of the original. Crucially, and as our examples from various novels have begun to show, the conceptualization of the paranoid chronotope centers on this disjunctive doubling of itself rather than on a fixed logic of either of its levels. This is significant for two reasons. To begin with, a focus on disjunctive layers—texts, meanings, realities, modalities—rather than on content illuminates a logic common to otherwise differing phenomena. The chronotope, according to Michael Holquist, can be usefully employed to study relations between texts and their times and thus acts as "a fundamental tool for a broader social and historical analysis, within which the literary series would be only one of several interconnected types of discourse" (2002, 111). Employed in this way, and as I will show, the paranoid chronotope not only enables a comparative study of phenomena in literature, society, and critique; it also helps us discern and better understand formal similarities between, for example, Cold War communist scares and twenty-first century conspiracy theories and between the logic of a neoliberalized public sphere and academic formulations of postcritique.

Second, and conversely, a focus on the changing and chafing logics of the respective sides can tell us something about the social, historical, political, and cultural developments of paranoia. For example, the fact that Ed Fletcher in "Adjustment Team" is ultimately reassured by a centralized and "fully licensed team" is symptomatic of the paranoid style of the 1950s. This was the Cold War atmosphere that relied on what were, ultimately, easily identifiable threats and oppositions—the commies, the coloreds, the homosexuals, women—in short, political agendas, identities, convictions, and institutions. There are enemies and a continuous and contiguous risk of infiltration and manipulation, but in the end the enemy has an identity (however distorted) and so does the individual subject (however deluded). Power still seems relatively tangible. The everyday life of lawns and buses and cafés is constructed by a logic of institutions, identities, systems, and national politics, but there is a dark, other side, one governed by control and manipulation. This side is parallel to the first and, like it, functions according to a clear and spatiotemporal logic. The Adjustment Team spatially exists above everyday life quite literally (Ed travels upward in a phone booth elevator for a meeting with them) and it seems to exert its power to orchestrate society primarily by making sure everyone is at the right place at the right time. The locus of power, once discovered, is a discrete unit, and so are the subjects being controlled. Essentially, what we see here is a disciplinary logic reflected in the paranoid chronotope as it plays out in Dick's story.

It becomes harder, looking toward the later years of the twentieth century and the beginning of the twenty-first, to pin down such power relations. As I discuss in Chapter 2, the "enemy" has become more difficult to identify and narrow down and so has the logic of power and control. Key descriptions of control and neoliberalism as they have developed and intensified since the Second World War, such as those by Foucault, Gilles Deleuze, and Wendy Brown, note how power becomes more minute and modulating, less interested in institutions and identities than in affects and desires. The autonomy of the political subject as a cornerstone of democracy is at risk or, some argue, seriously undermined. We move from a disciplinary logic of individuals and identities— most visible in the American Fordist production model and in the family as a financial institution—to a society in which control is less clearly distributed. This has fundamental implications for the spatiotemporal logic of relations between individuals and political governing. How, then, do we grasp the public sphere and our role as individuals in it today? This dilemma and its potentially paranoid effects are gruelingly represented in the novel I analyze in Chapter 2, *Your Fathers, Where Are They? And the Prophets, Do They Live Forever?* by Dave Eggers (2014). Here the protagonist abducts and locks up various representatives of society in separate barracks of an abandoned army base in a desperate but futile attempt to "see" power and (re)construct a disciplinary order. Perhaps, having left a Cold War paranoia and its collective psychopathology behind, we find ourselves perversely nostalgic "for a paranoia in which the persecutor had a more or less recognizable face and a clear geographical location" (Santner 1997, xiii). Perhaps, then, to venture a hypothesis of the resurgence of paranoid politics in the present, what we are witnessing in the twenty-first century is at least in part nostalgia for political power that might have been more solid but also more easily identified and resisted. Indeed, are not conspiracy theorists, nationalist parties, and alt-right movements the closest we come to the "fully licensed team" to organize our reality for us today?

The "disjunctive duality" of the paranoid chronotope as I have begun to outline it here makes visible negotiations of a challenging equation— how to hold on to a conception of a world governed by visible rules discernable for and negotiable by free inviolable subjects while simultaneously recognizing a world in which subjects are deeply immersed in and governed by the social and by the progressively complex political, economic, and technological mechanisms that make it up. Paranoia is not only about projecting a system and order outward but also, and quite centrally, about protecting the self or, crucially, a certain conception of the self. More explicitly, particularly in postwar culture, paranoia is the means to protect liberal individualism in a time when it is increasingly under threat.

The American Liberal Subject

While paranoia is intrinsically about conceptions and projections of how the world hangs together, one of its essential components is the agency that this perceived world does or does not bestow on the individual subject. Ed Fletcher illustrates what we might describe as the radical individualism of paranoia. The paranoid subject, as I have begun to describe it, typically sees itself as the only person—or group—able to identify this other layer. This is commonly seen as the reason that this individual or group feels special and explains why it is being pursued—as the protagonist in DeLillo's *The Names* puts it, "Sometimes I think I'm the only one who sees it" (1989, 179).

The legacy and tradition of liberal individualism constitute a major dilemma in the paranoid schemas I explore. Crucially, "liberal individualism" is not to be understood here as related to liberals or liberal politics in the contemporary sense of these terms. Rather, it refers to a modern Western conception of the self, of society, and of politics as relying largely on a free, autonomous individual responsible for himself and his own decisions (here the self is a he; bear with me—more on this in a moment). The thinking subject identified by Descartes, the individual in charge of his own destiny both posed and in different ways interrogated by Thomas Hobbes and John Locke in the seventeenth century, and the possessive individualism that C. B. Macpherson describes as developing from these philosophers have had immense influence over the development of societal and political beliefs and systems ever since then (see MacPherson 1962).

Interestingly, modern conceptions of the subject have also emerged in acute—one may even say paranoid—denial of its spatiotemporal conditions. In trying to ascertain what is indubitable, we may recall, Descartes strove to eradicate all that could not be established as absolutely true. Knowledge coming from the senses, he realized, is not necessarily true since it is not always possible to separate, for example, dream and reality. To push this as far as he could, he experimented with the idea of a malicious, cunning, powerful demon in the place of a benevolent and truthful God. If there were such a demon and, worse, if such a demon employed "all his energies in order to deceive me," all things external to himself must be regarded as potential "delusions of dreams" "devised to ensnare my judgment." To abjure the power and influence of such a demon—should it exist—Descartes forfeited the experiences and confidence of his own body, "I shall consider myself as not having hands or eyes, or flesh, or blood or senses, but as falsely believing that I have all these things." For Descartes, then, the philosopher who has come to be seen as standing at the pinnacle of the modern subject, paranoia constitutes a necessary step to achieve any kind of certainty (even if, famously, the certainty is precisely that he is capable of doubt: being aware of the possibility of deception itself becomes the key). As we see quite clearly here, it is specifically at the moment when the subject leaves its disembodied state and steps into the embodied, spatiotemporal world that the potential dual spacetimes appear and the paranoid chronotope becomes a possibility.

The liberal subject as animated and articulated by Hobbes and Locke continues this tradition of suspiciously guarding itself from its devious and unreliable surroundings. Unlike Descartes, however, for whom it was the self's own senses that were potentially deceptive, these political theorists worked primarily toward warding off the influence and will of others. Possessive individualism, as Macpherson theorizes it, centers on ownership, of the self if nothing else, and thus recognizes very particular spatiotemporal conditions of the subject. These conceptions of the individual, while thus tainted with paranoia, are often seen as proof of the integrity and inviolability of the subject of liberalism. In Chapter 2, I will outline and engage with these discussions in more detail, but what is central to my study as a whole is the lingering conceptions of liberal individualism. At the same time, such conceptions became progressively difficult to maintain after the Second World War. This is also when we see a consolidation of what Melley calls "agency panic." Agency panic arises from a disjunction between an enduring belief in liberal individualism and a growing albeit reluctant awareness of our inability to account for the social regulation of subjectivity. Melley links it to the postwar period in particular which saw a "troubled defense of an old but increasingly beleaguered concept of personhood—the idea that the individual is a rational, motivated agent with a protected core of beliefs, desires, and memories" (2000, viii). While it also changed over this period, as we will see, the paranoid chronotope—characterized, as I have begun to show, by a disjunctive dualism—developed in the second half of the twentieth century as a formation centering exactly on this ambivalence. I suggest that it is in the clash between the long tradition of beliefs and practices of the liberal individual and more recent threats against it that we find key answers to the particular paranoia growing strong and increasingly informing discourses and politics from the 1950s onward. As we have begun to see, paranoid fiction by writers such as Burroughs, Dick, Pynchon, DeLillo, and Gibson almost inevitably centers on a threat to a certain subject position, and, more precisely, to the idea of liberal individualism. This is equally true of the more contemporary heirs to the paranoid literature tradition that I analyze in this book, including Eggers, Flanery, and Ben Lerner.

A central dimension of the scope and force of paranoia in my study is the pervasive and foundational belief in the autonomous liberal subject in a specifically American setting. The liberal, and even more so the neoliberal, project is, of course, hardly exclusive to America. Especially toward the later parts of our period, it becomes increasingly problematic to identify the national borders of this phenomenon. Still, while the tension between conceptions of the autonomous liberal subject and its undermining in neoliberal control society needs to be seen as a cultural feature of the West more broadly, America can be seen as the most overt example. Melley underscores the cultural specificity of agency panic as he sees it arising from the crisis of "a long-standing national fantasy of subjectivity" (2000, 15). Similarly, Patrick O'Donnell notes that America has been "the visible site where the incongruities of subjectival fluidity operating within the prefigurative historical order of a national destiny are negotiated in the epoch of late capitalism" (13). America can, in this sense, be seen as a central venue for the drama of the autonomous liberal subject—its most hopeful endeavor as well as its most damaging fall.

The evolution of the autonomous liberal subject in America is historical as well as ideological, emerging from a distinct set of spatiotemporal conditions. Indeed, the nation itself materializes as a result of a spatial movement and the inauguration of a "new" time intended to better reflect the freedom of the individual. Hofstadter's account of the paranoid style in American politics begins with this and with the way the freedom available and under construction in this new space is under continuous threat from "wicked and artful men, in foreign countries" (1798 Massachusetts sermon quoted in Hofstadter, 9). This narrative continues through the centuries. Hofstadter's admittedly random examples, reaching from the 1700s to the 1950s, are nonetheless illustrative. In his example from 1855, Europe conspired and plotted destruction, "threatening the extinction of our political, civil, and religious institutions"; in 1895, "secret cabals of the international gold ring [were] being made use of to deal a blow to the prosperity of the people and the financial and commercial independence of the country"; and in 1951, Senator McCarthy saw the government as part of "a great conspiracy, a conspiracy on a scale so immense as to dwarf any previous such venture in the history of man" (7). What is significant in this last example, apart from the fact that it falls within my historical framework, is the way in which the threat was no longer seen as coming exclusively from abroad but now existed on the level of government itself: "A conspiracy of infamy so black that, when it is finally exposed, its principals shall be forever deserving of the maledictions of all honest men...." (7). In the twenty-first century, insinuations of this kind constitute a regular feature of Donald Trump's discourse, the most explicit example, perhaps, being his insistence on the existence of a deep state.

The drama of the autonomous liberal subject continuously playing out in America, then, bears its particular spatiotemporal marks. Historically, the autonomy of the free American subject was closely connected with creation of a space away from the conservative and regulating traditions of Europe. As American exceptionalism, isolationism, and expansionism all show, albeit in different ways, the autonomy of the free subject is associated with the nation and, more specifically, with America. Enemies from without have included the old systems and hierarchies of Europe, the alternative ideology of the Soviet Union in the twentieth century, terrorists, and a range of more or less clearly defined enemies—most commonly Muslims, Mexicans, or immigrants more generally in the twenty-first century.

When America as an idealized space has been threatened from within, as in the McCarthy era, this has often been seen as a conspiratorial infiltration of foreign persuasions, often in collusion with government officials, frequently with the goal of undoing the free subject and enterprise of the American way. When it is not the New World Order international elites or the Zionist Occupation Government or the Hungarian-American billionaire George Soros plotting to destabilize and control government, banks, and media, it is Barack Obama insinuating his way into the highest office on a fake birth certificate or Muslims infiltrating society and breeding, in a long-term plan to take over, possibly in collusion with those promoting abortion rights who thereby assist in minimizing the white population. The suspicion of government has also been perpetuated in theories of the government spraying chemical agents over the population (so-called chemtrails), elites promoting climate change in order to oppress workers, or, in 2020, the conviction that Covid 19 is a hoax purposefully designed for manipulative political ends and that its vaccine contains trackable microchips or alters DNA.

As I will show, what haunts the free American subject today is also, if perhaps less spectacularly, a "system" promoted by America itself. Globalization, digitalization, and communication systems, the proliferation of control and surveillance mechanisms, and the intensifications of neoliberalism put pressure on American liberal individualism from within. Such developments have produced progressively all-encompassing but increasingly ungraspable power mechanisms. Even the most mundane and minute details of our everyday existence are connected with multinational companies, with cyber networks, and with global geopolitical logics that we have no means of conceptualizing and situating ourselves in relation to. Already in the 1980s, Jameson recognized this inability of seeing the whole as generating a representational problem, one resolved by more or less perverted cognitive maps. According to O'Donnell, with negotiations of subjectivity come "the attendant phantasmatic remapping of national onto global orders and agendas" (13). The particularly American nature of paranoid subjectivity is emphasized by Emily Apter, who sees it as "a singularly American style of one-world thinking" (385). One-world thinking, or "oneworldedness," as she also calls it, is "a delirious aesthetics of systematicity" a "match between cognition and globalism," a sort of paranoid cognitive mapping that insists on everything being connected (366). And while this way of seeing the world is not unique to America, the proclivity to connect the dots and project a single world mapped with itself as a starting point does have a strong basis here, particularly among white men.

The centrality of an experience and conception of a subject position under threat at least in part explains the predominance of white male authors and thinkers in the paranoid literary tradition and white male agents in contemporary paranoid politics and practices in society. Numerous scholars have pointed out that the liberal conception of subjectivity as previously outlined and as implemented in social and political structures is premised on a Western, male subject position. It is this particular position and tradition that is at stake in the paranoid formations I analyze. Of course, women and racialized or otherwise "other" or "othered" subjects produce paranoid fiction and practices. Indeed, in many ways such historically precarious subject positions are more exposed to threats and persecutions and thus are potentially more prone to paranoia. However, this paranoia tends to have a different entry point; embodiment has distinct implications for those who have never been allowed to forget it. Simplified, we might say that while the paranoia developing from Cartesian and liberal traditions expresses itself as the reluctant admittance of spacetime and embodiment in the first place, the paranoia about sexual and racial bias, persecution, oppression, and violence is born from the very inescapability of spacetime and embodiment. The starting points and what is at stake, in other words, are dissimilar. Thus, for example, although paranoid fiction by women might "bear a structural and theoretical similarity to many of the male-authored texts," Melley suggests it comes with "radically different political implications" (2000, 34).

According to Melley, while gender very much depends on "who is articulating agency panic," a common denominator is "its tendency to romanticize the inviolate, liberal subject" (34). This is part of his analysis of the mechanisms of agency panic specifically, which makes these gendered disparities instructive. Here, I put a stronger emphasis on the masculinist and white tradition of the inviolate liberal subject to begin with. This is not to suggest, of course, that women or people of color have not, too, aspired to a free subject position, but rather that this position has always already been entangled in embodiment and in the social in much more concrete ways. This creates a different point of departure for how separate the subject is, and perceives itself to be, from its environment and therefore also a different historical and political starting point when it comes to its violations. Kathy Acker, for example, clearly wrestles with paranoid subjectivity, but her wrestling is unremittingly tied to its embodied and sexualized nature. Her rewriting of Charles Dickens's *Great Expectations* (Dickens's version originally published in 1860; Acker's, in 1982) and Cervantes's *Don Quixote* (Cervantes' version originally published in 1605/1615; Acker's, in 1986) show paranoia as explicitly related to how *Bildung* is enmeshed with gender and sex and with the impossibility of being an "I" without them. In novels such as *Play It As It Lays* (1970) and *The Last Thing He Wanted* (1996), Joan Didion's prose points to conspiracies that are not just national and/or abstractly political but deeply interrelated with gender and embodiment. In Diane Johnson's *The Shadow Knows* (1974), paranoia is profoundly linked to the physical and economic exposedness of being a young single mother. Marge Piercy's *Woman on the Edge of Time* (1976) uses the speculative format to construct an exquisite and painful paranoid chronotope in which sexist, racist, and classist oppression of society that nearly does away with a young Mexican-American mother is paralleled by a feminist utopia.

Ralph Ellison's classic novel *Invisible Man* (1952) also dramatizes the paranoid chronotope in an intensely physical way. Its protagonist is extremely visible and extremely invisible in his black skin: "a man of substance, of flesh and bone, fiber and liquids—and I might even be said to possess a mind. I am invisible, understand, simply because people refuse to see me. Like the bodiless heads you see sometimes in circus sideshows, it is as though I have been surrounded by mirrors of hard, distorting glass" (2001, 3). In John A. Williams's *The Man Who Cried I Am* (1967), the African-American writer Max Reddick's struggle not just to be a black writer but to even feel that he "is"—"Just tell me I am" (1971, 380)—is doubled with what he discovers to be a plot to exterminate all black people in America. For Ellison and Williams, the paranoia is masculinist but it remains markedly different from the paranoid tradition discussed here precisely because of the inevitability of embodiment and social construction as an entry point. The "other world beyond this one," which the icon of elevator construction who passes as white in Colson Whitehead's *The Intuitionist* (1999) tells the protagonist Lila Mae Watson is not a transcendent one. In fact, "his race kept him earthbound," but this world exists rather in the blackness of his skin that white people fail to recognize (240). A contemporary fictional example of racialized paranoid embodiment taking shape as a paranoid chronotope can be found in Jordan Peele's film *Us* (2019), in which the characters are haunted by their murderous doppelgängers, who can free themselves from their "tethered" state by eliminating the "free" version of their bodies.

Melley suggests that historical associations of women with a more contextualized, embodied, and socially interdependent subjectivity and the "masculine associations" of liberal and disembodied individualism explain why so much male paranoid fiction positions "social communications as a feminizing force" and includes narratives in which "dwindling human autonomy" is frequently connected with violent restorations of masculine individuality (2000, 14). Melley shows how social political theorists, too, such as Herbert Marcuse and William Whyte, point to ways in which "the prescription for ailing individual agency in America is nothing so much as a healthy dose of masculinity. What is so telling about this sort of struggle is the ease with which it becomes a struggle against social commitments of any kind" (57). Since Eve Kosofsky Sedgwick's theorizations of homosociality in the mid-1980s and O'Donnell's (2000) and Melley's (2000) acute observations about paranoia at the beginning of the new millennium, paranoid masculinity has reached new heights, or perhaps new lows, depending on how we look at it. Incel terrorist attacks, an online "manosphere" invested in aggressive abuse of women and vehement antifeminism—what Angela Nagle among others identifies as a high level of "cross-pollination between the manosphere and the alt-right" (2017, 98), strong links between alt-right websites such as Breitbart and Infowars and an overtly misogynist president from 2016 to 2020, and an increasingly loud and violent male-coded nationalism and conservatism—all contribute to a twenty-first century landscape pervaded by what seems to be simultaneously a crisis and a consolidation of a masculinity constructed largely on paranoid premises. As such, masculinity materializes as a key to understanding paranoia in America from the 1950s to the present.

In this book, I identify contemporary paranoia as linked to difficulties in identifying and understanding power and truth in contemporary society, and I am interested in the paranoid identity formations to which these difficulties give rise. To provide background and context to the analysis of power, truth, and identity in subsequent chapters, I discuss in Chapter 1 the concept of the public sphere, its role in understanding and negotiating power and truth, and the positioning of the individual in relation to it. In Chapters 2 through 4, I respectively focus on power, truth, and identity in three thematically related but independent sections. I begin with a look at how questions of power, truth, or identity are negotiated on a more general societal level in American society today and in what ways this may give rise to paranoia. Then I read one twenty-first century novel: Eggers's *Your Fathers, Where are They? And the Prophets, Do They Live Forever?* in Chapter 2, Flanery's *I Am No One* in Chapter 3, and Lerner's *10:04* in Chapter 4. I see these novels as carrying the heritage of twentieth-century paranoid fiction into twenty-first century problematics in thought-provoking ways. In the third and final section of each chapter, I address critique and postcritique so that I can identify and problematize conceptions and analyses of power, truth, and identity as linked to the public sphere and as they have been more or less implicitly raised in the previous sections. This arrangement allows two ways of reading: vertically, with attention to each thematic in turn, and horizontally, should the reader be particularly interested in one or the other perspectives on society, literature, and critique. The objective of this organization is the possibility it offers to deploy the paranoid chronotope across these dimensions and thus to elucidate the pervasiveness and recurrence of paranoid tendencies across multiple dimensions of American society, politics, and culture.

1

THE PUBLIC SPHERE AND PARANOIA / THE PARANOID PUBLIC SPHERE

Introduction

In order to understand the implications and complications of contemporary configurations of power, truth, and identity and their paranoid affects and effects in the following chapters, this first chapter will outline central conceptions of the public sphere and its developments in America, especially in terms of how they pertain to conceptions of the subject and critique. On the one hand, and as subsequent chapters will show in more detail, these developments might warrant considerable, justified suspicion. Indeed, perhaps they have rendered the paranoid imagination superfluous to some degree. In modern society, we really are, as John Farrell claims, targeted by "vast and anonymous agencies" that use and manipulate information and images in order to influence our political and economic conduct (2006, 3). On the other hand, there is a disjunction between developments in the public sphere and the lingering conceptions of the autonomous liberal subject that struggle to overview and accept these developments. How do these developments fit with the concept of a political subject with integrity, a subject capable of making informed decisions, a subject governed by mind rather than emotion, a subject with the capacity for critique? And how do they fit with the idea of a public sphere, not only or even necessarily as it was once idealized by Immanuel Kant, Hannah Arendt, or Jürgen Habermas, but at least the idea of a public of some sort, a public as something of which citizens—as political subjects—are a part and in relation to which they appear as political subjects in the first place?

The Public Sphere

It is helpful to think of the public sphere in chronotopic terms. This is in many cases an idealized chronotope—not least in the theories we are about to discuss—but it is ultimately also a matter of more concrete chronotopes—of actual spacetimes: the town squares in Roman times, the salons of the eighteenth century, the modern university, or the more complex digital spacetimes of the twenty-first century. In general terms, a first element of the public sphere as a chronotope is the basic principle that there are dimensions too vast or complex for individuals to grasp—truths, societies, political systems, worlds—but that individuals are nonetheless required to work toward comprehending. These are not transcendent dimensions in relation to which individuals must or should remain passively controlled, but concrete dimensions in which individuals are required to take active part. In the Kantian version, as we will see, critique emerges and is made possible precisely because a previous logic, according to which passive and ignorant individuals stand in relation to transcendent powers and truths, is reconfigured and secularized, paving the way for a configuration in which individuals actively share and participate in the responsibility for and the making of the truths, societies, systems, and worlds of which they are part. A second element, which at least in a post-Enlightenment context stands in logical relation to the first, is the postulation that there are individuals—free rational subjects—whose responsibility is to strive toward knowledge of these dimensions and to give legitimacy to these truths, societies, systems, and worlds by continuous interrogation. Because truth is not transcendent and eternal but among us and evolving, individuals are central to the striving for it at all times. Third, individuals and societies must continuously search for and find the spaces that make interrogation possible. Individuals must come together—as a public in a public sphere—to exchange and challenge their respective knowledges and views.

For a chronotope of the public sphere to become paranoid, not only must there be an uneasy tension between the conception of the subject and the conception of the public—such tensions, after all, are central to the modern Western imaginary in general and an American context in particular. The public must also be perceived as being fundamentally—sometimes even existentially—at odds with and perhaps even a threat to the subject. Conversely, if we accept that the public is part of who we are and become, we also need to accept that the subject is not fully transcendent and therefore also not fully in control of itself.

If one accepts and even takes as a starting point a conception of the subject as inextricably bound up with the public, the configurations of the public become very important and it is the subject's delimitations rather than the public's that are the threat. In short, if one accepts that the individual is not as free and autonomous as classic liberal theory would have it, then the chronotope need not be paranoid, at least not when it comes to the subject at its center. To make a very broad but crucial distinction among the considerable number of contradictory and often conflicting conceptions of the public sphere, we might say that this is a matter of the public as threat or as threatened.

The first approach is informed by liberal political theory. It is shaped, essentially, by the formative conception of the subject outlined in the Introduction. The individual who appears in Hobbes and Locke, says C. B. MacPherson, is on his own in the best possible way. He is the "proprietor of his own person." He owns himself and his capacities and owes "nothing to society for them" (1962, 3). The will of others is relevant only insofar as it is of interest to him. He is, in other words, characterized more by his own possession of himself and less by a relational and moral connection to the social whole. As grounds for liberalism, it becomes evident that such a conception of the individual requires that governmental interference in the life of individuals be limited. This conceptual reliance on the liberal subject has guided and influenced American history, culture, and politics in fundamental and lingering ways. The lineage of liberal and possessive individualism, in other words, balances a strong theory of the subject with a suspicious guarding of its integrity against outside influence.

For theoretical and political traditions that recognize that we are all inevitably part of a social and political context, on the other hand, and this represents the second approach, it is not the subject itself so much as the contexts and spaces in and through which it appears that need to be secured. Recognizing ourselves as part of a larger milieu—a community, a state, a globalized world—our sense of self is connected with our relative separateness and/or connectedness with it. In this context, a human subject is seen to emerge via a space in which experiences, thoughts, and knowledge are shared and negotiated: a public space. As Michael Warner puts it, "To address a public or to think of oneself as belonging to a public is to be a certain kind of person, to inhabit a certain kind of social world, to have at one's disposal certain media and genres, to be motivated by a certain normative horizon, and to speak within a certain language ideology" (2005, 10).

If the liberal individuality shaping American ideology stems from Hobbes, Locke, and MacPherson, this second tradition can be seen to develop rather from Aristotle and his idea of man as a political animal, *homo politicus*. To attribute to human beings or rather "man" or rather certain men fundamental qualities such as the capacity for moral reflection and association, the *polis*—the space in which, as Wendy Brown explains it "we realize and develop our distinctive capacities for association, speech, law, action, moral judgment, and ethics" (2015, 88)—is crucial. Those with a fundamental recognition of the subject as emerging with political life include Rousseau, who saw this as "self-sovereign through collective sovereignty" and Hegel, who saw "freedom [as] linked to equality, mutual recognition, and identification in belonging" (Brown, 95). Public space exists between and is constitutive of the individual and power and enables the sharing and conferring required to understand and negotiate the individual's position in relation to power.

The very idea that it is the job of individuals to engage with public issues—that it is not only within their capacity but also their duty as citizens—is commonly ascribed the Enlightenment project and its quite radical reevaluation of both the rights and the reason of individuals. Critique in its modern form takes shape at this point. Kant famously argued for the importance of individuals struggling against their own tendency toward self-imposed nonage—that is, the laziness and cowardice that not only prevent them from thinking for themselves but also make them susceptible to "guardians" who are more than happy to tell them what to think. People must fight against nonage, Kant insisted, and they must do so in a public manner. As functionaries in society, they must obey and follow the rules. Thinking for themselves does not mean renouncing their duties toward society in the everyday. It is equally their duty, however, to think about and express their critique of society in public. Only in this way, by public debate and, ideally new public understandings, can society advance.

Arendt, too, stresses this constitutive relation between the political subject and the public. She insists that the world can never be seen or even produced from a private position but is by nature shared, common to all, produced by plurality. The world exists in sharing our passions, thoughts, and experiences with those with whom we coexist. Plurality does not mean that the world is perceived the same by all or that it relies on a common nature. Quite the contrary, the common world relies on the public realm precisely because it is constructed by innumerable coexisting and irreconcilable perspectives for which it is difficult to devise a common denominator. In fact, "the reality of the public realm" relies on the lack of such common measurements. "For," says Arendt, "though the common world is the common meeting ground of all, those who are present have different locations in it, and the location of one can no more coincide with the location of another than the location of two objects. Being seen and being heard by others derive their significance from the fact that everybody sees and hears from a different position" 1998, 57).

A third key figure in this tradition, Habermas, sees the public sphere as central to the development of modern life in and after industrialization. The public sphere flowered, in his view, with the emergence of the middle classes in the eighteenth and nineteenth centuries. For him, famously, the public sphere exists between the state and civil society and is where citizens can critically discuss power and its effects. As such, the public sphere and the critique it facilitates are cornerstones not only of the social or the political generally but of modern democracy itself. The emergence of the public sphere in its modern form is historically determined by an educated and literary middle class, the bourgeoisie, and liberal society. The bourgeois public sphere, then, is a category "typical of an epoch" (1991, xvii); more specifically, it is "a child of the eighteenth century" (xviii). With the rise of the modern state and a civil society separated from it, the public sphere gains its modern, liberal, bourgeois, and legally institutionalized form (4). Habermas traces the development of this modern public sphere from the marketplaces, salons, coffeehouses, and art journals, as well as the world of letters, of the seventeenth and eighteenth centuries onward, and via its roles and challenges to liberals like Locke and dialectical thinkers like Hegel and Marx.

Habermas is aware that his nonetheless enormously influential conception of the public sphere arises from an idealized situation that has not quite made it through capitalism's infiltration of the state. When he wrote about the public sphere in the 1960s, it was precisely because he worried about its disappearance. Still, according to Manuel Castells, the notion of the public sphere remains "a useful intellectual construct—a way of representing the contradictory relationships between the conflictive interests of social actors, the social construction of cultural meaning, and the institutions of the state" (2008, 80). Crucially, it continues to be an important organizational principle despite its destitution. This approach, in which the concept as well as the existence of the public sphere is questioned but nonetheless regarded as a significant principle for discussion as well as political action, is a common one in post-Habermasian debates. The public sphere, says Bruce Robbins, is both impossible and necessary. It has, he argues, never really existed and as such is a phantom that haunts modern society. At the same time, Robbins says that he is one of many who share a "qualified but steadfast commitment to the concept of the public that any supporter of democracy *must* share" (1993, xii). For it to be anything more than a phantom, however, we must move away from ideals of a single public and recognize "the actual multiplicity of distinct and overlapping public discourses" (xii). This may be seen as a call to pay closer attention to precisely the chronotopic dimensions of the public sphere and the ways in which they have been and are actually instantiated.

Recent theories of the public sphere underscore how it is of vital importance to critical theory as well as democratic practices while pointing to the necessity of revising it, of making it a tool, as Nancy Fraser puts it, in "actually existing democracy in late-capitalist societies" (1990, 77). Fraser's basic account of Habermas's public sphere is simple and to the point:

> [it] designates a theatre in modern societies in which political participation is enacted through the medium of talk. It is the space in which citizens deliberate about their common affairs, hence, an institutionalized arena of discursive interaction. This arena is conceptually distinct from the state; it is a site for the production and circulation of discourses that can in principle be critical of the state. The public sphere in Habermas's sense is also conceptually distinct from the official-economy; it is not an arena of market relations but rather one of discursive relations, a theatre for debating and deliberating rather than for buying and selling. Thus, this concept of the public sphere permits us to keep in view the distinctions between state apparatuses, economic markets, and democratic associations, distinctions that are essential to democratic theory. (57)

What we discern here is the public sphere carved out and separated from the state and from market relations—an arena, a site, a sphere that allows joint but independent debate and deliberation. For the public sphere to remain useful, Fraser argues, we must first recognize that, for four main reasons, its utopian potential was never realized. First, access to political processes was not as open as would have been necessary for the public to debate them. Second, the social order did not differentiate as sharply between the state and the (newly) privatized market economy as would have been required for discursive deliberations to move beyond private financial interest. Third, "the social question" fragmented this ideal public into conflicting groups such as workers and women, undermining the notion of *a* public. Fourth, society and state became increasingly intertwined in a "welfare state mass democracy" in which critical scrutiny was largely replaced by public relations (58). According to what Fraser calls a revisionist historiography, it has also been suggested that Habermas's public sphere is not only determined by idealized, masculinist, and class-blind dimensions; it is also an ideological notion serving "to legitimate an emergent form of class rule" and, as such, is "an instrument of domination" (62).

Plenty can be and has been said to problematize the notion and centrality of the public sphere more generally. Theories have been haunted by nostalgia, Seyla Benhabib suggests—a sense that there once was a public sphere "of action and deliberation, participation and collective decision-making" but that, to the extent that it still exists at all, is now profoundly debilitated and degraded (1997, 1). Walter Lippman's 1927 study *The Phantom Public* expressed disillusionment with the viability of democratic ideals of sovereign citizens and representative democracy. John Dewey's response in *The Public and its Problems* from the same year insisted on the significance of civic participation but was also concerned with the detrimental effects on the public sphere of industrialization and modern society. Dewey asked if it still existed at all (2012, 105). Benhabib, appropriately for the present context, quotes Dewey: "If a public exists, it is surely as uncertain about its [own] whereabouts as philosophers since Hume have been about the residence and make-up of the self" (1).

The anxieties that I have noted as expressed in conceptions of the autonomous liberal subject for which the public becomes a threat are paralleled, then, by an anxiety in those who believe in the importance of such a public. Benhabib argues that "the increasingly desubstantialized carriers of the anonymous public conversation of mass societies" have generated a hiatus and that this hiatus has transformed "the regulative ideal of the public sphere into a *constitutive fiction*" (2). This hiatus and tension, she submits, creates a state of permanent anxiety in those political theoretical traditions to which the public sphere is central, as what they see as being at stake is nothing less than the viability of democracy itself (2).

Let us pause for a moment and consider the implications of these foundational theories of the public sphere for the relation—or perceived relation—between the individual subject and society. For Kant, Arendt, and Habermas, the public sphere is essential to the, necessarily conjoined, emergence of a political subject. And while Kant nursed hopes for the surfacing of constructions of such spheres and subjects as an effect as well as a cause of the Enlightenment,

Arendt and Habermas explore the increasingly tenuous nature of this relation in modernity and late modernity. Already at this point, it seems possible to see how the loss of a common world in Arendt and the deterioration of the spheres of nongoverned critical exchange in Habermas may ultimately lead to the paranoid configurations of subject and world today. In addition, public space and the public sphere have changed considerably since the 1950s—the time of Arendt's and Habermas's influential work on the public sphere. Globalization, economic developments, and technological and digital revolutions have radically altered the way we communicate with and visualize our relationship to each other. We share and negotiate experiences across multiple, often unintelligible and unintelligibly connected spaces. I will look at some of these contemporary spaces and spheres in relation to questions of power, truth, and identity in subsequent chapters.

The analyses in Chapters 2 through 4 will also bring out the concrete and chronotopic configurations of and challenges to the public sphere today. In recent decades, Kant's Enlightenment questions about what we can know and on what bases we can make judgments or act have become more clearly and blatantly relatable, not just for philosophers but also for citizens. Questions of identifying and comprehending power, truth, and identity, in other words, are not only of obvious relevance to philosophers, academics, and theorists; they are more obviously relevant to a larger and more general audience. Most are now aware of, even if we do not fully grasp, the surveillance and control mechanisms that monitor our movements and the algorithms and filter bubbles that determine what we see and hear and what others see and hear from us. But most of us are not quite clear on precisely how this affects our subject positions and our political agency. Indeed, what can we know for certain in a contemporaneity in which we have access to an endless and unceasing mass of information that we struggle to conceptualize and, crucially, that we do not necessarily have common platforms from which to appraise, understand, debate, critique?

The Covert Sphere

While the state of affairs just described is common to the connected world generally, America has its own relation to the public sphere, particularly as it pertains to questions of security. Ever since the CIA was established in 1947, Timothy Melley suggests, the U.S. government has institutionalized a strategy of public deception (2012, 3). From 1947 onward, and intensifying enormously with the war on terror, we see what is in effect a modification of the social contract. Being open about being secretive, which is an essential part of U.S. policy, relies on trading "democratic oversight for enhanced security" (7). Citizens are informed that intense work is being done in the name of security. They also "know" that much of this work would be unacceptable to them and to a general public, if not to America's legal system. The fact that much of this work remains undisclosed is therefore in part a blessing, at least seemingly foreclosing complicity and assuaging guilt. Being publicly deceived, simply put, becomes part of the social contract. This means that significant aspects of American political work, primarily security, are beyond the public sphere. Melley relies on Habermas's basic conception of this sphere "as a forum for the rational, public discussion of state policy" (2), but notes that security work is not hidden from view in the sense that the public knows nothing of it—it is rather that, in terms of content, there will be little for the public sphere to discuss. Or as then vice-president Dick Cheney put it shortly after 9/11: "A lot of what needs to be done here will have to be done quietly, without any discussion" (quoted in Jane Mayer 2009, 10).

"Quietly" does not mean that the public sphere remains quiet. Rather, the postwar public sphere has been profoundly transformed alongside the development of the national security state (Melley 2012, 33). What emerges is what Melley calls a "covert sphere" that is not, as we might think, meant to account for the sphere in which secret business is conducted. Rather, it is one in which the public *imagines* that secret business is going on. If we recognize, as does Melley, quoting Fraser, that the public sphere is where "political participation is enacted through the medium of talk," then the covert sphere is where "the public can 'discuss' or, more exactly, fantasize" about the secrets of the state. More specifically, the covert sphere, as Melley defines it, "is a cultural imaginary shaped by both institutional secrecy and public fascination with the secret work of the state" (5). The covert sphere is different from the public sphere centrally in that the latter is ideally based on rational and critical dialogue and the former is shaped by "narrative fictions" (6). These fictions—literary and visual cultural expression in its various forms—are a complex amalgamation of fantasies of secret government action and policies, reflections of "real covert actions," "strategic fictions" through which some secrets can be disclosed, and "compensatory fantasies" invented to appease critique and unease on behalf of a public who might feel bereft of their own agency (5, 25).

Via this covert sphere—defined also as "the sum of public discourse about secret government" (23)—the public comes to "half-know" about U.S. political strategies and actions. Some facts are dug up by journalists, activists, and other "aggressive guardians of the public interest"; others are intentionally exposed by the clandestine operators themselves in order to encourage public support for continued secrecy. Primarily, however, as Melley suggests, the public comes to "know" about the covert actions of its government via popular fiction (9). Much more than a source of entertainment for those interested in this type of fiction or even fiction in general, Melley argues, the covert sphere has profound political and cultural implications for American society at large. The covert sphere, in fact, has contributed to cynicism and skepticism about government as well as about historical narrative (6).

In other words, the covert sphere fills the postwar public sphere with concrete spacetimes—with narratives that take the abstract security work of the postwar public sphere and transform it into more tangible and more easily identifiable stories and persona. Creating this imaginary but more substantial layer becomes a way not only of filling an otherwise unknown sphere with concrete scenarios and characters but also of retaining a subject position endowed with knowledge and agency. What makes the covert sphere distinct in relation to a cultural imaginary more generally—indeed, what makes it a paranoid chronotope—is precisely the way it stems from and is motivated by insecurity and suspicion. It is both a way of imagining a world that is larger than the self and a way of imagining a world that is threatening to undermine it.

Melley identifies three defining features of the narratives that make up the covert sphere. First is the overwhelming predominance of white male writers and protagonists. From the Cold War onward, a sort of "rugged male agency" has been constructed in a "hypermasculine imaginary" that "remasculinizes" America to protect it from "creeping socialism," from "'leaky' forms of identity," and from "enemy 'penetration,' 'thought-control,' and subversion" (23). Second is the way it is organized around two competing anxieties—threats to the nation and threats posed by the nation itself as a security state. Either the enemy is externalized, and often racialized, in the shape of communists, immigrants, or jihadists, or it is a narcissistic and demonized symbol of the astounding power of the security state (27). Third is the prevailing sense of epistemological uncertainties. Skepticism, suspicion, even paranoia regarding what we can know and how we can know it are predominant (28). One result of these uncertainties and their direct relation to the national security state, Melley argues, is transformations in the conditions of public knowledge, marked by the increasing prevalence of skepticism as well as irrationalism. In more recent terminology, these transformations lay the groundwork for post-truth society and post-truth politics in which "large swaths of the public feel that one story is as good as another" (34).

Such suspicious dispositions and performances of mistrust can be identified as what Christopher Castiglia calls "critiquiness." Critiquiness comes with predetermined opinions and expectations that preempt if not actively prohibit alternative political possibilities. Castiglia traces the historical development of critiquiness back to the Cold War. He points out that, while the war effort on behalf of the community during the Second World War included factory work, rationing, and knitting, the industry of the Cold War required a consolidation of "affective orientations.... Along with suspicion, citizens were encouraged to feel indignation, anxiety, and self-satisfaction toward the Soviet Union and its hidden domestic agents, enemies that, shifting location continually, might be anywhere and everywhere." With help from John Lewis Gaddis's argument that the Cold War was "a war of orientations," Castiglia shows how, more than anything, civic participation came to be associated at this point not with what citizens were asked by their government to do but what they were asked to feel and think (215). This disposition remains in and reaches even more into our contemporary moment. Via Donald Pease, Castiglia argues that the replacement of communism by terrorism as an abstract enemy has perpetuated if not multiplied suspicious dispositions in America. (216). According to Pease, by positing Islamic terrorism in the position of menace if not fundamental threat to the American way of life—the world that communism previously inhabited—U.S. foreign policy has "conjoined the totalization of danger in the external realm with a reorganization of domestic civil society" (2009, 99). The reinforcement of such dispositions has allowed the government to perpetuate the war on terror and continue building the security state in the name of safety, and it has continued to encourage critiquiness as a sense of participation in the public sphere.

There are clear similarities between the disposition of critiquiness during the Cold War and the suspicious temperament of the contemporary moment. As Castiglia suggests, the resemblance between the dispositions required during the Cold War—suspicion, indignation—and the critiquiness of contemporary critique should "give us pause" (215). Both Castiglia and Pease point to a commonality in the projection of threat onto first an external and then an internal "enemy" based on a predetermined political position. These different historical contexts—the Cold War and contemporaneity—powerfully position citizens in relation to their own nation and in relation to what is seen to threaten it. An enemy is envisioned as distanced from America both geographically and ideologically, but it is also seen as continually working to infiltrate and manipulate and thereby threaten the American way. Classic Cold War novels such as Jack Finney's *Invasion of the Body Snatchers* (1954) represent this duality on the one hand by positioning the enemy as alien and on the other by portraying the way it threatens to highjack the bodies and minds of American citizens. Much of Philip K. Dick's fiction follows this basic pattern, perhaps the most famous example being *Do Androids Dream of Electric Sheep?* from 1968, not to mention its adaptation into the film *Blade Runner* in 1982 in which replicants and humans are increasingly difficult to tell apart. The enemy is thus emphatically external and at the same time threatening to what is often seen as the most American, and thus the most internal feature—the autonomy and freedom of the individual subject.

The critiquiness that Castiglia and Pease describe emerges from and makes visible a paranoid chronotope in American politics, the primary characteristic of which is the continuity of spatial configuration. Despite, or perhaps because of, the escalating complexity of the world spanning the 1950s to the present, the continuity of a rather simple configuration is worth noting: An enemy stemming from an alien space, geographically and ideologically but always also potentially close, necessitates constant vigilance and security measures whose own threats to freedom are secondary. The more directly temporal dimension of this paranoid chronotope is the way in which it always places individual freedom in the future. During the Cold War as well as in the present, and because the disposition of critiquiness positions citizens as anxious and suspicious of an external threat, citizens are expected to accept escalating encroachments on their civil rights, increasing surveillance, and a perpetuation of a state of exception in the name of security. To bring shape to the paranoid chronotopic dimension of this more clearly, to the ideologically dominant conception of reality in which Americans are free citizens in the greatest democracy in the world, these citizens are expected to add another conflicting conception of reality that stipulates their freedom and democracy be put on hold.

The balancing of these disjunctive levels of reality is further aggravated by what Emily Apter sees as the "conspiratorial logic of supranational oneworldedness," narrative articulations of which she discovers in literary authors such as Thomas Pynchon, Don DeLillo, and Philip Roth (Apter 2006, 367); in films such as *The Manchurian Candidate* (1962), *The Parallax View* (1974), and *All the President's Men* (1976) (368); and in American public and political spheres more generally. According to this logic, American citizens are encouraged to connect some dots but not others:

> We have been exhorted by Washington to connect the dots, to posit connections between weapons of mass destruction in Iraq and the World Trade Center attacks, to see "shadowy" global networks of jihadists masking themselves as ordinary citizens, to upgrade Palestinian terrorist groups to the status of international terrorism, or to decipher what Richard A. Clarke called a "worldwide political conspiracy masquerading as a religious sect" (quoted in Raban, 24). In this scheme, what we are told *is* connected is rivaled only by what we are asked to believe is *not* connected: there is apparently *no* link between oil and the Iraq invasion, *no* coincidence between electioneering politics and war, *no* cause-effect relationship between the media-hyped epistemology of insecurity and the abrogation of civil liberties, *no* common thread of sadism between Iraqi and US treatment of prisoners at Abu Ghraib. This logic of non-connectivity condemns *you* as a paranoid if you suspect that the case for war is less than solid, and doubts *your* credibility if you fail to see that only when it comes to terrorism are all the dots connected. (369)

In other words, Americans are encouraged to see and not see at the same time. What we observe here is the disjunctive doubling of two spatiotemporal logics: a paranoid chronotope.

There is a sense in which the concept of the chronotope itself stems from a disjunctive relation. As I noted in the Introduction, the Kantian underpinning of Bakhtin's concept of the chronotope lies in the recognition of time and space as crucial categories of perception as well as cognition. For Kant, this understanding stemmed from his then revolutionary epistemological claim that we cannot have knowledge about things in themselves but can only perceive them as representations, representations that are themselves shaped by concepts and intuitions coming from the outside world. A gap is thus introduced, one that separates mind and world. Radically, as Holquist observes, Kant thereby also recognized a split in the subject—between the perceiving, "empirical I" and "a 'transcendental I' that is able to organize such responses into a coherent mental representation on the basis of which the mind can then make judgments." Making judgments "is how Kant defined thinking, the action of understanding"

(2010, 22). Because this thinking is inescapably co-constituted by the outside world, it is constitutively contingent on it. The subject, as we have seen, becomes such in and of a public sphere.

In Bakhtin's ambition to investigate the historical and formal conditions that shape both the individual subject's conception of the world and the world's conception of the individual subject, the concrete configuration of such conditions becomes crucial. Building the chronotope on recognition of the co-constitution of the I and the world, Bakhtin rejects Kant's understanding of space and time as transcendental forms and suggests instead that these are "forms of the most immediate reality" (1981, 85n.). As Holquist explains it, "the site we occupy in being is not merely a site we occupy in space and time, but a *task*, the obligation to forge relations within ourselves and with the world we live in that will keep all the separate elements from devolving into chaos" (2010, 25). I rely on Kant's gap between mind and world, but I also emphasize the exposedness of the split I to particular and evolving spatiotemporal conditions. Thus, I see Bakhtin's chronotope as already potentially disjunctive. But the chronotope that Bakhtin accounts for, developed as it is to recognize forms and genres, is geared largely toward identifying historical but singular and material spacetime configurations. It is also underwritten, according to Holquist, by remaining with and insisting on this divided subject (rather than denying it and striving toward a new unity, as did the German idealists) (25). The chronotope is "an instrument for calibrating existence," calibration being understood here in a technical sense as "to adjust experimental results, to take external factors into account or to allow comparison with other data" (31). In this sense, the gap between mind and world that the chronotope takes off from receives attention not so much in terms of an imbalance or anxiety but mainly in the ways in which this relation is configured and (albeit temporarily) stabilized by differing spatiotemporal relations.

But how do we forge relations within ourselves and with the world—how do we "think" or "make judgments" and affirm the divided self when the public sphere is not just full of inevitable inconsistencies but actively functioning according to mutually incompatible or even hostile logics? In the late twentieth century and early twenty-first, paranoid chronotopes at least seemingly helped stabilize this relation. The paranoid chronotope of the American public sphere, as I have begun to show, allows the combination of an entire set of irreconcilable truths. To begin with, there is the circumscription of individual freedom in the name of freedom. Only by means of twenty-four-hour surveillance can we ensure your freedom, only by means of collecting all your data can we ensure data security, and so on. Then there is the already noted construction of one map that should be believed and one that should not. Between some dots, causal connection is endorsed; between others, it is repudiated. The organization of everyday life in the twenty-first century, which is increasingly shaped by surveillance and security, takes place in the shadow of a set of "truths" that only the "wrong" sort of paranoids would question. Finally, and inversely as well as ironically, this paranoid chronotope helps maintain a sense of liberal individuality in the face of all encroachments upon it. Here we come back to critiquiness and to the alluring simplicity of paranoia. Only by stabilizing these conflictual dimensions by means of a paranoid chronotope—that is, only by identifying, fleshing out, and producing a world around a set of particular and preferably external and coherently evil enemies—is it possible to retain this otherwise impossible configuration of a free subject in highly governed times.

Critique

Clearly at stake are the practices of interpretation, critical thinking, and critique. That our confidence in such practices is unsettled today is less than surprising when we consider how the multiplication and polarization of spheres, the affect economies and troll factories, the demise of facts and truth as major players in political discourse, and so on, complicate the conditions for as well as the status of subjects involved in critical discourse. Unfortunately, however, these practices have not only lost some of their standing but have come under heavy barrage from several directions at once. First, we have witnessed a critique of critique emerging from within the field of critique itself. Many scholars in the humanities are questioning the function of critique in contemporary society. Second, the neoliberalization of the public sphere in general and the university in particular aggravates the possibilities of critique. Third, we are witnessing a right-wing identitarianism increasingly and harshly attacking what it tends to see as the left-wing elitism of humanities research. I will address these three contexts in the course of this book. In what remains of the present chapter, I introduce the first one.

Both crisis and the tendency toward self-criticism are virtually characteristic of critique historically, but one feature stands out in this most recent version, which is often labeled "postcritique." This is critique's materialization out of a distinctly American academic context. Many find the first concomitant formulations of critique and its crisis as evolving with Kant's articulations of the Enlightenment in the eighteenth century and in key references in the subsequent history of critique, including Matthew Arnold's in the nineteenth century and Walter Benjamin's in twentieth. These central moments of critique as well as crises arise, then, from an historical and distinctly European context. In the twenty-first century, however, the crisis seems to be surfacing mainly in and relating to America in general and American academia in particular. More specifically still, it emerges primarily from university literature departments.

Centrally geared against the forms of suspicious reading that have shaped many interpretative practices in the humanities for the past fifty years or so, this most recent crisis somewhat ironically but perhaps also somewhat symptomatically takes the form of a new suspicion. A central target of this new suspicion is Paul Ricoeur's hermeneutics of suspicion, as articulated in his book *Freud and Philosophy: An Essay on Interpretation* (1970) via a synthesis of the writings of Friedrich Nietzsche, Sigmund Freud, and Karl Marx. More precisely, the target is the major influence such hermeneutics have had on ways of reading and interpreting texts in American universities. But it is also geared toward the "moods and methods" of suspicion more generally, according to Rita Felski: the symptomatic reading developed by Louis Althusser, Fredric Jameson, and others, New Historicist readings influenced by Michel Foucault and others, and theoretical schools such as postcolonial and queer theory. These diverse methods and theories are identified by Felski as "an orientation in the phenomenological sense, a constellation of attitudes and beliefs that expresses itself in a particular manner of approaching one's object" (2015, 21).

The new suspicion is geared not only toward our ways of understanding and interpreting contemporaneity but also toward what these understandings and interpretations themselves will do and may have done to the world. Repeatedly expressed is a concern that critique has contributed to the bleak status of facts and knowledge and to the polarized and paranoid climate of the public sphere in the present moment. Bruno Latour is frequently taken as a symptomatic instance of "the loss of confidence in the very gesture of critique" (Noys, 2011, n.p.). In his famous 2004 *Critical Inquiry* article "Why has Critique Run out of Steam? From Matters of Fact to Matters of Concern," he argues that critique as we have known it has become superfluous and has proven downright dangerous. Critique prevents us from dealing with present, pressing matters such as, most essentially, climate change. Critique has been adopted by our enemies and has helped them dismantle the world. Critique has infected the relationship of people in society and the humanities. Critique has added deconstruction to destruction, added ruins to ruins, "even more smoke to the smoke" (225, 228).

In itself it is unsurprising that critics feel required to interrogate their own function against real and concrete threats such as the increasing peril of democratic values, the dwindling role of truth and facts, and the deteriorating integrity of political discourse. So far, however, the crisis has been a pronounced need to revisit, reconsider, and perhaps also reject modes of critique and ways of reading as they have been practiced primarily in the humanities from the 1970s onward. Reasons given for revisiting, reconsidering, and possibly rejecting critique today include the fear that it has contributed to the dismantling of truth and facts as central bearers of society as we see it today, that it is no longer doing the political work its early proponents thought it would, that it has contributed to a destructive mood in literary studies, and that it has exacerbated the undoing of humanities departments and research.

As I will show in the critique sections of Chapters 2 through 4, the articulated crisis in critique partly misses the mark when turning back on itself. More specifically, and as I will further develop in later chapters, the crisis results at least in part from a paranoid configuration of the complex relations between intellectual work, digital communications, and neoliberalism in America in past decades. Distinctions between private and public, between experts and opinion makers, between liberal education and training, between education and profit making have become increasingly hard to maintain in a society shaped both by groundbreaking changes in forms and channels of communication and by neoliberal principles. This is true of society at large. and, as we will see later, these progressively fluid borders generate paranoia on many levels. Discourses on postcritique suffer, I will show, from such muddled distinctions between private and public, between experts and opinion makers, between education and training. Pointing to the close links between what American scholars call critique and what they also call "Theory" or "French Theory," as well as to the relative disconnect of this critique from a tradition of critique formulated in the Kantian Enlightenment and European twentieth-century traditions, I will show that what these latter traditions emphasize, but what is curiously absent from the former, is a recognition and problematization of the fundamental significance and nature of the public sphere.

The critique sections in Chapters 2 through 4 in different ways develop and bring together discussions of the public sphere with current debates on postcritique. By linking postcritique to the problematics of power, truth, and identity, as they are addressed in each chapter, and to the larger configurations of the public sphere via neoliberalism and technology, I am able to position it in larger cultural, societal, and political challenges in a different way from how it has tended to do itself. At least if we follow the Kantian and Habermasian traditions, critique and the public sphere are inseparable. In this sense, and in light of a reconfigured and heavily diminished public sphere, the postcritics are right—we are indeed facing a crisis. But does this not also suggest that it is highly problematic to discuss the crisis of critique without also acknowledging and engaging with the crisis of the public sphere? Little attention has been given to this development from those dealing explicitly with postcritique debates in the literary context, however. In fact, there is a marked absence of such discussions. Thus, while contemporary debates on postcritique do follow squarely in critique's tradition of self-reflexivity—in this sense, postcritique can be placed squarely within critique rather than beyond it—they tend not to interrogate their own conditions that relate to the conditions of critique when it comes to the current state of the public sphere.

Contemporary debates on critique, while expressly aiming to take the world around them seriously, seem intriguingly uninterested in the economic and political conditions surrounding them. In fact, inadvertently incorporating neoliberalism's insistence on productivity, reinvention, immediate relevance, and individual responsibility, postcritique tends to neglect what I see as one of its fundamental problems—how neoliberalization of public space in general and of the university as a space for critical thinking in particular threatens to undermine the very conditions of critique. In other words, I, too, believe that there is a crisis in critique, but I suggest that it emerges for different reasons and therefore needs to be articulated otherwise; that another response is necessary.

It seems crucial that the revisiting and renegotiation of critique be linked to an awareness and critical analysis of the status and effects of the spaces where critique and society meet—that is, to the public sphere generally and in America the university specifically. For this to be possible, we need tools to interrogate the relation between the logics of the new public sphere and the continual configuration of opinions and emotions central to neoliberal power. Postcritique in its American instantiations, as I will show, is shaped by distinct, rather narrow spatiotemporal conditions. Examining these conditions in relation to the larger spatiotemporal conditions of neoliberal contemporaneity and its configuration of the public sphere makes apparent a disjunctive doubling not dissimilar to what I described in the Introduction as represented in the fictional universes of

Dick, Pynchon, Gibson, and DeLillo. What my analysis will elucidate, then, is a chafing logic between critique as it has been articulated primarily by American literary scholars on the one hand and the conditions and effects of neoliberalism and the new public sphere on the other. In the critique section of Chapter 4, I will articulate this in terms of the paranoid chronotope of critique.

2

POWER AND PARANOIA / PARANOID POWERS

Introduction

Regardless of how the relation between individuals and their environment is posited or imagined—and this relation will clearly vary across different cultural, religious, philosophical, and political convictions and conventions—it seems a neutral suggestion that any conception of the individual subject relies on how the relation between the individual and its surroundings is conceived. This conception takes place within an individual consciousness, but it is also inevitably and influentially filtered via transindividual spaces, crossing and connecting social, cultural, and political spheres in which relations between the individual and the larger forces of society and the world are explicated, consolidated, and negotiated. Today, and whoever we are, however well aware, and whatever our political convictions, we all unremittingly live in and negotiate the implications of information, surveillance, security, control society. The increasing difficulties in identifying the locus of power that these configurations have entailed generate uncertainties at best and full-blown paranoia at worst.

This chapter outlines and discusses shifting modes of power in terms of discipline, control, and neoliberalism. Acknowledging the sense of a decreasing visibility of power structures expressed in society and fiction alike, it illuminates the chronotopic dimensions of these configurations of power in the hope that this will help specify and explain the increasing difficulties subjects have in recognizing power as well as their difficulties in accounting for and representing it culturally. A first section on power and society is thus followed by one that reads Dave Eggers's *Your Fathers, Where are They? And the Prophets, Do They Live Forever?* Quite explicitly showing entanglements of power and the novel form, Eggers's novel helps us understand a paranoia emerging from the challenges of understanding as well as representing contemporary power. The final section of the chapter identifies this reading as based on a hermeneutics of suspicion and thus resumes the question of critique. It tries to identify the specifics of critique as it has been articulated in postcritique and to show how the latter is informed by a very specific American academic context that has its own problematic relation with the public sphere.

Section 1: Power, Paranoia, Society

Introduction

There is nothing new about an American paranoid mindset. Indeed, according to Richard Hofstadter's influential take on American history and culture, the "paranoid style" is part and parcel of the very mentality of American culture all the way back to its seventeenth-century formations. The paranoid mindset or style or "frame of mind" is recurrently about "a conspiracy against a way of life" (2008, 19). In Hofstadter's 1950s contemporaneity, this conspiracy is, of course, seen as a communist one. He identifies three key elements of the contemporary paranoid imagination: first, a conspiracy, beginning already with the introduction of the federal income tax in 1913 and peaking with Roosevelt's New Deal in the 1930s, to emasculate free capitalism and lay the groundwork for socialist or communist rule; second, the infiltration of top government by communists craftily maneuvering to dump national interests; and, third, infiltration of communist agents (much like Jesuit agents before them) into education, the press, mass media, and so on, with the aim of paralyzing American resistance (25). Since Hofstadter, the list is long of the people or groups that have been identified as constituting a threat to American individuals of a certain, dominant kind. African Americans, feminists, homosexuals, Muslims, Mexicans, immigrants, elites, deep state agents, and of course George Soros, have all been identified as conspiring against what are seen as core American beliefs and values.

In the twenty-first century West, the shape of power has become more difficult to discern and the borders of individual knowledge, agency, and rationality are under constant pressure from algorithms, data management, and neoliberal quantifications, as well as affective economies. Who are we under such conditions? What constitutes a liberal subject? The emergence and effects of the rapid economic and technological development that America has itself strongly contributed to—information society, surveillance society, security society, control society, whatever we want to call it—in some ways seem to conspire against the very beliefs and values from which such advancements have been born—freedom, productivity, progress. Surveillance and control mechanisms, the digitization of knowledge, the transformation of communication technologies, and neoliberal rationalization of human and nonhuman life do threaten to undermine conceptions of the autonomous subject that sit at the very core of American culture. These threats are harder to identify and pin down than the specific ideologies or identities seen to threaten American individualism in earlier periods: communists, a threat to the free market; homosexuals, a threat to conservative Christianity; independent women, a threat to traditional family values. What is more, the very acknowledgment of the effects of control, security, surveillance, and capitalization mechanisms on individuals come with profound implications for conceptions of the individual as a free subject in possession of itself, its thoughts, and its capacities that is so central to the American "way of life" in the first place.

The disjunction between lingering beliefs in certain liberal conceptions of the autonomous individual and the realization that we are being controlled and regulated in ways that we struggle to account for is, as I began to note in the Introduction, quite usefully captured by Timothy Melley's conception of agency panic. Agency panic is an "intense anxiety about an apparent loss of autonomy or self-control—the conviction that one's actions are being controlled by someone else, that one has been 'constructed' by powerful external agents" (2000, 12). For Melley, agency panic has two main characteristics: it speaks to an anxiety about the cause of one's own actions, and it takes shape through the attribution of agency and intentionality to nonpersonal agencies and entities (12). Conspiracy and paranoia provide "an odd sort of comfort" to such panic, as they become a means for individuals to comprehend a virtually incomprehensible system while warding off threats to the integrity of the self (8). Already Hofstadter saw this mechanism as he traced his paranoid style through the history of American politics, but Melley points specifically to the upsurge of paranoia and conspiracy theory in a postwar context in which mass control became possible to imagine alongside technological progress. This period, he argues, saw a shift in how political power and conspiracy were envisioned, from being a matter of private messages from distant places to being enabled by mass communication on home ground. The possibility of mass control or, more specifically, the notion that individuals can be made subject to and manipulated by mass control, implies that individual autonomy is perhaps not as strong as American ideology has maintained (3). Agency panic, then, is essentially the conflictual realization that social relations and communications affect individual agency and autonomy combined with a continued insistence on such agency and autonomy (14). Of course, the levels and intricacies of social relations and communications have continued to develop enormously in the two decades since Melley made this observation.

Melley also observes how theoretical engagements with power, language, and subjectivity during the latter parts of the twentieth century by theorists such as Jacques Derrida and Michel Foucault tended to relocate agency from the autonomous individual subject to discursive or social systems. Such moves, he suggests, in themselves provoked agency panic in vehement defenders of the liberal subject insofar as they perceived this as a dichotomy, or an "all-or-nothing" relation between human agency and power (40). In identifying power as existing everywhere, Foucault does not give it subjective agency exactly, but, Melley insists, in imputing to it tactics and strategies and "aims and objectives," power seems to gain "the rhetoric of subjectivity, as if it constituted a higher form of consciousness, a 'Them'" (101). Theories of this kind may themselves have contributed to agency panic, Melley and others have proposed, and I interrogate this possibility in terms of fictional wrestling with such theories in self-conscious paranoid fiction and also to some extent when looking at ways in which critique and postcritique negotiate such tensions. At the same time, I want to examine the underlying power structures actually interrogated by Foucault's theories to understand not how these theories but how the configurations of power they identify may have given rise to a more general sense of paranoia in society at large. I want to shed light on this tension between the sense of autonomous individual agency characteristic, if not constitutive, of American culture and increasingly intangible political control. More precisely, in what follows I explore how shifting relations between discipline and control from the 1950s to the present have generated paranoia on a societal level.

The changing—but, crucially, also coexisting—techniques of power during this period are in central ways about shifting modes of organizing space and time. It is therefore quite useful to outline conceptions and perceptions of discipline and control as different and, to some extent differing, chronotopes. Envisioned as chronotopes, it is easier to see the mechanisms upon which they rely and also, more precisely, to see why the one is harder to grasp than the other. A preliminary and preemptive account indicates that, whereas the chronotope of disciplinarity relies on a temporally successive and long-term construction of individuals in organized and tangible space, the chronotope of control works according to nonlinear, fast, and fluctuating temporalities in discontinuous and largely imperceptible spaces. Developing this reading, I will suggest not only that the chronotope of control is less visible and less tangible than its predecessor but also that the centrality of the disciplinary chronotope to modern Western culture—as seen not least in the analysis of the novel later in this chapter—contributes to this poor visibility. The result takes us back to Melley's agency panic and to what Wendy Brown identifies as an intensification and perversion of liberalism and neoliberalism in the twenty-first century (2019). I briefly expand on Melley's and Brown's explanatory models by rearticulating and recognizing these parallel and interlinked developments as emerging from a disjunction between the older and more identifiable disciplinary techniques of power and our reluctant and ill-equipped recognition of more diffused and pre-emptive techniques of control. The result is a paranoid chronotope of power.

The Chronotope of Discipline

Foucault famously outlines three forms of power—sovereignty, discipline, and security—sketching their historical development while also stressing their coexistence. Recognizing differences between these forms of power with the help of the chronotope elucidates what is ultimately the pivotal questions of this chapter: What is the relation between individuals and power, how is it imagined by individuals, and what kind of paranoia does it have the potential to generate? Chronotopically, one might say that sovereign societies, associated mostly with pre-eighteenth-century governing, establish a spatiotemporal relation between subservient subjects and a centralized, highly visible, even spectacular, power. Sovereignty, represented as religious, feudal, and royal power, centers on the importance of hierarchy. The spectacular, territorial power techniques of these earlier modes are gradually replaced by more discreet, continuous techniques centering not so much on deterrent and formidable displays of power as on the more subtle molding of subjects. The chronotopic dimensions of discipline—associated, rather, with modernity—structure space less by hierarchy and more by lateral division, a distribution of elements, an institutionalization and individualization of multiplicities (Foucault 2007, 12, 20). Or, as Gilles Deleuze says, "Power is no longer the right to make perish"; rather, it "organizes and compels production and multiplies what is produced through its gridding, its organization, power no longer makes die; it takes as its aim the management and control of life" (1985b, 15). In this new "age of governmental reason," government becomes internalized to itself, to society, and to subjects. Put differently, what this "age of critical governmental reason" establishes is a system in which everyone, at least theoretically, has equal rights and is equally accountable. Notably, this accountability is not based on religious beliefs, feudal power, or sovereign legitimacy but on an internal logic of the political system itself. This is essentially a system emerging from a notion of equal rights as systemized by the writings and responses to Thomas Paine via various constellations of Rousseau, Locke, Hobbes, and Bentham.

As power is configured in relation not to external hierarchical sovereignty but to internal regulations, as Foucault explains it, governmental practices cease to be moral and become exclusively practical. The freedom of individuals and markets must be secured, but at the same time individuals and markets must be protected from the interests of others. Liberalism, Foucault suggests, thus consumes as well as produces the manifold freedoms of the individual, of expression, of the market (2008, 63). In this way, it displays a paradoxical but foundational interconnectivity between freedom and control. A subject in and of this logic develops a rationality of negotiating between the limits agreed upon in the societal contract and the possibilities and freedoms that the contract leaves open. At the same time, a new regime of truth surfaces, one in which truth is associated less with God or the King or the Law and more with the market. We will return to this in the next chapter.

Discipline, then, perhaps recognized as the dark underbelly of liberalism, constructs individuals and identities in order to ascertain the freedom necessary for liberal democracy. The subject of rights, according to Foucault, is enabled via a contractual negotiation through which its liberty is possible by the very same means that limit it. The individual is subjected to correction and training by institutions but it also has, at least in theory, the possibility of renegotiating, or even overthrowing, the terms according to which these power relations are constructed.

Chronotopically, a key distinction between sovereignty and disciplinarity is that sovereign societies establish a spatiotemporal relation between obedient subjects and a centralized and manifestly visible power, whereas disciplinary modes work "to distribute in space; to order in time; to compose a productive force within the dimension of space-time whose effect will be greater than the sum of its component forces" (Deleuze 1992a: 3). In this sense, the disciplinary chronotope of power is more discreet than its predecessor. Individuals are divided and constructed in relation to distributed modalities of power. With discipline, in other words, power is not over there, in the tower, in the castle, in the church, but in here, on every level of an individual life. At the same time, spatial control becomes central as discipline works to organize space via "hierarchal and functional distribution of elements" (Foucault 2007: 20). What can be seen, said, and known is organized via relatively tangible players and components: institutions, identities, and individual bodies and subjects. Centrally, for clarification of the role of the individual in the chronotope, the disciplinary chronotope binds the regime of enunciation to identifiable institutions and the construction of a delineable subject. Subjects of discourse are constructed, a process linked, of course, to the lines of subjectification. The production of subjectivity is shaped, under discipline, by the modes of enunciation available via fairly perceptible actors in society.

Foucault locates disciplinary power as particularly characteristic of the period from the seventeenth century to its ultimate heights in the first half of the twentieth, followed by a marked demise alongside the rise of security and control after the Second World War. In an American context, discipline is frequently associated with Fordism and thus with the early and middle decades of the twentieth century. As an economic program, Nancy Fraser suggests, Fordism came along with, was embedded in, and was dependent upon a much broader set of mechanisms: "a facilitating shell of social, cultural, and political arrangements" (2003, 161). Not just factories but also hospitals, prisons, schools, welfare agencies, and families generated a form of governmentality that trained and organized individuals in a national context. The totalizing ambitions of Fordism as a project intent on "rationalizing all major aspects of social life" constitute one key similarity to discipline; a second one is the technology of self-regulation in everyday life. Coercive modes of power are replaced by the production of subjects well trained to self-regulate. A third defining feature, the national focus of discipline, is also present, but here Fraser emphasizes a difference, not in the precedence of the national itself but in the way disciplinary agencies that have been largely state run in France, have been nongovernment in America (164). In other words, while disciplinary power tends to be associated with state-run and government agencies in Europe, its American variants have emerged to a larger extent from corporations. Michael Hardt and

Antonio Negri see the New Deal of the 1930s as producing "the highest form of *disciplinary* government" in an American context:

> When we speak of disciplinary government, we are not referring simply to the juridical and political forms that organize it. We are referring primarily to the fact that in a disciplinary society, the entire society, with all its productive and reproductive articulations, is subsumed under the command of capital and the state, and that the society tends, gradually but with unstoppable continuity, to be ruled solely by criteria of capitalist production. *A disciplinary society is thus a factory-society.* (2000, 242)

Hardt and Negri's description, while pointing to the centrality of state power also in America, further underscores the capitalist and production-based nature of disciplinary power in this context.

Looking at these techniques of power via what Foucault and Deleuze call the *dispositif* illuminates their implications for the visibility of power. A *dispositif*—often translated as "apparatus"—maps the constituents and coordinates of power while acknowledging that they are always temporary. In other words, it constitutes a way of accounting for the specific assemblage of techniques of power at any one time. Deleuze identifies the lines of the Foucauldian *dispositif*: visibility, enunciation, force, subjectification, and, finally, fracture. The first he describes in terms of a structuring of lines of light—the way it falls and is allowed to fall, making certain elements visible or invisible but also, via this process, stimulating the birth of some aspects while allowing others to perish (1992b, 160). Seeing, as Deleuze puts it in his first Foucault seminar, "is not a behavior among other behaviors, it is the condition for any mindset in a period" (1985a, 5). The second line pertains to the limits and possibilities of enunciation. Multiple regimes of enunciation—for example, science, law, a literary genre—determine what can be said and, perhaps even more crucially, how it can be said at any one time (1992b, 160). Speaking, according to Deleuze, "is not an expression of the mindset" but is "a condition for the mindset in a period" (1985a, 5). Deleuze identifies these first two, seeing and speaking, as central, "as if each period defines itself above all by what it sees and makes seen and by what it says" (5). Lines of force are the dimensions of power internal and variable to the apparatus out of knowledge. They pass through the apparatus connecting seeing and speaking in various ways. The lines of subjectification are the limitations and possibilities of the production of subjectivity specific to the apparatus. They arise from what Deleuze calls "a sort of surplus-value" that has the potential of escape (1992b: 161). These lines push the boundaries of the *dispositif*, repeatedly "tracing paths of creation" until the apparatus breaks down. Thus they also pave the way for the lines of fracture, which form the potential for a new *dispositif*. The various lines also group into two lines that are different in kind: lines of stratification and lines of creation. These make it possible, indeed necessary, to distinguish between "what we are (what we are already no longer) and what we are in the process of becoming" (164).

Considering the lines of the *dispositif* of discipline—its visibility, enunciation, force, subjectification, and fracture—in terms of a chronotope demonstrates how there is at least in theory the possibility of identifying and culturally integrating disciplinary processes and the sources and entities enabling them in cultural representations of space and time. The subject moves from one space to another—from the family to the school to the army to the factory—and although subjectification ensures that power is internalized in its very being, this is still a spatiotemporal construction of power that is quite recognizable, and representable, as such. The regime of enunciation is bound up more directly with these spaces. In a factory society, Hardt and Negri say, "productive subjectivities are forged as one-dimensional functions of economic development" (243). Discipline, as Deleuze reminds us, is analogue: it relies on spatiotemporal continuous transmission, and its power is transmitted via analogous spaces.

The lines of creation are possible exactly for this reason—although the subject cannot be separated from its own construction, it still has the potential, not least because of the lines of visibility also characterizing this *dispositif*, of identifying and widening the fractures of this same *dispositif*; the identification of power, of potential resistance. Indeed, disciplinary power is a regime that, when "pushed to its highest level and most complete application" is also "revealed as the extreme limit of a social arrangement," thus making resistance possible (Hardt and Negri 2000, 243). In the chronotope of discipline, then, individuals have reason to ponder the nature and extent of their autonomy as subjects. But they are also still positioned in relatively clear relation to the spatiotemporal arrangements of power that constitute them. Some light still falls, as Deleuze might say, on the power mechanisms themselves.

The Chronotope of Control

After the Second World War, the continuous evolution of disciplinary power accelerated. Foucault theorizes this further dissemination of power in terms of "security"; Deleuze sees it in terms of control. This is of course not a clean break or a directly comparable relation—techniques of power coexist and overlap—but during this period, fast-developing technologies and neoliberal agendas paved the way for more adaptable arrangements. As Deleuze puts it, "as soon as there is a variation in the statement regime and the fields of visibility, you can say: we are entering another historical formation" (1985a, 18). In chronotopic terms, we see that security centers on a much more fluid and flexible spatiality than does discipline. Rather than distributing and training subjects via preorganized spaces, it centers on a milieu capable of regulating possible and unpredictable events and elements "within a multivalent and transformable framework" (Foucault 2007, 20). Apart from a more distributed spatiality, then, security also comes with new ways of negotiating and preempting temporality and uncertainty (20). Deleuze, building on Foucault, recognizes that the more spatially organized power of molding disciplinary subjects is replaced by incessant and fluctuating modulations. Rather than the training of individuals under discipline, control functions via the continuous, disseminated, and fragmented capture of "dividual" components and, in the neoliberal logic, with the individual as enterprise. This makes neither the source of nor the resistance to power easy to pin down. The chronotope of power has become less stable and solid.

Fraser shows how each of the three main features of Fordism she identifies and associates with discipline—its totalizing ambitions, its technologies of self-regulation, and its national qualities—changed in a post-Fordist context. In terms of social regulation, we are now working with a vanishing distinction between nonmarketized and capitalist regimes. In this "de-statized governmentality," social regulation is more privatized and more dispersed. In terms of the subjectifying and individualizing logic of disciplinarity, this too is disappearing as a control mechanism. A post-Fordist subject is neither "the Victorian subject of individualizing normalization nor the Fordist subject of collective welfare" (168). Rather, the post-Fordist subject is one supposed to self-realize by means of self-investment. An important difference here is that the universalizing ambitions of the Foucauldian counterpart, perhaps captured better in terms of his theories of biopower and populations, are replaced by "a new kind of segmented governmentality" where those in a position to self-invest remain in tracks of efficiency and risk prevention while others are subjected to "brute repression" (169). The third difference between Fordist disciplinarity and post-Fordist "flexibilization," as Fraser calls it, is the national context, which can no longer be maintained in a global present. Governmentality becomes transnational, broken up locally, nationally, and globally in terms of functions, agencies, and entities that are no longer nation or state centered (168). Notably, this is not about a decline in state sovereignty but about fostering government practices that rely on individual responsibility and privatized risk management, and that encourage the extension of market forces and entrepreneurial models into many and diverse social domains (Lemke 2012, 84). It is, as Thomas Lemke, says, "not a diminishment or reduction of state sovereignty and planning capacities but a displacement from formal to informal techniques of government" (2012, 84).

The chronotope of control, then, allows for a multiplication and diversification of regimes of enunciation. This type of power has nothing to gain from delimitation and normation. On the contrary, lines of force function to proliferate rather than demarcate subjective interest. In place of the training and disciplining of subjects in accordance with preset norms and in line with stipulated spatiotemporal structures, normalization under security adopts a more flexible and fluctuating conception of norms based on whatever works whenever—that is, what is most advantageous under any given circumstance. "Just-in-time" capitalism informs not just production lines but every level of existence as we become also just-in-time subjects—called for and made to fit particular and temporary contexts rather than ascribing to longer and more stable continuities. The subjectification processes in this logic take place not by controlling individuals so much as by controlling environments; it is not the individual so much as a multiplication of sources of enterprise, affect, and desire that is constructed; it is not individuals of society so much as "dividuals" of the market that are of interest. Increasingly, and in the place of more long-standing political convictions and social norms, what citizens "feel" or how they react to information itself becomes a great resource for economic gain and political power. In the chronotope of control, in other words, power is more directly and fluidly incorporated into events themselves.

In the chronotope of control, and to continue thinking in terms of the *dispositif*, one might say that the light falls everywhere but also nowhere in particular. According to Jeffrey T. Nealon, in the face of disembodied control exercised via browsers, bankcards, credit reports, and DNA, a panoptic surveillance relying on more concrete objects—photographs, surveillance tapes, and the like—appears "positively quaint" (2008, 68). In fact, the developments are fast enough to make some of Nealon's examples from 2008 themselves seem quaint. How do we know what we are looking for, or even looking at, when power resides less in institutions and the individuals emerging from them and more in the algorithms, data management, and surveillance systems that now inform if not shape everything we do? Both the spatial and the temporal dimensions of the chronotope have changed quite radically. Where disciplinary techniques produce molds, "distinct castings," or "individuals as a single body," control relies on modulation "like a self-deforming cast that will continuously change from one moment to the other, or like a sieve whose mesh will transmute from point to point" (Deleuze 1992a, 4). There is no beginning or ending in control, you are never, as Deleuze puts it "finished with anything" (5); you are perpetually "in orbit, in a continuous network" (6). Or as Luciana Parisi puts it, under control our spatiotemporalities have been "glue[d] together" into "uninterrupted relationality" (2013, 102).

Chronotopically, and like the key difference between sovereignty and disciplinarity outlined previously, a key difference between disciplinarity and control is a continued and accelerated distribution of power in space and time. The chronotope of power almost seems to be disintegrating: lines of visibility, enunciation, force, subjectification, and fracture disseminate beyond the boundaries of concrete spacetime and beyond the boundaries of perception and cognition. Today, according to James Bridle, the entire world has become "code/space" and its ubiquity actually prevents us from comprehending it, from understanding its impact on our sociality and even our ways of thinking (2018, 38). For Bridle, computation reconfigures our social lives, alters our way of moving in space, reforms our understanding of time, refashions our cognition, "*becomes* culture" (39–44). But of course the chronotope of power has not and cannot vanish. It has just become even more difficult to discern. And, as I said earlier, it is hard to see not only because it is infinitesimal and disseminated but also because, I will argue, it is overshadowed by the lingering and formative influence of the chronotope of discipline. Importantly, this disjunction between current mechanisms of power and power's culturally embedded conceptions means not only that power has become less visible but also that we as subjects have become less visible to ourselves.

The Chronotope of Contemporary Power

What we see of security and control in the twenty-first century fits well with while far surpassing Foucault's and Deleuze's descriptions in and of the second part of the twentieth century. Already Deleuze had observed that the computer is significant to control, but what it can do—its "passive danger is jamming" and its "active one is piracy and the introduction of viruses" (1992a, 6)—does seem both a little unspecific and a little outdated. Since these descriptions, technological advancement and the broadbanding of contemporaneity have fundamentally transformed the spatiotemporal conditions of power. As many theorists of control in the twenty-first century have recognized, digital communications and information technologies are not just tools for human knowledge and progress but have changed our modes of being and thinking. One may turn to Eugene Thacker and Alexander R Galloway's conception of the "Network," Galloway's "protocol," Wendy Hui Kyong Chun's "fiber-optic networks," Antoinette Rouvroy's "algorithmic governmentality," Benjamin H. Bratton's "machine as the state," Tiziana Terranova's "information overload," Safiya Umoja Noble's "algorithmic oppression," and others to better understand how to account for control as it has developed in recent decades. Here, it suffices to note what these all point toward: the increasing indiscernibility, speed, and nonhuman nature of the contemporary chronotope of power.

To this we must add the continued development of neoliberalism during the last parts of the twentieth century and the first of the new millennium and how it has contributed to an implicit but ultimately concrete undermining of the function of a liberal subject. Brown shows how the liberal rationality of safeguarding the individual and its right to negotiate the market is gradually reversed, placing the market first. One might say that the liberal chronotope is flipped: rather than placing the human subject at the commanding center of economic rationality, the subject is expected to adapt to this rationality. Thus, the relation between interiority and exteriority becomes even more complicated. The autonomy of individual sovereignty as articulated by Kant, the Lockean and, since Locke, liberal promise "that popular and individual sovereignty secure one another," and John Stuart Mill's wish that each be "entitled to 'pursue his own good in his own way'" are all overridden by a capital logic of investment and divestment, performance and assessment (Brown 2015, 109). In short, norms of the social and political are replaced by norms of "market conduct" (108). Brown identifies two major reorientations: that of the subject's relation to itself and that of the state's relation to the citizen. In both cases, the rationality of the subject is no longer based primarily on rights or sovereignty (109). Neoliberal rationalities are harder to grasp than its liberal predecessors, then, not only because the identifiable identities and institutions of earlier modes of power are replaced by digital control but also because the function of the liberal subject as a social and political entity itself is unsettled and undermined.

In both the Introduction and Chapter 1, I noted the centrality of the liberal subject to American culture. This is a conception of liberal individuality originating, as we saw, in Hobbes and Locke and delineated subsequently by MacPherson (1962) as pertaining in essence to the modern individual's relation to and possession of himself as primary, and relational and moral sociality as secondary. Such conceptions not only have been foundational to American culture generally but have been formative in the Western imagination and novelistic tradition as a whole. In fact, it is difficult to even imagine the formation of political and civil society as well as that of the modern novel without a conception of the free individual and its transcendent rights and role in society from the seventeenth century to the present. With sometimes considerable variations between such conceptions, a recurring and central component is the individual subject as in charge of itself in terms of both rights and responsibilities. However, and as this chapter has begun to show, developments of security and control during the second half of the twentieth century forced even staunch believers into anxieties over the stability of the subject's integrity and autonomy.

Although she does not frame it in these terms, Brown's two books on neoliberalism in the twenty-first century clearly speak to a paranoid rejoinder geared toward the social as that which delimits and interferes with the true freedom of liberal individuals. Theorists of the liberal subject central to American history and conceptions of self certainly display a degree of paranoia regarding the influences on the subject by forces from the outside, as we have seen, but neither they nor their progeny in theories of neoliberalism such as those of Friedrich Hayek and Milton Friedman or the ordoliberals desired the level of detachment of "human capital" that we see in "actually existing neoliberalism" today. Indeed, if we do not see ourselves as part of the social fabric at all but as "responsibilized," entrepreneurialized and capitalized individuals (Brown 2019, 29, 38), inferences of the social or the interferences of society ultimately work to prevent the true freedoms of such individuals— the freedom of tradition and markets.

On the one hand, the promotion and perversion of neoliberal agendas have entailed a strengthening of conceptions and positions of the individual. Supposedly not part of the social—not subjects of gender, race, class, sexuality but "human capital and moral-economic familial units"—both the individual and the family have been recuperated from the otherwise "disintegrating forces of late modernity" 39). These conceptions and positions are fundamentally "denaturalized," Brown suggests, but also potentially more powerful than earlier versions (39). The neoliberal aggression toward the social, as we will see, of course seems to work to benefit precisely the white male individuals who have seen themselves disenfranchised and dispossessed by these very same agendas, those who have not only lost jobs to overseas cheap labor but who might also feel that they have lost their "pride of place" to blacks and Latinos (3). Ultimately, "freedom without society" has given license and voice to white male supremacists (44). On the other hand, we have cause to wonder to what extent subjects, even of the kind who seem to benefit from rejections of the social—centrally male and white U.S. citizens—manage to fully dismiss it. The increasing pressure postmodernity puts on long-standing conceptions of the liberal individual as rational, agential, and with a protected core of inner life is met, as Melley notes, with an ambivalent acknowledgment of such pressures combined with a disavowal (2000, 14). What we can also see is how such anxieties have intensified not only alongside further intensifications of control during this period but also with the intensification and, as Brown argues, perversion of neoliberal rationalities in the twenty-first century.

Conceptions of individual agency, as I suggested in the beginning of this chapter, depend on the perceived relation between individuals and their surroundings. This perception takes place not only within individuals but also, centrally, via social, cultural, and political representations of these relations. Such representations can be elucidated by different configurations of the individual's relation to space and time—that is, by chronotopes. The distribution of agency, in other words, depends on actual spatiotemporal conditions of power, but it also depends on how these conditions are culturally imagined and represented. Is space navigated or even molded by individuals or are individuals molded in or by space? Is time governed by the timeframe of individual or human destiny, or do individual or even human destinies seem transient and perhaps immaterial as subsumed by the immensity of geological time?

The chronotope of discipline has informed Western culture and cultural expression in fundamental ways. We have been interpellated as disciplinary subjects—constructed and addressed as individuals with specific identities. An entire cultural tradition, not least the modern novel, has been shaped by and contributes to such construction. In a European context, disciplinary identities have been more strongly associated with a particular place and time. Class and gender especially have been more clearly marked as constitutive of the individual subject and its opportunities for navigating and negotiating its place in society. In an American context, the subject has been conceived of as more mobile—as fundamentally free and capable of pursuing liberty across the board of power if inclination and work ethic so enable it. In American history, this can be traced back to the rejection of hierarchal, religious, feudal, and royal powers of Europe, and the idea of individuals negotiating their own freedom by mastering their own spacetimes, which established a starting point for the nation itself. The "new" and "free" space and time offered by America seemed to match the freedom of individuals who abandoned the conservative and regulatory traditions of Europe. The freedoms of individuals and markets constituted the very shaping of the country's distinctive disciplinary chronotope as one in which the liberal subject answers not to the king or even to the state but to the family or the business. What Fraser describes in her account of Fordism as discipline is the expansion and systemization of this disciplinarity on a larger scale (162). And, as we will see in the next section, the cultural imaginary of the novel seen as a cultural form closely aligned with discipline also contributes to strengthening this imaginary. This cultural heritage and economic and technological expansion feeds straight into the agency panic Melley sees in the postwar period, when corporations were often imagined as possessing extraordinary, nonhuman powers, "like self-motivated agencies, repositories of secret intentions, with the capacity for astonishing control of consumers and workers" (2000, 188).

This is why the social can be perceived as a threat—an undue interference with the freedom of individuals and markets. But while this threat has been a constant, if evolving, presence in American history, challenges to the subject presented by the control mechanisms of the last few decades are less established. A social associated with clear institutions—the state and its agencies; indeed, "society"—and with identities—claims to equality and justice by women, African Americans, Gays, Hispanics—is more easily distinguishable and constructable as an enemy to the free (white male) subject. This can be contrasted to the subtle ways in which the milieus of security and the algorithms of control shape our conditions for action while not being so easily identifiable. Indeed, as I have begun to ask, how do you recognize your own free agency in relation to spatiotemporal conditions that you cannot grasp? To the milieus and algorithms we must add the way neoliberalism itself contributes to this indistinctness of power. Arguments that *neoliberalism* is an awkward and insufficient term for what is really a multiplicity, says Brown, misses the point that "inconstant, morphing, differentiated, unsystematic, contradictory, and impure" is precisely its modality. It is simultaneously ubiquitous and diverse in that it weaves itself into existing and nonidentical cultural and political traditions (2015, 48).

The *dispositifs* of security and control are, however, not completely indiscernible. If they were, then perhaps we would not be so concerned but could live on in blissful ignorance, convinced of our own unadulterated agency. Security and control seem, in fact, to be just discernable enough to foster paranoia. For example, most of us are quite aware of at least some of the ways in which our choices online generate filters, the way our cellphones monitor our every step, and the way our data are exploited. On the one hand, we seem to have grown fascinatingly accustomed to this in a very short time. Bridle argues that "computational thinking has triumphed because it has first seduced us with its power, then befuddled us with its complexity, and finally settled into our cortexes as self-evident" (44). Some even suggest that we welcome the pleasures and distractions of control with open arms. Bernard E. Harcourt points out that the new power structures are ever so much more pleasant than the old disciplinary ones. Our pleasures have become interweaved with coercive surveillance technologies, making it hard to differentiate them (2015, 21). On the other hand, and while I do not disagree with Bridle and Harcourt, I want to emphasize the ambivalence and potential for paranoia generated by these developments. As Jessica Johnson notes, routine state and corporate surveillance via computers and cell phones with their simultaneous modulations of habits and tracking of consumption and movement patterns contributes to an increasing mistrust in both the media and the government (2018, 102). And as we will see in Chapter 3, the dynamics of the new public sphere generate mistrust—to the point of misgiving—in the possibility of establishing truth and facts.

Where, then, does the American subject look for an image of itself, for a mirror in which the free liberal subject can be identified—and recognize itself—as such? As I have begun to argue here, and as will be developed further in the next section, we cling to conceptions of the self and freedom by clinging to the frames of a disintegrating but culturally prevailing disciplinary chronotope of power. In this chronotope, the subject has a relatively distinct identity and is at least to some extent capable of identifying and navigating the spatiotemporal logics of power. Behind it lurks the chronotope of control that threatens to undo this imaginary. Control society does not rely on identities and stable logics. Quite the contrary, it thrives precisely by being diffused and flexible, by resisting spatiotemporal stabilization. This potentially puts pressure on the cultural forms in which the white male subject is constructed as in charge.

Section 2: The Disciplinary Tradition in Dave Eggers's Your Fathers, Where Are They? And the Prophets, Do They Live Forever?

Introduction

Placing its rather drawn-out birth in the time between the mid-sixteenth century and the start of the nineteenth, Guido Mazzoni sees the novel entering its modern phase as "the existence of private, common individuals secured an unprecedented linguistic space in European culture" (2017, 18–9). This space is opening up as the novel progressively frees itself from allegory and morality, from requirements of style and demands on spectacularism. Human characters and narratives no longer have to mean or represent or teach anything other than what they themselves are—stories of particular individuals in everyday settings. In place of allegorical heroes and virtuous exemplars, the novel makes space for the contingent, private life of characters in a "middle station of life" (219) and for "the disenchanted analysis of human beings" (187).

Understood in terms of generic chronotopes, we can distinguish between an earlier literature that binds characters to a set of transcendent principles and a novelistic logic that binds them to their "own" space. In an elementary way, this distinction is suggestive of two underlying chronotopes, or different "image[s] of man" as Mikhail Bakhtin puts it. Bakhtin's neo-Kantian approach recognizes that time is organized by convention, which in turn means that the mediation of spatiotemporal conditions is crucial to how those conditions are understood (Holquist 2002, 113). This mediation varies not only across genres, as we have seen, but also across time and cultures. The way in which any mediation, or plot, shapes any story therefore depends "not only on formal ('made') features in a given text, but also on generally held conceptions of how time and space relate to each other in a particular culture at a particular time ('given' features)" (114). In other words, and although the modern novel will come to include numerous chronotopes, it is possible to see it as reflecting a more general secularization of spacetime—a "formally constitutive category of literature" according to Bakhtin, or "abstract *generic chronotopes*" that speak to a general categorization of larger sets of works (Bemong and Borghart 2010, 7).

In other words, in a secular modernity and in the novel that emerges with it, common individuals are exposed to themselves and to their immediate surroundings in new ways. In earlier literature, Mazzoni says, "a prioris bound the narrative of ordinary lives to an apparatus of ideas and principles that came prior to the disorder of ordinary lives" (18). Whatever concerns and anxieties may have afflicted such ordinary lives, characters and readers could rest assured that, whether accessible or obscure or even unfathomable, there were higher ideas and principles to explain or to justify the state of things. In the modern novel, however, the chronotope is largely reduced to the everyday; it becomes "flat" as its transcendent levels fall away. Left to their own devices, modern characters must navigate space and time using their own capacities and moralities, and they must rely on their own agency.

With this secular reliance on the self, the liberal subject materializes. The co-constitutive relation between the emergence of the subject, the disciplinary chronotope, and the modern novel is considerable. As modern politics and civil society took shape during the eighteenth and nineteenth centuries, a novel form developed built on and grappling with the realizations and limitations of individual subjects in relation to institutions, economies, and laws. Nancy Armstrong establishes and confirms the importance of the novel to the formation of individualism in the West, which she says develops via a negotiation of and, perhaps primarily, a defense against and abjection of alternative conceptions of the individual (2005, 10). Indeed, she argues that the novel cannot be separated from its project of "universalizing the individual subject" (10).

As soon as we take a closer look, however, we are forced to notice certain cracks in the burgeoning shape of the liberal subject. The central view to be defended and consolidated in the novel that Armstrong describes tirelessly protects the idea of self-enclosure as derived from the philosophical lineage of Locke, Rousseau, Hume, and Adam Smith. In different ways, these philosophers account for the transfer of information and emotions between bodies and minds while retaining the idea of clear subjective boundaries and man's "capacity for judgment" (Armstrong 2005,11). Armstrong ascribes the importance of these boundaries as they are established in the novel to an historical context in which growing masses of poor people in urban areas, colonial insurrections, and new mass media threatened to engulf and obliterate the boundaries of the individual (24). Other boundaries that required protection, she says, included those against the nonhuman or inhuman, the unnatural or aberrant, overpopulation and degeneration, desires that threatened the coherence of the social, and, not least, the excessive individualism so foundational to earlier fictions. At the same time, the novel was born exactly by giving "narrative form" to a "wish for a social order sufficiently elastic to accommodate individualism" (139). Armstrong, in other words, finds in the formation of the European modern novel a paradox similar to that Melley finds in American individualism more generally: a strong conception of the individual subject that becomes so precisely by imagining itself at risk or, as Armstrong puts it, "in opposition to an engulfing otherness, or mass, that obliterated individuality" (25).

One potentially engulfing otherness to be negotiated can be found in the power structures of a fast-developing industrial society. The "bourgeois morality" as identified by Armstrong, is centered on the individual and his right to assert himself, but which also must be coordinated with a social contract that secures a functioning society. How, in other words, to continue insisting on the rights and freedom of individuals while also insisting on their subjection to the contract? Referring to Althusser's reading of Rousseau, Armstrong observes that this is solved for Rousseau by seeing the individual's subjection as a subjection to himself and his own authority and by conceptualizing "an entirely new kind of individual, one endowed with the natural ability to understand the advantages of becoming a citizen" (30). Reading novels such as Daniel Defoe's *Robinson Crusoe* (1719) and Jane Austen's *Pride and Prejudice* (1813), Armstrong shows how bourgeois morality becomes a negotiation between individual desire and social authority (50). In fact, she leans on Foucault and Bentham to maintain that the novel becomes nothing less than "a ubiquitous cultural narrative" of this negotiation. As such, it also becomes a sounding board for historical changes in which the limits of individualism can or must be drawn (51).

In a specifically American context and history, the individual defending herself against the encroachments of society is integral to culture. It is also, as we began to see in the previous section, one intimately connected with liberalism and, down the line, with neoliberalism. As Foucault shows, negotiations of freedom and the encroachments on it are less spectacular than in earlier (and perhaps pre-American) sovereign models. Instead of overt demonstrations of power, freedom emerges as a continuous and more internal negotiation of the balance between individual freedom and the (minimal but essential) regulations required to protect that freedom of both the self and others. The freedom that liberalism consumes as well as produces is precarious and must constantly negotiate the balance between freedom and the security required to protect it. It must determine, according to Foucault, "the precise extent to which and up to what point individual interest—that is to say, individual interests insofar as they are different and possibly opposed to each other—constitute a danger to the interests of all (2008, 65).

In an American framework, as we approach the neoliberal era, the critique of government and the prioritization of the economic entails a suspicion of any kind of social intervention because it potentially interferes with the freedom of subjects as economic agents. Melley suggests that this "vision of an autonomous self beleaguered by society" speaks to liberalism and conspiracy theories alike (2000, 11). Actually, Melley argues, the two are intimately linked: the broad appeal of and to liberalism and a sense of the individual as being in antagonistic opposition to a society broadly but monolithically conceived pave the way for the elusive but menacing and controlling powers envisioned by conspiracy theories (11). Both longstanding conceptions of selfhood and conspiracy theory favor "an all-or-nothing conception of agency, a view in which agency is a property parceled out *either* to individuals like oneself *or* to 'the system'—a vague structure often construed to be massive, powerful, and malevolent" (10). Such conspiracy theories are not only vague, favoring "the system" or "society" as the threat rather than more carefully conceptualized interests and problems within it; they also tend to be flexible in their political applications. Especially during the final decades of the twentieth century, as Melley notes, conspiracy theories were coming from the left as well as the right, from Packard as well as Hoover, from African American as well as white racist groups (10). It was not so much about a vindication of a particular and clearly articulated political position, but about defending individualism "abstractly conceived" (11).

While I agree with Melley about this broad and vague application historically, in Chapter 4 I will elucidate how conspiracy theories characteristic of the new millennium are increasingly entangled with identity politics and are mobilized among groups such as the alt-right and white supremacists specifically, and how this is at least in part linked to implicit white masculinist assumptions of the liberal conception of agency in the first place. In other words, the individualism of the twenty-first century is not abstractly conceived at all. On the contrary, it is overtly configured in terms of distinct identities and subjects. Yet the mass manipulation of the Cold War that Melley describes is undoubtedly easier to envision and incorporate into the human-sized narratives of the novel. It relies on more recognizable ideological tensions as well as senders, recipients, and methods of communication. This, as my reading of Eggers is about to show, can be partly explained by the novel's long-standing and lingering reliance on disciplinary power. The reading will demonstrate how shifts from a more visible disciplinary power to a chronotope of control create a crisis in both the individual subject and the novel form.

Your Fathers, Where Are They? And the Prophets,
    Do They Live Forever?

Its title, *Your Fathers, Where Are They? And the Prophets, Do They Live Forever?* positions Eggers's 2014 novel in an historical and formal homelessness. The tension between the epic quality of the title's Biblical quote and Eggers's contemporary and formally uncomfortable novel can be seen to eclipse the entire history of the Western novel that I just pointed to. The development of this tradition is, as we have begun to see, intimately connected to the modern period and also closely connected to the rise of modern capitalism. The technological and political developments of the Industrial Revolution establish a middle-class readership and lay the groundwork for an individualism that the novel comes to reflect and develop. The "formal realism" specific to the novel, according to Ian Watt, relies on its aspirations to give "a full and authentic report of human experience" (2001, 32). This is an aspiration new to the period as it departs from earlier literatures that were typically formed by conceptions of ahistorical truths and that therefore tended toward type characters, vague temporalities, and unspecified settings favorable to underlying timeless ideals and values. In other words, we have begun to see a new chronotope materialize with the modern novel, one in which time and space have become concrete, and man- or at least society-sized.

The new chronotope allows the construction of the specific via individual experiences in particular times and places. What was new about the novel as it emerged with the Industrial Revolution in the West was precisely its interest in the particularities of specific individuals in a context in which these particularities were subject to sociopolitical molding. Thus, for example, D. A. Miller (1998) and Jeremy Tambling (1995) emphasize the extent to which the Victorian novel was informed by (or, as Tambling puts it, "aware of") evolving forms of power during this period (1995, 23). The molding belongs to the *dispositif* of discipline. Disciplinary power, Miller argues, "provide[d] the novel with its essential 'content'" as protagonists were trained and placed under social surveillance and "normalizing sanctions" (1988, 18–9). Few dispute the relation between Victorian literature and Foucauldian discipline (although Lauren Goodlad does suggest that the common focus on "discipline and punish" has produced a slightly twisted view of the Victorian period, which can be amended by greater attention to Foucault's work on governmentality (see Goodlad 2003, 539), However, some question Miller's rather pessimistic readings of Charles Dickens as providing "disciplinary closure" (see David Ben-Merre 2011, 47) and repudiate the idea that fiction from the period was "wholly determined by and complicit with disciplinary strategies" (see Pam Morris 2004, 224.)

Leaving the question of complicity aside and returning to *Your Fathers*, we see that here the disciplinary strategies are painfully present in their absence. In creating a direct link between Zechariah 1:5 and its setting in an abandoned army barracks in twenty-first century America, the novel effectively parenthesizes centuries of such novel tradition. Without this tradition, both the novel and its protagonist implicitly ask: Who is the subject? The predicaments of Thomas, the young man around which the plot revolves become the identity crisis of the novel as well as the identity crisis of the white male American subject of the new millennium. In *Your Fathers*, the disciplinary chronotope upon which both a certain subject position and a certain novel tradition have relied seem to have broken down. Without it, power becomes harder to grasp, truth becomes more difficult to establish, and identity, at least as associated with an autonomous individual subject, becomes a precarious affair.

The novel helps us to see how "the gates" of the chronotope—in our case the disciplinary chronotope—serve as the necessary "entry into the sphere of meaning" (Bakhtin 1981, 258) and how its time and space, as Holquist emphasizes, become "the fundamental constituents of understanding, and thus provide the indices for measuring other aspects of human existence, first and foremost, the identity of the self" (2010, 27). Unable to grasp meaning or understand himself without it, Eggers's protagonist desperately attempts to put the disciplinary structure back together again. In doing so, he exposes the novel's structural alliance with and reliance on the chronotopic shape of discipline. The disciplinary chronotope, as we saw in the previous section, is organized around analogous and relatively identifiable spaces as well as a temporally continuous development—a subject constructed and becoming itself in relation to institutions through which it passes: family, school, hospital, military, factory. This is a governmentality, according to Fraser, intent on rationalizing social life in all its major aspects and formations.

The breakdown of this structure is clearly signaled in the distinct awkwardness of the novel's formal organization. The chapter titles reflect the names of barracks in an abandoned military base—apparently mimicking the real-life

Fort Ord—on the California coast. The titles run as follows: "Building 52," "Building 53," "Building 54," "Building 55," Building 52," "Building 52," "Building 55," "Building 52," Building 52," "Building 57," "Building 52," "Building 57," "Building 53," "Building 57," "Building 55," "Building 60," "Building 53," "Building 48," "Building 53." As the narrative proceeds, Thomas successively kidnaps characters and installs one in each barracks: an astronaut (building 52), a Vietnam veteran and retired congressman (building 53), a former teacher of his (building 54), his own mother (building 55), a policeman (building 57), a hospital administrator (building 60) and "the woman of [his] dreams" (building 48). Each chapter is a dialogue between Thomas and one of his victims, who is chained to a concrete post. This staccato structure slices up the reading and shapes the narrative by foregrounding repetition both with and without difference. Thus formally regulated, the plot itself is chained to this organization. One reviewer remarked that a novel written solely in dialogue form creates its own and "unique technical challenges" (Edward Docx, 2014, n.p.); Another pointed out that, with one character in each chapter always chained to a post, "not much can happen" (Phil Klay, 2014, n.p.), but this is only partly true. The novel does have a very particular pace that is compulsively circular; a new dialogue is initiated each time Thomas collects a new person, and each encounter has similarities with the others—confusion, explanations. At the same time, each encounter is emotionally linear; Thomas is driven both to the past—he has an idea of a glorious American past that he has missed out on—and to the future—what he hopes to extract from the interviews with his victims is a sense of goal and meaning in his life and in American life in general.

The novel's chained progression mirrors a lack of goal and meaning, which is also reflected in the way in which the narrative *is* allowed to progress. The placement of different representatives of society in numbered barracks does seem methodical, but the logic by which Thomas selects his targets is governed by impulse. Thus, the narrative comes to be organized in accordance with the unclear motivations that seem to transpire as he goes along. An exception is his choice of the first victim, an astronaut who used to go to the same school as Thomas but does not remember him. The kidnapping takes place on same day that Neil Armstrong passes away and has been elaborately planned. For Thomas, the astronaut symbolizes a period in the recent history of America when individual as well as national identity was characterized by both potential and determination. The astronaut embodies an American ideal in terms of his glorified occupation and in terms of what Thomas sees as the true grit required to achieve it—"for a while there you were a god. You promised you'd become an astronaut and you became one" (15). To Thomas, the NASA program where the astronaut worked represents a government agency at its best as well as its worst—the hope and pride of America as well as their breaking. The decommissioning of the shuttle and the termination of the space program meant "the inevitable collapse of anything seeming solid. The breaking of every last goddamned promise on Earth" (15). As we will see in Chapter 4, space is considered a final frontier to which the young self-made man of the American dream can aspire and thus lay claim to the masculinity associated with it. With the closing of such frontiers, white American men are, Michael Kimmel observes, forced to seek and restore their masculinity from the past (2017, 19). The astronaut embodies precisely a nostalgic ideal of personal and societal progression as well as its forced demise. Thomas wants to extract this "narrative" to better understand the deterioration of order and identity that has deprived him and men of his generation of their sense of purpose and direction.

After his first well-rehearsed and premeditated kidnapping, Thomas conducts the ensuing kidnappings in an increasingly arbitrary and spontaneous fashion. This off-the-cuff progression is articulated by Thomas himself when he explains to his next captive, a former congressman, why he was chosen: "Once the astronaut and I started talking, in the back of my mind I thought, Well, I bet Congressman Dickinson would have something to say about this" (31). Toward the end of his conversation with the Congressman he declares: "As we've been talking I've been thinking of someone else who should be here. I think I should get him while there's time" (52). Talking to his former teacher, whom he abducts next, he says that the congressman "gave me the idea to find you, indirectly at least" (55). And so Thomas's undertaking develops. Gradually, his mission to comprehend and perhaps amend the decline of "grand human projects" (212) is sidetracked by a more personal investigation of the killing of his friend, Don Bahn. This alternate direction is itself activated by a seemingly accidental turn (or is it?), when the astronaut mistakenly and, he maintains, accidentally, calls Thomas "Don" (21). Convinced that the astronaut's misstep is not coincidental, Thomas brings up Don's fate in, and in some cases even as a cause of, most of the ensuing "interviews" and this strand progressively emerges as a key to the narrative.

Chance, as I noted in the Introduction, is not an acceptable feature of life for a paranoid mind. Neither is it a tolerable explanation of plot events in the paranoid novel, which are driven precisely by the lack of chance—whether perceived by a paranoid protagonist or by the paranoid construction of the narrative itself. Indeed, as the disciplinary system slips through his fingers, Thomas compensates for his cumulative loss of focus with a paranoid consistency. His incentive to know what went wrong with American society and his ensuing pursuit of an explanation for Don Bahn's death are both ultimately relegated to secondary relevance after he meets a random woman on the beach and becomes convinced that she is the woman of his dreams. Thomas announces to the astronaut: "Maybe this is what this was all about. You, the congressman, my mom, Hansen, maybe it was all meant to lead me to this woman in the sweater" (111). Talking over this event with his mother in barrack 55, he suggests that there is a "divine purpose" and that meeting that woman must be a sign: "I mean, here I am in the middle of nowhere, and you're here, and the astronaut is here and the congressman, and then I see this woman who has been in my dreams since I was ten or so. It all has to mean something" (116).

Thus, the repudiation of chance comes to seem even more imperative than the interrogation of the decline of grand projects and universal struggles, of "some cause greater than ourselves" (36). Rather than accept the vacancy of the disciplinary system and the identity and purpose he had hoped to recuperate from this system, Eggers's protagonist dives into an increasingly paranoid romance. Toward the end of the novel, as he is planning an escape from the military base with the woman before the police arrive, she, or their imaginary union, is provided as the rationalization for the entire adventure. He explains to her:

> For once in my life there was logic, and an orderly procession of events, one leading to the next, every time I had an idea it worked out. I wanted the astronaut and found him. I wanted the congressman and I found him. And the cop—I mean, it couldn't be chance. It couldn't be random, especially given at the end of it all I found you. I didn't even seek you out. I didn't know I wanted you, but it's all so obvious now that it was all leading up to this, to us. Now we just have to complete it. (196)

Stitching coincidences as well as his own more or less random actions into a seemingly meaningful narrative, Thomas escapes his original, failing project of facing and negotiating the vacuity of the power system and reinscribes it with a more individualist meaning and purpose.

A second feature of the paranoid novel discussed in the Introduction is the precarious connection between the character and the chronotope that enfolds him. Distinguishing between novels based on "the *ready-made* hero" and those centering on "man's essential becoming," Bakhtin describes how the former moves the hero in space—up and down social ladders, away from or toward his goal, through events and escapades—without the hero himself being changed. The hero is "a *constant* in the novel's formula" which means that all other quantities can be "*variables*" (1986, 20). Of more interest to Bakhtin, and to us, is the second kind of novel, which he calls "the novel of human *emergence*," that allows, or even centers on, developments in the hero. In other words, here it is the hero who becomes the variable, which requires a reinterpretation and reconstruction of the plot. Time enters into the image of man and, because human beings emerge in different ways, this type of novel also has various subtypes (Bakhtin, 21). Where these subtypes typically reverse the order of novels of the ready-made hero—making the spaces through which the hero moves more or less unchangeable while the hero becomes dynamic—Bakhtin hones in on the type in which the hero's emergence "is accomplished in real historical time, with all of its necessity, its fullness, its future, and its profoundly chronotopic nature" (23). Here, the hero "emerges *along with the world* and he reflects the historical emergence of the world itself" (23). Because he changes with a changing world—in fact, these changes are "accomplished in him and through him"—the problems of man's potential, freedom, initiative, and reality appear with full force. In this type—that is, in what Bakhtin sees as the realistic novel of emergence—man moves on from the purely private and enters "a completely new, *spatial* sphere of historical existence" (24).

In Eggers's novel, however, the hero seems to be simultaneously steeped in but out of sync with historical existence. It is as if he balances precisely on the cusp of a historical shift between discipline and control and is indisposed to take the leap. Bakhtin suggests that the hero of the realist novel of emergence is positioned exactly "on the border between two epochs . . . forced to become a new, unprecedented type of human being" (23). But Thomas is resisting; he is trying quite concretely to reconstruct the emergence of himself as a disciplinary subject even as the power structures through which he is supposed to materialize prove increasingly unable to acknowledge or account for him. Thomas seems to perceive his own agency as in precise correspondence with this fading disciplinary chronotope—the spatial division, the temporal repetition, the institutional focus—if only they all align, he will "come to." This desperate hope directed at institutions can also be seen, as Jon Doyle points out, in David Foster Wallace's novels *Infinite Jest* (1996) and *The Pale King* (2011), in which characters strive toward "some semblance of order" by turning to organizations (Alcoholic Anonymous in the former and the Internal Revenue Service in the latter), hoping that they will "fill the void left by postmodernism's negation of values" (2018, 260). We will return to this hope and its slightly different role in Foster Wallace's work in Chapter 4, but for now let us note that in *Your Fathers*, this is a precarious conception upon which to entrust one's sense of agency in that this chronotope seems to be evacuated. Pursuing individuals as representatives of larger societal institutions of power, Thomas fails to extract answers, which points simultaneously to the failing system and to its fundamental and essential emptiness.

Visibility, Deleuze proposes via Foucault, constitutes "the general condition under which all behaviors of a period show themselves" and it is "the conditions for visibility, the conditions for statability, which permit the definition of a period" (1985b, 3). Thomas's strategy seems to be recreating those conditions in order to force them to "show themselves" as they once were. But they cannot show themselves because they are no longer the same. As long as they were representatives of a disciplinary system at work, the mother, the teacher, the policeman, the politician, and the astronaut had functions that could wield power and yield identity. But without such functions, they cannot give Thomas any answers or help him recover his sense of self. Thomas desperately attempts to excavate the central components of the disciplinary *dispositif* as well as the novel tradition: the individual, the family, the community, and the interaction between them. However, he finds in their place evacuated spaces, empty shells. What is produced instead is a disjunctive layering of power where there is on the one hand a governing but largely invisible layer and on the other a perception of power that seems concrete enough to hold on to although it is progressively impotent. What is produced, in other words, is a paranoid chronotope.

This in turn speaks to a third feature of the paranoid novel I discussed in the Introduction, the lack of a sense of shared reality. If novelistic success after Henry James and Percy Lubock has come to mean the ability "to maximize the novel's generic disposition to embody social relatedness" as Dorothy Hale suggests (1998, 14), Eggers stages the decline of disciplinary models, leaving characters unmoored from individuality, family, and community. Whether this is a paranoid staging of what happens as such entities decline or a reflection of societal change, it does speak to the difficulties some critics have discerned when it comes to the novel form's negotiations with contemporary society. Armstrong, for example, argues that the novel form needs to unleash itself from its formal reliance on conceptions of individuals and their relation to community. To continue to offer ways of imagining ourselves, she says, the novel needs to reimagine our conceptions of both individuals and community that exist in the contemporary world. "In years to come, the novels that matter [will be . . .] those seen as having prepared us for an epistemic shift in how we imagine ourselves as human beings" (2011, 8). But *Your Fathers* cannot matter in this sense. It matters rather by pointing to the difficulties in overcoming such epistemic shifts within the novel form. Centrally, it also speaks directly to the paranoid effects such shifts might have on young white American men who no longer feel supported by it.

Observing Thomas walk from barrack to barrack and from authority to authority to seek answers about society, we might wonder if he is haunting the novel or if the novel is haunting him. Miller shows how the modern novel emerges as an effective practice of active but discrete social discipline which comes to regulate both working- and middle-class subjects, assigning the first to a more overt policing power while the latter, openly disavowing policing forces, comes under the control of a Foucauldian micropolitics that, via the most "trifling detail" regulates social behavior. Thus, a middle-class readership is exposed to the ideology of the novel via its very form: "Whenever the novel censures policing power," Miller argues, "it has already reinvented it, in the very practice of novelistic representation" (20). That Eggers's setting mirrors a declining analogue mode of power is underscored not only by the fact that the action takes place on an abandoned military base but also by the fact that the different barracks come to play a central role on the narrative level and on the level of form. Thus, the setting accentuates the way characters and their stories desperately try to speak to and for the disciplinary *dispositif* inherent in the novel form.

The alignment of the crumbling scaffolding of discipline on the narrative level with the collapsing scaffolding on the level of form accentuates narrative and form's shared investment in this *dispositif* while pointing to its breaking lines. As Deleuze notes, a set of "vast spaces of enclosure" organize the disciplinary societies that Foucault theorizes. "The individual never ceases passing from one closed environment to another, each having its own laws: first, the family; then the school ('you are no longer in your family'); then the barracks ('you are no longer at school'); then the factory; from time to time the hospital; possibly the prison, the preeminent instance of the enclosed environment" (1992a, 3). In this light, Thomas's enforced spatial and temporally concurrent distribution of parents, government representatives, teachers, policemen, and hospital workers in barracks appears as a fraught attempt to mimic this system. He has, he says, "stopped time and asked questions" (194) and for a moment this seems to result in "alignment and order and a coming-to" (202). That he yearns for this system to make sense can be seen in the way he projects the abandoned army base as a place of potential rescue and escape for young misguided men like himself (49), as if the disciplining mode that he yearns for can be reinscribed upon this otherwise lost generation. Actually, in his interpretation this generation yearns for order and purpose and will self-destruct without it: "If you don't have something grand for men like us to be part of, we will take apart all the little things. Neighborhood by neighborhood, Building by building. Family by family" (211).

The Chronotope of the Paranoid Threshold

Thus *Your Fathers* actively stages the tension between the *dispositifs* of discipline and those of control. In its overt attention to the failing of institutions and identities, it articulates the tensions of a shifting political landscape. For Foucault, Deleuze remarks, historical formations are "thresholds of knowledge" and because there is nothing prior to or beneath knowledge, to know is "always to produce the non-relation between the visible and the statable [l'*énonçable*] it is to combine the visible and the statable, to produce mutual captures of the visible and the statable" (1985a, 19). In Eggers's novel, this threshold takes on flesh and blood; as Bakhtin would put it, it becomes chronotopic. The threshold, one of the minor chronotopes Bakhtin outlines, is a chronotope of crisis and fracture. It comes with emotion and significance, but falls outside biographical time. Instead of duration, it is filled with potentially portentous decision and indecision. This contrast between the chronotope of biographical time and the chronotope of the threshold is significant—in the former, time is continuously tied to private life and its spaces and, to the extent there are historical forces and crises, these spaces are closely interwoven with the biographical. In the latter, such forces and crises profoundly affect characters but they occur instantaneously and befall them from the outside and push them toward resolutions (Bakhtin 1981, 248–9).

In *Your Fathers*, we can see how the larger paranoid chronotope is repeatedly—indeed, almost compulsively—organized around the minor chronotope of the threshold. Each chapter and each barracks add to a stack of thresholds that require but fail to enable transcendence. Nothing much happens, as critics of the novel argue, when the narrative is chained up alongside Thomas's hostages. The empty shells that Thomas finds instead of reliable disciplinary representatives speak to a space that it is time to leave behind. But Thomas is unable to leave it behind. He is caught up by this threshold. Unlike biographical time, which "does not take into account the forces from the historical environment that act on a consciousness and that orient the consciousness toward the future," the chronotope of the threshold, Bart Keunen says, present a subject "closely involved with the world" and "'caught' by (or 'up in') things" (2010, 43). In Thomas's case, the historical forces that he hopes to make sense of and "align" turn out to be petty, impotent, biographical. His increasingly confused wanderings reflect a subject deserted by the disciplinary moldings that have constructed it and that would have been invested in binding it into place.

That there is nothing before or beneath knowledge for Foucault means that this knowledge is not of an object by a subject but a continuous and historical formation (Deleuze 1985b, 5). But what can Thomas know, and how can he identify the truth—of himself and the system—when the visible and the statable do not seem to add up in the ways he expected? Foucault proposes that the "individual is no doubt the fictitious atom of an 'ideological' representation of society; but he is also a reality fabricated by this specific technology of power that I have called 'discipline'" (1977, 194). Eggers's protagonist comes across as the embodiment of such a fictitious atom having his reality removed from him as disciplinary technologies—societal institutions as well as the novel form—are losing its fabricating powers.

Historically, Armstrong argues, "the novel provides a means of mediating between individuals (presumably capable of self-government) and a human aggregate made of such individuals; the modern household (also known as the family) has served as an apparatus of and the model for a modern liberal society" (2011, 8). And as we saw in the previous section, the family is but one of the many institutions that construct and train the disciplinary subject. As the novel's portrayal of the literal caving in of disciplinary structures is reflected in its clipped formal constitution, *Your Fathers* invites us to ask what happens to our conception of the individual and to our expectations of the novel form as we face the gradual decline of the disciplinary *dispositif* of which they have been an integral part. Clearly, both conceptions of the individual and those of community are at stake. Eggers's novel appears as an experiment balancing on the cusp of such transition. The "lines of splitting, breakage, fracture," which, according to Deleuze, always coexist with the lines of visibility, enunciation, and subjectification of the *dispositif* (1992b, 162) are here both thematically articulated and formally realized. By means of content as well as form, the novel suggests that the crumbling model of liberal society needs to be urgently and physically reinforced, as if the *dispositif* could be reassembled and coerced back into structured distribution.

Although *Your Fathers* is very specifically geared toward a contemporary moment, and although its depiction of a disciplinarity haunting the self is explicitly staged, the ambivalence whereby the modern subject is subject of and subjected to power in the Foucauldian sense is intrinsic to the novel form more generally. At the beginning of this section, I noted how the modern novel emerges with the secularization and modernization of society. The chronotope begins to mirror everyday life and ordinary people subjected to themselves and others without recourse to higher, religious or sovereign, powers. Under sovereign power, subjects can and are, of course, pursued or haunted in various ways, but what is particular about disciplinary power is that the subject is now increasingly pursued or haunted by himself. Being made subject, he is part of power and has rights of his own, but there remains the sense that he has been made subject—that power has been internalized. Power will never again be quite what it seems. The subject will never again be quite what it seems. If always partly you and always partly the disciplinary power that has made you into you, how will you know the difference? Who is making your decisions? Are you haunting yourself? This is a paranoid chronotope of disciplinarity—an agency panic, if you will, for the nineteenth century.

Indeed, disciplinarity opens the door to a paranoid chronotope that recurs in the modern novel more generally. While not explicitly paranoid in the same sense as in the postwar culture I explore here, negotiating the tension between the idea and ideal of the liberal subject and his social contract on the one hand and the disciplinary power developing alongside industrialization on the other is constitutive of the form. Relying on Bentham as well as Althusser, Armstrong emphasizes the crucial role of fiction in negotiating the social contract. To begin with, the modern nation needed a "cultural apparatus" to make sure that "many different individuals imagine their relation to the real in approximately these terms" (2005, 50). In addition, shaping an individual into a modern citizen required the individual's voluntary attention to the social contract—making it see itself both as a free subject and as a functioning citizen-subject. "In this respect," argues Armstrong, "fiction itself began to operate as the additive responsible for kicking the history of the modern subject into successive historical gears" (52). As our reading of *Your Fathers* has suggested, however, Thomas is caught at a chronotopic threshold, unable to go back or move forward. This ultimately feeds into the larger, paranoid chronotope that supposedly explains his predicament in the present.

Readings of the kind just completed are exquisitely suspicious, of course. Associating novels with underlying power structures takes us right to the heart of the suspicious hermeneutics heavily critiqued in the past decade. Foucault and new critical scholars such as D. A. Miller are certainly prime suspects in postcritique. According to Rita Felski, Foucauldian readings insist that power is "diffused throughout society via undetectable capillaries of control: a micropolitics of discourse that molded the contours of personhood all the way down." Pointing specifically to Miller's analysis of the novel, she shows how it contributes to extending the notion of "policing" beyond institutions and the law and into the disciplines of reading (Felski 2015, 97). Miller's study of the novel and the police is also identified by Eve Kosofsky Sedgwick, along with Judith Butler's 1990 *Gender Trouble*, as constituting a central critical example of a kind of paranoid reading that we are perhaps ready to problematize (2002, 129).

Section 3: Critique

Introduction

Postcritique is directly aligned with questions that are the crux of this book: How are relations between the individual and its surroundings envisioned? What is the agency of the political subject under surveillance and control? Where might one identify facts and truth in contemporary society? The phenomenon of postcritique is approached and analyzed in terms of its chronotopic conditions. Centrally, this means reminding ourselves of the foundational link between critique and the public sphere that I began to outline in Chapter 1, and how the relation between the critical subject and this sphere—and, of course, the imagined relation between the two—affects understandings of critique and its intermittent crises. A primary purpose of the present section as well as critique sections in the chapters that follow is to highlight the somewhat constricted spatiotemporal context in which postcritique has been built and how it is haunted by much larger and more complex sociopolitical conditions. This disjunctive layering, I will ultimately argue, is nothing less than a paranoid chronotope. It will take a while to get there, however, so the current section serves mainly to outline the historical context of postcritique.

Critique/Literature

To begin, let us take a few steps back and situate critique in literature in relation to critique conceived more broadly in a philosophical and social context. In Chapter 1, I began an account of key thinkers of critique and the public sphere such as Kant, Arendt, and Habermas. A necessarily incomplete but hopefully indicative continuation of such an account historically would also include Marx, Nietzsche, and Benjamin as well as more central Frankfurt school thinkers such as Theodor Adorno and Max Horkheimer and post-Marxist scholars, not least the Italian thinkers such as Antonio Negri and Roberto Esposito. As the list suggests, these are primarily European political and philosophical thinkers. As postcritique has developed during the final decade of the twentieth century and the first decades of the twenty-first, however, as we have already begun to notice, it has materialized largely in an American context and has primarily been pursued in literary studies. So, what is the relation between the expansive and sprawling political history of critique and critique and postcritique, as articulated in American literary studies today?

Admittedly, there has never been a sharp distinction between literature, especially the more philosophical kind, and critique. Charlie Blake says that the intellectual, ethical, and fundamentally antimetaphysical investigations portrayed in Voltaire's *Candide, or, the Optimist*, published in 1759, helped to establish some of critique's basic conditions as they were to be articulated just a few years later by Kant. Kant, as we have seen, formulated the basis of modern critique as essential on the route toward Enlightenment. Critique emerged here as a vital dimension of a society in which eternal or divine subjects or truths could no longer be taken for granted and individuals were obliged to shoulder the responsibility of knowing and mobilizing reason as it related to particular historical situations and challenges. Without eternal truths, what can we know and say about the world and how we should act in it? How do we establish clear distinctions about what is true or false, valid or invalid, justified or not, in general terms? And how do we establish "the conditions that make true or at least reliable knowledge possible?" (Blake 2020, n.p.). Such investigations cannot be limited to philosophy-as-epistemology but necessarily also rely on aesthetics and politics and the various narratives that make up our historical and situational consciousness. According to Blake:

> what all three of [Kant's] critiques (of pure reason, of practical reason, and of judgment) are centrally concerned with are a quest for a stable and consistent response to the three questions he poses for any future philosophy, these being the questions of what can be known for certain, how moral and political actions can be determined, and on what basis valid judgments about actions and experiences can be made, whether individually or collectively. (n.p.)

In the nineteenth century, such questions were further and quite radically problematized by thinkers such as Nietzsche, Freud, Darwin, Marx, and Engels. If it was already hard for Kant to establish the foundations for a rational subject, these later thinkers in various ways enabled and practiced critique as an interrogation of individual knowing and of the societal, cultural, and political powers forming this knowing. Nietzsche, Freud, and Marx were of course the masterful trio that came to underlie the hermeneutics of suspicion as formulated by Paul Ricoeur. This made for a form of critique that, unlike Kant's, would come to have a considerable and more direct influence on literary interpretation. Indeed, as I noted in Chapter 1, the crisis in critique as it is now formulated is largely associated with the questioning of the hermeneutics of suspicion and its role in literary studies today.

Interested in the influence of psychoanalysis on interpretation, Ricoeur interrogates contrasting ways of understanding what precisely is to be interrogated. Looking at historical modes of interpretation, he points to two main traditions, one more semantic and one more symbolic, but both building on the belief that true meaning can be found but that finding it requires interpretation through language structures or exegetical interrogation. Thus, hermeneutics is essentially "understood as the manifestation and restoration of meaning" (Ricoeur 1970, 27). To find this meaning, the object must not be reduced to something that occurs if we try to understand it causally, individually, historically, affectively, or ideologically. Rather, it must be accessed phenomenologically described, drawn out from that fullness of language in which its truth resides. This, Ricoeur says, requires faith in meaning and confidence in language.

With modernity, however, and its concomitant crisis of meaning and language, a more humble approach evolves. Both language and consciousness are put into question, and interpretation becomes a matter of approximation, of "demystification, as a reduction of illusion" (27). Interpretation changes focus because what is of interest is approximating not only the object, meaning, and truth, but also the forces that affect that striving: the unconscious, the fallibility of language, and power. While suspicion is not in itself new—indeed, an awareness that things might not be what they seem has been present in philosophy at least since Descartes, as Ricoeur acknowledges—what is new is the questioning of consciousness as coinciding with itself, or rather that "meaning and consciousness of meaning coincide" (33). The blow to this one refuge, then, that pries open this unity, is the work of the "masters of suspicion," who turn consciousness, too, into an element to be interrogated. With these three—who are similar primarily in the way they oppose the notion of the truth of consciousness—interpretation changes drastically. For the emerging hermeneutics of suspicion, interpretation cannot be a matter of spelling out the truth of consciousness. Rather, consciousness is seen to work according to a logic of what it shows and what it hides or, in more Freudian terms, what is manifested and what is simulated. Interpretation becomes "suspicious" because it knows that consciousness is constantly configured and ciphered by false consciousness, by ideology, by the will to power (34).

This does not mean that there is no truth, however. Rather, there is "a new reign of Truth" that requires demystification to "clear the horizon for a more authentic word" (33). For interpretation to be valid according to this new "interpretation of interpretation," it must take into account a much broader field than before (32). Interpretation is exposed to time and space in a more concrete way: it becomes chronotopic. First, this reconfiguration greatly affects the temporality of meaning. Without belief in an eternal meaning to be drawn out, a "recollection of meaning" as Ricoeur would say, the stability and continuity of meaning are lost. In other words, meaning becomes historically configured. Second, meaning is spatialized in that it is necessarily situated and becomes part of and within social, historical, and political dimensions. In short, meaning is inevitably implicated in and by its temporal and spatial location. As Ricoeur stresses, though, Freud, Marx, and Nietzsche did not aim to diminish the importance of consciousness but rather strove to extend it beyond individual consciousness as it had been previously conceptualized (34).

With the focus on interpretation comes a heightened focus on reading itself as a critical practice. Understanding becomes intimately associated with interpretation, the latter becoming not just a "method" but, according to Drew Milne, "a necessary dimension of understanding as such" (2003, 6). This constitutes an important background for understanding why Ricoeur and the hermeneutics of suspicion are frequently positioned as a key to understanding critical reading as it was conducted in universities in the late twentieth century. Reading practices in English and comparative literature departments and a entire generation of scholars have been shaped either by this Ricoeurian conglomeration specifically or by a more general practice of suspicious reading, of looking behind and beyond the text for clues to a bigger picture. The hermeneutics of suspicion produced "very productive critical habits" that, Kosofsky Sedgwick suggests, by the late 1990s were "perhaps by now nearly synonymous with criticism itself" (124). Similarly, Felski calls the interpretative practices associated with the hermeneutics of suspicion a "thought style" and notes how it has shaped literary as well as more broadly humanist modes of interpretation since then.

Kosofsky Sedgwick was one of the first to signal disenchantment with this "intellectual baggage" (124). Her seminal essay, "Paranoid Reading and Reparative Reading, or, You're So Paranoid, You Probably Think This Introduction Is about You," published in the late 1990s, can be said to have kick-started debates that would continue and intensify over the following decades. Suspicious reading, Kosofsky Sedgwick insists, really is paranoid reading. As she sees it, critical inquiry and paranoid inquiry have become virtually coextensive and practically mandatory in literary studies (125). Alternatives are excluded and "anything *but* a paranoid critical stance has come to seem naïve, pious, or complaisant" (126).

But paranoid reading not only constitutes a "uniquely sanctioned *methodology*" in the American academy, according to Kosofsky Sedgwick (126). Michael Warner claims that it also functioned to "legitimate the profession" in the twentieth century. In a period characterized by "a widely felt disenchantment with the idea of literature," literary departments nonetheless positioned themselves as providing, via critical reading, "a basic element of education" (2004, 14). In the process, however, critical reading was positioned as in stark opposition to what must then have been "uncritical reading" which in turn was associated with naivete, unreflectiveness, and unsystematicity, with "identification, self-forgetfulness, reverie, sentimentality, enthusiasm, literalism, aversion, distraction" (15). Referring to Kosofsky Sedgwick, Warner says that critical reading has grown into what is in effect a paranoid suspicion of attachments to the text as an object of study (16). Kosofsky Sedgwick, Warner, and several others have since argued that the centrality of distantiation is not to be underestimated: the critical reader must continually anticipate manipulations by the text and its contexts.

Warner's essay was published in Jane Gallop's edited collection *Polemic: Critical or Uncritical* (2004), which evolved from a 2002 symposium. This collection and its "reconsideration of the opposition between critical and uncritical reading" (6) thus represent a relatively early intervention in the formation of what is not yet called postcritique. Indeed, Gallop and her contributors do not position their project in an acute relation to the present but rather investigate "the formulation of our ongoing sense of the critical" (6). This involved investigating deeply historical conditions and conceptions of critique and critical reading, ultimately reaching back to medieval texts and reading practices and then forward to religious wrestling with the relation between reason and faith, to Samuel Johnson's eighteenth-century conception of a "common reader," and to more modern and secular conceptions of reason and its limitations from Kant to Habermas to Foucault. Such a perspective reminds us, as does Amy Hollywood in her contribution to *Polemic: Critical or Uncritical*, that confronting what we perceive as uncritical modes of reading may force us not only to revaluate them but also to interrogate our conceptions of critical reading in the first place (2004, 45). A wider historical as well as postcolonial perspective also enables a critical revaluation of assumptions about the reason of the critical subject itself, as well as of the imperialist underpinnings of conceptions and formations of the public sphere and their seemingly inextricable links to critique as formulated in the post-Kantian tradition (see Spivak and Gallop 2004, 179). *Polemic: Critical or Uncritical* as a whole gives us a sense of the importance of historical as well as cultural and political contextualizations of critique and critical reading as well as of the absolute necessity of problematizing our capacity for pursuing them and relating them to our own time. As such, the collection is untimely in the productive, critical sense. As Gayatri Chakravorty Spivak says, "I am still putting together the ingredients for our historical moment. I don't yet have a definition" (181).

The closer we come to contemporary debates on postcritique, however, the more the spatiotemporal framework starts tightening up, narrowing down, and closing in. The context and the debates become increasingly centered on a more limited and more contemporary context. In a 2009 special issue of the journal *Representations* (evolving from a 2008 symposium), editors Stephen Best and Sharon Marcus and their contributors explore "the way we read now," "we" reminding us of the positioning and periodization of this form of hermeneutics which the editors explicitly specify to mean themselves and their contributors as purportedly representative of scholars receiving doctoral degrees in English or comparative literature after 1983 (2009, 1). This "we" is specific and at least in the first instance limited to the issue's contributors, but it is intended for a certain generation and period for which suspicious hermeneutics has been naturalized. Like the Gallop collection, although now rather more polemically (ironically), the aim of the Best and Marcus collection is to reconsider the overwhelming formative influence of "symptomatic reading" on the discipline during this specific period.

"Symptomatic reading" has several things in common with the hermeneutics of suspicion because, according to Best and Marcus, it is essentially of "a specific type that took meaning to be hidden, repressed, deep, and in need of detection and disclosure by an interpreter" (1). This strategy comes from Althusser, however, who, inspired by Marx, Spinoza, and psychoanalysis, deploys it by reading Marx himself. This reading makes it possible to recognize inconsistencies and absences in Marx's oeuvre (and ultimately in other texts) caused by contextual and ideological underpinnings that remain unconscious or unacknowledged. In Althusser's formulation, symptomatic reading "divulges the undivulged event in the text it reads," (quoted in Best and Marcus, 5) or, as Best and Marcus put it, "assumes that texts are shaped by questions they do not themselves pose" (5).

As arguably the most prominent inheritor of symptomatic reading in America, Frederic Jameson sets the stakes for literature as the inevitable expression of the political unconscious, developing a critical method vehemently Marxist but also more historicist, more psychoanalytical, and more literary. For him, symptomatic reading is a way of recognizing a literary or cultural text at first not as individual so much as connected with a larger mode of production, and then as reflecting "a fundamental dimension of our collective thinking and our collective fantasies about history and reality" (1981, 18). Symptomatic reading in general and Jameson's work in particular became enormously influential in America during the final decades of the twentieth century. According to Best and Marcus, this popularity may be explained by its seeming endowment of literary criticism and the literary critic with an aura of strenuous labor and activism (5).

The prominence of symptomatic reading can be recognized in the way Jameson associates it directly with challenging readers to comprehend the spatiotemporal and economic conditions of late capitalism. For him, symptomatic reading unveils the return of the allegorical in postmodernity as a figurative machinery employed to grasp totality in globalization, as a method for thinking a system vaster than what can be "encompassed by the natural and historically developed categories of perception with which human beings normally orient themselves" (1992: 2). In a postmodern context, the allegorical also becomes the conspiratorial as the difficulties in obtaining an overview come to be aligned with a sense concealment and impersonality (2). Thus, Jameson finds it necessary to interrogate paranoid fiction but also, undoubtedly, to become a suspicious reader himself.

Responding to what they recognize as a current tendency to move away from symptomatic reading, Best and Marcus and their contributors survey alternative ways of reading. This is in line with the move away from suspicious or symptomatic readings as a whole, which comes also with proposals for new ways of reading. Kosofsky Sedgwick's early essay had included not just a critique of suspicious hermeneutics but also a proposition for an alternative: reparative reading, which she constructs via Klein. Best and Marcus formulate their project in terms of various modes of "surface reading." Rather than always suspiciously looking beyond the text, they suggest we pay attention to "what is evident, perceptible, apprehensible in texts" (9). Other alternatives in this move away from symptomatic reading include Timothy Bewes's "generous reading," or "reading with the grain"— "thinking the text inseparably from the text . . . thinking its singularity" (2010, 24).

In *The Limits of Critique* (2015), Felski provides a thorough account of what she sees as the stakes in these debates. Noting the "avalanche" of arguments regarding depth versus surface reading, she is positive about the new, postcritical directions in which Best, Marcus, and other participants in the discussions lean, but she is skeptical of the metaphor of the surface. As she points out, depth versus surface does not necessarily correspond to suspicious versus nonsuspicious reading (54). More generally, and important for our purposes, this is when the various practices of the hermeneutics of suspicion and symptomatic reading become more explicitly and systematically positioned as a genre. While critique in a more general historical sense is recognized as an eclectic assortment of philosophical, political, and hermeneutic tenets, ideologies, and modes, as I have suggested, it is positioned here as "a specific genre of writing: the rhetoric of suspicious reading in literary studies and in the humanities and interpretative social sciences generally" (187). Terry Eagleton notes the humorous ring to Felski's title, saying that, while it points out that critique, at least in the Kantian tradition, is fundamentally about setting limits— "distinguishing what a form of inquiry may legitimately address from what is off-bounds to it" (2017, n.p.)— it perhaps signals not only the limits that Felski sees in the field but the very perimeters she herself sets on what constitutes critique in this context.

However, the delimitation of critique is not her doing, Felski argues, but rather that of literary scholars, as they have preferred to engage with the loftier-sounding "critique" even though the subjective and affective "suspicion" may be a more accurate description of their practice. Critique, she, says, endows scholars with "a sense of philosophical weightiness from its proximity to the tradition of Kant and Marx" (7). In Felski's historical lineage, then, "critique" mainly refers to the reading practices that literary scholars have purportedly been engaging in over the past decades when they have actually been engaging in the less grand-sounding "hermeneutics of suspicion." By preferring "critique," she submits, literary scholars have accumulated an underacknowledged debt to the hermeneutics of suspicion (2) and so the "specialness" of critique can be downgraded because it can be acknowledged to include diverse practices of suspicious reading such as "symptomatic reading, ideology critique, Foucauldian historicism, various techniques of scanning texts for signs of transgression or resistance" (2). In this way, Felski hopes to reveal similarities between the climate change skeptic, the criminal detective, and the literary critic to show that suspicious reading is not necessarily oppositional, transformative, or radical (3).

Striving to articulate a distinction between what she sees as a "tradition of *philosophical suspicion*"—Descartes, Kant, Freud, Marx, Nietzsche, the Frankfurt School, "post-'68 Parisian thought"—and "a *literary suspicion*," Felski points to the way literary works themselves may be instigators of suspicion (40). With the assistance of critics such as Ricoeur and Margot Norris, she claims that modernist literature resists easy reading and straightforward meaning, effectively provoking readers to become suspicious (42). It invites, demands, and even effectively trains readers in a hermeneutics of suspicion, the logic of which can and is turned against them (43). While pointing to a common methodological humdrum of the usefulness of a critique already present in the work at which it is aimed, Felski also shows how critique is "enmeshed in the world rather than opposed to the world." For her, this proves that critique "offers no special guarantee of intellectual insight, political virtue, or ideological purity" (51).

It would be difficult to see anyone in the philosophical tradition Felski describes pretending to offer such guarantees. Quite the contrary, it seems fair to suggest that critique in a more general philosophical sense has long—perhaps always—existed precisely in its entanglements with rather than opposition to the world and that no historical formulations of critique offer guarantees of insight, virtue, or purity. Indeed, critique in this sense is always already chronotopic—it is intimately associated with its contemporaneity and with finding a space—a sphere—in which this present can be thought. This is one of the many reasons that critique is most often seen as an absolutely crucial but also forever failing process—a Beckettian striving toward always failing better. I do not suggest a gap or flaw in Felski's argument. Because she has already announced her take on critique as a genre specifically associated with literary studies in America after Ricoeur, such a suggestion would point to what she sees as the failed promises of this particular context.

With Elizabeth S. Anker, Felski cultivates the description of critique as a genre. As such, it is seen as "a form of rhetoric that is codified via style, tone, figure, vocabulary, and voice and that attends to certain tropes, motifs, and structures of texts" (Anker and Felski 2017, 3). While acknowledging the fluidity of genre, Anker and Felski identify what they see as its key modalities. One is its diagnostic quality, derived from psychoanalysis, from Foucault's problematization but ultimate reinforcement of the diagnostic by adding the knowledge-power relation, and from a Marxian, in America largely Jamesonian, symptomatic reading of texts as fragments of larger social and political totalities. A second modality is allegory. Here, Anker and Felski trace various submodalities—the text read as manifesting and perhaps naturalizing a larger sociopolitical reality; the reader as identifying indexical functions of particular characters and thus detecting various modes of oppression; literature itself as staging the impossibility of its own reading (à la De Man); critics themselves as stand-ins for larger oppositional frameworks. A third modality is critique's self-reflexivity. Critique targets what may otherwise be taken as natural, transparent, or taken for granted, including its own practices, a reflex that leads to metacritique. There is no end to suspicion, as each new suspicious reading must lead to a suspicious reading of that reading. And so on and so forth. According to Anker and Felski, this has led to an attraction to self-conscious literary texts as objects of study (6–9).

Considered as a genre, then, with its principal features being diagnosis, allegory, and self-reflexivity, critique is centrally about turning in on itself. And, indeed, what is it exactly that the diagnostic, allegorical, and self-reflexive qualities are supposed to speak to if the larger oppositional frameworks are put to the side? Whether these are the limits of critique in America or the limits of Felski's conception of it, such articulations intimate that it is possible to conceive of critique as a genre in which the literary text ultimately speaks inwardly rather than outwardly and where the oppositional mode is not seen to be actively and meaningfully linked to a larger historical sociopolitical context.

Felski's brief engagement with the role of literary texts as forming and expressing a tradition of suspicion is itself indicative of the rather narrow and specific context that is seen to fail with the postcritical turn. Allotting approximately one page to this modernist context, she marks an implicit acknowledgment of a larger historical cultural, social, and political context in which critique, not just in the philosophical tradition but also in the literary tradition, is nothing like its enforced polarized and negative practice that she spends most of the book interrogating. In this larger and more nuanced context and understanding, suspicion and suspicious reading raise questions about epistemology and ontology and about modernity and literary form that are much more extensive than the distinct genre that she addresses in her argument as a whole. This suggests either that critique as it developed during the final decades of the twentieth century really is negative and limited and/or that Felski's conception of critique during this period is negative and limited.

With their 2017 edited collection *Critique and Postcritique*, Anker and Felski are ready to prefix the term "critique" with "post." Both "post" and "critique" raise the stakes on the general trend of "flourishing alternatives to a suspicious hermeneutics" (1). Although "post" is taken to stand for "a complex temporality" that looks forward as well as acknowledges its dependency on the past (1), it clearly positions Anker and Felski's discussions against what they see as the "adversarial stance" of critique and its inability to defend and justify the importance of literary studies in the present (19). With Anker and Felski surfaces more explicitly what seems to have been implicitly haunting at least some of the earlier readings—anxiety regarding the status of literature and literary studies in an American contemporaneity characterized by a continuous decline in and even attacks on the humanities. This is a significant dimension of my argument, and we will return to it in the critique section of the next chapter.

Essentially—and unsurprisingly when it comes to the new ways of reading but also more opaquely and problematically when calling it "postcritique"—this understanding of critique is strongly linked to literature and to reading practices that, as we have seen, are inspired by various forms of suspicious and symptomatic reading. What is at stake here is critique not only as what Anker and Felski call "a distinct academic genre" (2) but also as a distinctively literary practice. The critique discussed by Felski is not only determined by a literary discipline but also situated in relation to a specific geographical and historical context—the American academy in the final decades of the twentieth century. The "critique" that the "post" hopes to problematize, in other words, and as I have outlined, is not primarily formulated or inspired by Kant or Hegel, Marx, Arendt, Benjamin, the Frankfurt School, Negri, or others, but is specifically a theoretical conglomeration of mainly French theorists that was consolidated in American humanities departments during this period. In fact, and as names such as Ricoeur, Althusser, and Foucault indicate, critique in these terms is often concomitant with the curious phenomenon called Theory or French Theory, as it became such in American universities. Indeed, in this context the two phenomena are rarely easily or even possibly separated.

Critique/Theory

Theory with a capital *T*, or "French Theory" certainly has its own chronotopic conditions. It has its modern starting points in 1960s and 1970s France, but became "Theory" only once it was imported to America in the 1980s and 1990s. As such, it is a particularly American phenomenon and, according to François Cusset, a particularly academic phenomenon. The work of French thinkers—central to Cusset are Foucault, Derrida, and Deleuze along with Jean Baudrillard and Jean-François Lyotard among others—was appropriated, decontextualized, "domesticated," "homogenized," given "a political use-value that was specifically American" (2008, 10). The focus truly was French, says Milne, with German sources of critique largely neglected (3). Thus, as Eric Hayot points out, theory of this kind began not quite with the Russian formalists in the 1910s nor with Freud in Vienna in the 1920s nor with Marxists scholars between the wars nor with New Criticism after the war nor even in and with French thinkers in the 1950s and 1960s. These were all beginnings of a sort, but Theory as such did not begin until all these and other influences came together in American universities in the 1970s (2017, 279).

The influence of "the Theory era" on American academia was considerable. Hayot claims that it changed not only ways of thinking and teaching or only what to think and teach but also the very structures of teaching and thinking. To the extent that we now live in a post-Theory era, he argues, we do so because Theory had transformed the intellectual and the social completely (280). Both Cusset and Hayot point to ways in which Theory changed structures of research and teaching not least by enabling or necessitating a new interdisciplinarity. Thus, despite the emergence of Theory as such, Hayot says that one of its major strengths lay its diversity and internal incompatibility (280). Structuralism, Marxism, deconstruction, psychoanalysis, feminism, New Historicism, cultural studies and materialism, sociology of literature, and queer theory formed different schools. Some overlapped nicely and others did not, some more or less disappeared, and some thrived and/or transformed with time. An example of such interdisciplinary and theoretically informed work, as well as a prominent and almost inevitable reference in discussions of postcritique is Kosofsky Sedgwick's aforementioned revaluation of her own "paranoid" reading practices in the late 1990s.

If one article is cited as frequently as, if not more than, Kosofsky Sedgwick's in discussions of postcritique, it is Bruno Latour's article in *Critical Inquiry* (2004), which obviously positions itself in a discourse on "critique" although its discussions exclusively pertain to what I describe as "Theory." Latour argues that critique prevents us from dealing with pressing matters of concern in the present, that it has been adopted by our enemies, that it has helped them dismantle the world, and that it has poisoned the hearts of the people against the humanities. But, again, it is not primarily Kant or Arnold or Marx or Arendt or Benjamin who are his prime targets. Rather, it is "French generals" like Foucault, Pierre Bourdieu, and Baudrillard ("a French general, no, a marshal of critique" [2004, 228]) who are the culprits. It is the French generals who are apparently always one war late (225). Latour claims that politeness makes him stick with the "French field commanders" (229), but the fact remains that his target is quite clearly French Theory in its particularly American articulations. It is symptomatic that Latour's essay has become an ever-present reference point in postcritique debates and discussions although his institutional belonging is in science studies. That Latour's essay is generally quoted in debates on critique and postcritique is both indicative of the fluid distinctions between Theory and critique and, by virtue of its importance to literary discussion of postcritique, indicative of the centrality of Theory to literary studies in America.

Milne holds that the term "theory" risks obscuring the philosophical traditions from which terms and concepts are derived (3). The process of transforming a broad set of French thinkers into Theory required taking much of Theory out of context and domesticating it to fit an American setting, a process which included many adjustments but most centrally, Cusset argues, cleansing it of its attention to market forces and capital (xv). This argument comes with a qualification. Theory did entail a politicization of American academia. In its early days, French Theory first came into its American being in the temporary blurring of the borders between campuses and political upheaval in the 1970s—it intervened, as Cusset says "precisely on the border separating the counterculture from the university" (69). However, he notes that it soon became a more purely academic enterprise. Despite the initial interest and dissemination of then new French ideas among young Americans, theory of this kind never had quite the same grounding in society and the public sphere as did its French originators. In fact, Cusset maintains that Theory as a phenomenon stemmed from what was essentially a "creative misunderstanding" crucially related to differences in how French and American intellectual spheres were organized internally (5). In France, thinkers were active and actively engaged in public and political debates of the moment. Critique, Didier Fassin says, was "more than an intellectual exercise" for the French scholars whose involvements included student protests, worker strikes, and anti-apartheid struggles among others (2017, 18). The public intellectual is an important figure in France and as the then recent events of May 1968 gave witness to, students as well as professors where taking their theories to the streets. This is also, arguably, why the influence of French theories and theorists gradually diminished in France after these events—the political climate changed.

Yet when Cusset encounters a twenty-first century American academia filled with despair and self-criticism, he is surprised. One might have expected, he says, that the crises in the world—not only 9/11 but the wars after, including the war on terror and the surveillance and security measures coming with it—would have led to some reconsideration of Theory's reluctance to address the role of markets and capital; European and Asian academia expected some sort of awakening of American liberals (xiii). What seems to have happened instead was largely the inward-turning self-criticism that is now called postcritique. In American academia, as we have begun to see, this trend came in many guises and built on slightly different starting points, but identifying it as intimately linked with French Theory and its seeming fate allows us to recognize the continued ambivalent relation to the market and capital in this field.

Crossing the Atlantic and becoming Theory, the conditions of French theories and theorists changed radically. On the one hand, they radicalized academic discourse and played "an often crucial role in the social and political debates in contemporary American culture" (7); on the other hand, they were to be shaped by the relative isolation of American students and academics and the relative absence of the public intellectual (36). Cusset points to a number of ways in which Theory has been more secluded than the theoretical interventions of the French in the decades before. On a practical and social level, there is the common geographical isolation of university campuses along with a general view of the college years as set apart from larger social structures and the rest of the students' and the nation's life. On a more general and political-historical level, America's political history has looked upon intellectuals in general with suspicion and has not given them or the public sphere much ground. This has caused a lack of conceptual as well as substantial bridges between academic and public debate. Since the 1950s, demands for specialization and productivity have increasingly characterized university life, widening the distance between intellectual and public (36). Cusset shows how these factors contributed to Theory becoming highly specialized and caught up in the politics of academic life through career investments, publication routines, and star theorists.

A key question, therefore, but one that is seldom asked, is how Theory as critique as expressed in American academia has and can fare in its relative disconnect from, and radical transformations of, a public sphere. We need to remind ourselves here of the foundational relation between the public sphere and critique as pointed out in Chapter 1. For Kant, as we saw, it is our duty to society not only to think for ourselves but to do so in a public manner. Only by claiming our freedom to think and critically interrogate society together and in the open can we as individuals and as a society, move toward Enlightenment. Only by public scrutiny can political power gain legitimacy. Only by public debate and, ideally, new public understandings, can society progress. As we have seen, modern thinkers such as Arendt and Habermas point back to the public sphere of Greek and Roman times and articulate the centrality, and problematics, of the public sphere in modernity. We have also seen how the concept and instantiations of the public sphere have continued to be problematized—in its Enlightenment presumptions as well as in its later idealist, bourgeois, masculinist assumptions. Moreover, contemporary scholars have shown that new forms of communication and neoliberal practices pose challenges to the public sphere today. Frequently pointed to as the main challenges are the largely failed potential of the Internet as a space for the democratization of debate, the infiltration and predominance of capitalist principles in state politics, and the transnationalization and globalization of people and markets.

It is indicative that most discussions of postcritique, even as they address the problem of the relevance of critique to society at large, do not consider the role the public sphere and its current challenges in the exercise of critique as well as in its appraisal. In fact, disregard for the role of the public sphere in critique is a fundamental problem facing the contemporary debate on postcritique. It is also where the tension between Theory as it has been institutionalized in America and critique in its broader historical and largely European tradition becomes more acute. In fact, the lack of in-depth consideration of the public sphere and the absence of the sphere itself may be seen as a dimension that is haunting critique and postcritique.

One of the key spaces identified as a public sphere in America is the university. I will develop my conception of postcritique in relation to the university in Chapter 3 and as a paranoid chronotope in Chapter 4, but for now let us briefly summarize the tensions that have emerged between power, literature, and critique in light of such a notion. The period of the mid-1900s to the present shows shifting modes of power, from the more tangible and spatiotemporally identifiable disciplinary modes of power to the more spatiotemporally dispersed power of control and security. Institutions spanning the family, the school, the factory, and the hospital no longer perform the same continuous and formative role when our desires and affects are continually anticipated and modulated via neoliberalized and disseminated modes of control. These gradual shifts between what I call chronotopes of discipline and chronotopes of control respectively generate a paranoid response, especially among those who previously felt relatively safe in their subject position. Such a response was exemplified in *Your Fathers* in the way these chronotopic shifts unsettle not only the young white male protagonist but also the very novel form that maintains him. The role of the modern novel in fashioning and maintaining a certain conception of the liberal subject in disciplinary forms has been brought up as an explanation for this paranoid shaping of subject and form alike.

In the final section of this chapter, I exposed this understanding as itself potentially paranoid via the recent critique of critique. In subsequently identifying the historical background and incentives of this postcritique, I suggested that it is shaped by conditions particular to the American context. These conditions have, at least up to a point, been characterized by the lack of a self-evident connection to the public sphere both as a space for its articulations and as a target for its problematizations. Thus, suspicious reading can be seen as a mood and method in literary studies before it can be seen as critique in the broader sense discussed in Chapter 1, that is, as a crucial element in critical thinking together in public. In this way, and in anticipation of my conclusions, a paranoid chronotope has been constructed, one in which larger structures of the social and power are disavowed and reinterpreted as a more local concern.

3

TRUTH AND PARANOIA / PARANOID TRUTHS

Introduction

As we have noted, theories of the public sphere take very seriously the notion of political subjects who have both the capacity and the duty to think for themselves and to do so by reasoning with others in public. This is particularly clear in the Kantian subject's attempted consolidation of various Enlightenment trajectories of self and reason, of course, but it is also central to Arendt's appearance of the political subject via plurality, as well as to Habermas' educated liberal subject's appearance via communicative rationality in the public sphere. For all these in their diverse ways, a significant responsibility is assigned to individual subjects at the same time that a considerable accountability is allocated to the society in which they live for providing the spaces in which these individual responsibilities can emerge, and merge, as the political. While configurations of these relations have differed considerably over time, making it impossible to grasp them as one self-identical and consistent chronotope—the old market squares, the coffee houses and salons, the cultural arenas and universities—we can nonetheless turn the process and patterning of figuration on itself to discern two crucial components of this spatiotemporal arrangement: first, a subject of reason and, second, a public sphere in which this reason is called for to make judgment and ascertain what is true or at least reasonable. In chronotopic terms, we may say that the unstable messiness of the embodied world with its differing perspectives and experiences finds its arbiter in the less unstable and less messy—because more intellectual and organized—political subject in and of the public sphere. In terms of truth, specifically its contours, or at least its conditions, have been seen as separable from individual feelings, bodies, and desires as well as from the economy.

In this chapter, I do not deal with truth as the immense philosophical notion it is but rather trace some contemporary challenges to truth. I do so first by outlining some of its configurations in the current mediascape and under recent technological and economic conditions. In this initial section, I grapple with the ways in which truth does not seem to matter much to contemporary public debate, and identify two trends—a post-truth trend in which affect and cognitive bias trump truth and a neoliberal trend in which precise measurements and data are supposed to remedy precisely such affective economies. Foucault's theorization of truth regimes helps in situating these configurations historically and in the present. In the second section, I read Patrick Flanery's novel *I Am No One* to see how a truth that seems to come from nowhere disconnects a subject of judgment not only from others' truth but also from its own capacity for it. Employing the paranoid chronotope, I identify the disjunctive realities of the novel and show how an awakening to the "true" state of things contributes to a lack of shared reality. In the critique section that closes the chapter, I elaborate on questions of who will or is supposed to know the truth. The dwindling role of the expert in the present is situated in relation to what is sometimes seen as an inbuilt psychopathology, or even paranoia, of expertise. Positioning such perennial uncertainties about the possibility and status of knowing in relation to a contemporary deterioration of the university as a public sphere, I give a broad and critical context to postcritique.

Section 1: Truth, Paranoia, Society

Preliminaries on Truth

Truth, as Michel Foucault has taught us, is not best approached with the aim of establishing its universals—a futile task, he says—but to identify and perhaps negotiate its entanglements with power. Foucault distinguishes between two Enlightenment approaches to truth. The first approach works toward establishing formal conditions for truth and universal norms for distinguishing between rationality and irrationality. The second labors to analyze the historical conditions of and for truth and the rationalities put to work to establish it. Unlike the former, for which formal conditions and universal norms may appear accessible to rational inquiry alone, the latter recognizes that the question must be a "genealogical enterprise" that interrogates universals as "effects of historical practices" (Lemke 2012, 63). Of course, it is the latter that Foucault develops in his study of historical regimes of truth. Truth, as he puts it, "is a thing of this world." Truth is not generated by free spirits or protracted solitudes but produced by various constraints at various points in time. As such, it is necessarily within power. "Each society," he famously says,

> has its regime of truth, its "general politics" of truth—that is, the types of discourse it accepts and makes function as true; the mechanisms and instances that enable one to distinguish true and false statements; the means by which each is sanctioned; the techniques and procedures accorded value in the acquisition of truth; the status of those who are charged with saying what counts as true. (2000, 131)

So, then, what techniques and procedures are used to acquire the truth in the twenty-first century and who is charged with saying "what counts as true" today? A first observation here must be that what counts as true seems to be pulling in two directions. On the one hand, aspirations to truth seem to have become increasingly impotent as a deciding factor in politics and society generally. When Oxford Dictionaries Online identified "post-truth" as the word of the year in 2016, this was certainly a sign of the times, the most obvious reference points then being the Brexit referendum and the election of Donald Trump. Defining post-truth as "relating to or denoting circumstances in which objective facts are less influential in shaping public opinion than appeals to emotion and personal belief," *Oxford Dictionaries* noted that "post" refers not to a point in time when truth is gone but rather to a point at which it does not matter much. They also note that post-truth can be understood as an extension of Stephen Colbert's "truthiness" not only to a particular situation or assertion but to "a general characteristic of our age" (*Oxford English Dictionaries Online*, 2016). *Truthiness*, as Christopher Castiglia clarifies it, is the production of something that sounds true to those already in agreement without having recourse to logic or fact (2017, 214). This comes with a heavy recalibration of what counts as expertise and the value of academic, scientific, and intellectual labor. The "who" charged with saying what counts as true, in other words, is not a delineable and rational subject or institution so much as a conglomeration of affects, emotions, and convictions.

On the other hand, and seemingly counteracting such post-truth conglomerations, the final decades of the twentieth century and onward have seen the development of highly measured techniques and procedures to secure the acquisition of truth. Such empiricist and positivist strategies run across social institutions demanding "data accumulation, data display, data-driven leadership, and data-driven accountability regimes" (Kenneth J. Saltman 2018, 2). Measurements, rankings, numbers, and algorithms are mobilized and seem to bulwark society against the fake news and post-truth strategies of major contemporary politicians and parties and to counteract the devaluation of truth and the conspiratorial formations it contributes to. This firm preoccupation with numbers and measurements is closely aligned with the developments of neoliberalism as a governing rationality, a rationalization and marketization of the human and society that holds that everything can—and should—be measured. "All conduct," Wendy Brown says, "is economic conduct; all spheres of existence are framed and measured by economic terms and metrics" (2015, 10). This not only transforms all components of society into businesses; as I will discuss later, it also releases truth from any foundations other than its current contractual and economic relations. Truth, in other words, becomes instrumentalized.

What we are witnessing is thus a curious arrangement of truth techniques that seems to pull not only in different but in opposite directions. In one direction, truth seems increasingly irrelevant to individuals and political systems; in the other, there is an obsession with numbers and measurements. Neither, arguably, lands us in ourselves as political subjects of reason and judgment. The truth that is felt to be right speaks to the affects, emotions, and desires that have constructed and continuously construct us less as individual subjects and more as "dividuals" in the Deleuzian sense discussed in Chapter 2. This is a truth that binds us to certain opinions, people, and groups while constructing others as enemies via cognitive bias at best and fear and paranoia at worst. It is a truth that binds us to ourselves and assembles those "dividual" bits and pieces into a sense of wholeness and identity. In the face of the unoverviewable control, which I also discussed in Chapter 2, and the chaotic overload of information and disinformation that I will speak more about later, such truths help construct a shield—an identity—through our truth. In this way, the truths of others become not merely different from ours, or even just opposite from ours, but opposed to ours. By the same token, others become not merely different from us, or somehow just opposite to us, but opposed to us: a questioning if not persecution of our selves as truth. We will see this more clearly in my discussion of the perversion of identity politics in Chapter 4.

The truth as numbers, in turn, seems to anchor indistinct power and informational chaos into tangible rationality, but this is a rationality that ultimately tells us little about ourselves, inadequately mirrors our experiences, and deprives us of our own and our joint capacity —however incomplete and faulty—for judgment. Judgment, Kant taught us, is far from infallible but it nonetheless constitutes an absolutely essential practice for enlightened subjects. Judgment in its general post-Kantian sense is based on cognition combined with experience and knowledge as well as on a constant interrogation of our own capacity for it. We must continually ask ourselves what we know and on what basis we make our judgment. This points back to judgment as relying on public reasoning—on the deliberations of a public sphere—which, as we saw in Chapter 1, is essentially what makes us political subjects: individual judgment exercised via critique in the public sphere. For this to be feasible, however, there needs to be a public sphere that both enables and demands this of us, a public sphere that interpellates us, if you will, as political subjects, a public sphere that not only enables public debate and deliberation but relies on us as political subjects in the first place. In recent decades, the state of the public sphere has not mirrored this ideal well. In what follows, I will show how the seeming disjunction between post-truth emotions and positivist neoliberal measurements is born of a changing public sphere and how it contributes to a spiraling paranoid chronotope of truth in contemporary Western society.

Truth Media

We have become strangely used to the prevalence of blatant falsities and deliberate lies in politics. Most of us are conscious of at least some of the ways in which "news" is manipulated or even fake, how facts may, in fact, be "alternative," and how "information" reaches us in individualized and biased spurts. The borders between what counts as news sources and what counts as conspiracy theorist sources are increasingly blurred. Online troll factories are not only or even primarily identifiable as occasional misguided youths or extremists in cellars, as we might have imagined them, but are frequently large organizations with paid employees, such as the Russian "Internet Research Agency," that produce whatever "news" they are paid to deliver or quite simply jam the system with too much information or hate mongering. At the same time, algorithms contribute to the consolidation and radicalization of our own existing perspectives. What kind of public sphere is this?

The media, of course, is a central dimension of the public sphere. Indeed, the "structural transformations of the public sphere" that Habermas described in his famous 1962 book of that name are largely about changes in the press: from the smaller privately governed public institutions that he associates with the liberal model of the public sphere to the expanded, commercialized, and societally powerful institutions in which private ownership becomes a problem. As smaller media outlets grow into mass media outlets, journalism turns to public services heavily shaped by the commercialization of the press in general and economic interests in particular. The media as supportive of the public sphere as a meeting place in which critical subjects debate becomes the media as governing those debates in the first place. "Whereas formerly the press was able to limit itself to the transmission and amplification of the rational-critical debate of private people assembled into a public, now conversely this debate gets shaped by mass media to begin with" (1991, 188). Even if Habermas thus identifies a central problem in the relation between media and the public already visible in the 1960s, and although the media has continued to develop beyond the "new media" he has in mind for that time, it continues to be regarded as a salient dimension of the public. And as Sophia A. McClennen notes, the media is "one of the main forms of public pedagogy—shaping the national consciousness in ways that directly influence the health of democracy" (2016, 32).

Looking at more recent developments in the relationship between the media and the public, McClennen observes ways in which developments in the media and media platforms work toward disintegrating rather than strengthening the public sphere. Cable television, for example, and the 24/7 news cycle that it has consolidated, brings viewers "less facts and more punditry." In addition, "the ratings-driven market mentality of news shows has favored scandal and sensation over investigative reporting of key issues" (32). It also favors strong emotion and polarization. In fact, the media environment of the twenty-first century is, Sarah Sobieraj and Jeffrey M. Berry claim, "uniquely supportive of outrage-based political discourse" (2011, 22). Their investigation of this outrage relies on a definition that highlights mechanisms linking contemporary news dynamics and the paranoid mode today. Outrage, they say,

> [demarcates] a particular form of political discourse involving efforts to provoke visceral responses (e.g., anger, righteousness, fear, moral indignation)

from the audience through the use of overgeneralizations, sensationalism, misleading or patently inaccurate information, ad hominem attacks, and partial truths about opponents, who may be individuals, organizations, or entire communities of interest (e.g., progressives or conservatives) or circumstance (e.g., immigrants). Outrage sidesteps the messy nuances of complex political issues in favor of melodrama, misrepresentative exaggeration, mockery, and improbable forecast of impending doom. Outrage talk is not so much discussion as it is verbal competition, political theater with a scorecard. (20)

Noting that outrage in political discourse is obviously not new, Sobieraj and Berry compare their study of present-day outrage in political journalistic discourse with that of syndicated columnists from 1955 and 1975. They find that even in those years of "impassioned politics of protest," American journalism remained considerably more restrained than it is today (34). They say that in an earlier period in which three major networks competed for dominance and thus for the largest portion of a mass audience, the strategy had to be one of avoiding offense. In our more recent narrowcasting environment consisting of numerous programs, talk shows, blogs, and other modes of online communication, it has become not only possible but desirable to home in on and speak to more homogenous groups. Outrage connects niche audiences with appropriate advertisers (22). Radio talk show hosts such as Rush Limbaugh, Mike Savage, and Sean Hannity divert the grief and anger of frustrated citizens to appropriate enemies. Outrage media, Michael Kimmel observes, has risen alongside the construction and mobilization of eroded entitlement among white men in the twenty-first century (2017, 34).

The most extreme case in contemporary mainstream television is, of course, the right-wing network Fox News, founded in 1996. Fox News has grown not only into the most watched cable network in America but also increasingly from a conservatively oriented network into "an active and unapologetic mouthpiece for the Republican Party" (Brock and Rabin-Havt, 9). You do not need to be an investigative and progressive journalist dedicated to monitoring misinformation in conservative media—as are David Brock and the nonprofit Media Matters organization he founded—to perceive the profound and rather flagrant disjunction between the Fox News motto—"fair and balanced"—and the unabashed promotion of "politically motivated misinformation" they engage in (Brock and Rabin-Havt, 2012, 11). Comparing the Fox News motto with Orwellian "Newspeak," David Neiwert says that the network and other right-wing media increasingly eschew journalistic standards while claiming to speak truth to power (2017, 9). Indeed, a successful strategy of such media is to position itself as the truth teller up against the corruption and conspiracies of the deep state and the "liberal" and often "global" "elites" controlling other media as well as scientific discourse. With its rhetoric of violence and demonization, its equating of the "truths" of lobbyists and politicians with the truths proposed by scientific experts, and its frequent accommodation of conspiracy theories, this media has contributed incalculably to a disdain for truth in general and a polarized and paranoid climate in American society in particular.

The construction of alternative truths by news outlets of this kind is aided by the ways in which online technology is mobilized to generate opinion with and for a specific agenda. One example is the more than 13.000 automated Twitter accounts (for both sides but more for the pro-leave position) in connection with the Brexit referendum, or the automated online debate surrounding the US election of 2016 (see James Bridle 2018, 237). It is also abetted by the active dissemination of conspiracy theories via message boards such as 4chan and 8chan and by sites such as Breitbart and Infowars. The latter, reported in 2017 to have over 10 million visits monthly, has as its primary function to produce fake news and spread conspiracy theories. And what does it matter that it has been banned by several major social media platforms when President Trump gladly retweeted its content while accusing "radical left-wing media" such as *The New York Times*, the *Washington Post*, and CNN of producing "FAKE NEWS"?

One response to such configurations of "truth" is a "willing suspension of belief," which Geoffrey Kabaservice sees particularly in populist conservatives and Trump voters who consume online alt-right "news" and other right-wing media (Kabaservice 2017, n.p.). He suggests that a suspension of belief becomes possible either because people on the right simply appreciate provocations of Democrats and liberals, intellectuals, and pretentious commentators, or because they see in fake news the "underlying symbolic truths" that none of the Democrats and liberals, intellectuals, and pretentious commentators are willing to articulate. They might not actually believe that Barack Obama is a Muslim, that Democrats run sex rings, that climate change is a conspiracy created by China and/or scientists, but they do believe that Obama has a racial otherness that puts him in an uneasy relationship with "real America," that a corrupt government exploits exposed people for its own enjoyment, and that climate change science serves the globalists who are fine with sacrificing the working class (2017, n.p.).

The appeal of "underlying symbolic truths" can at least in part be explained by cognitive bias, particularly in the shape of confirmation bias, a phenomenon that is not paranoid in itself but makes us more likely to believe in information that corresponds with our existing beliefs. While there is nothing new about confirmation bias itself, the onslaught of information and disinformation today is likely to push us further in its direction. We are constantly subjected to news, opinions, views, and conspiracy theories, either via "fair and balanced" media such as Fox News or via forums without journalistic or scientific gatekeepers such as social media. In this new public sphere, holding on to our existing beliefs is like clinging to the ship's mast during a storm. During a storm, few people would spend time checking on the boat or even the mast itself. The skepticism required to negotiate the information/disinformation onslaught can protect us from lies and fake news, but it can also foster our inclination toward certain "truths" and our disinclination toward others. In extreme cases, according to Neiwert, the healthy skepticism most people have toward the current media landscape has been elevated to incredulity toward all more official sources and a "self-reinforcing form of highly selective skepticism" (32).

And what a formidable mast the alt-right universe has come to erect. This universe is broad and sprawling, but may be defined as "an international set of groups and individuals, operating primarily online though with off-line outlets, whose core belief is that 'white identity' is under attack from pro-multicultural and liberal elites and so-called 'social justice warriors' (SJWs) who allegedly use 'political correctness' to undermine Western civilization and the rights of white males" (Hermansson et al. 2020, 2). Despite its eclectic character—including, according to Patrik Hermansson, David Lawrence, Joe, Mulhall, and Simon Murdoch, three broad and frequently independent groupings that they identify as "the European New Right and Identitarian Movement, the American Alternative Right, and Online Antagonistic Communities" (3)—what unites them is rejection of the "the 'dangerous myth' of equality," according to leading alt-right figure Jared Taylor (2). The rights of women, minorities, the LGBT+ community, and the movements promoting them pose a serious threat to white people and therefore need to be aggressively opposed. This means a vehement rejection of what these groups see as left-wing, liberal democratic hegemony in the West (2), a central dimension of which is, of course, the mainstream media.

Neiwert, picking up the Orwellian strand, argues that what has been created is not only an "epistemological bubble" that generates, reconfirms, and strengthens alt-right and extremist values but, more than that, "an alternative universe."

In this America—"Alt-America"—global elites conspire to make the Muslim and non-American Barack Obama the president, to force ordinary people off their land and out of work by pushing the great hoax of climate change, to ban guns in preparation for a tyrannical dictatorship, perhaps a New World Order or a Sharia law caliphate, to import illegal immigrants to win their votes, and to shame increasingly terrorized white people via "political correctness" (2017, 28). "Established facts, supported by concrete real-world evidence are," Neiwert declares, "inconsequential to people inside the Alt-America universe." Indeed, such facts tend to be interpreted as yet another proof of "the conspiracy and its efforts to hide 'the truth'" (28). In alt-right circles, in other words, selective skepticism has turned into a more directed, purposeful, and systematic distrust. Or, as these people might put it themselves, gullibility has been transformed into active resistance to liberal mind control.

Exploring the concept, practice, and invocation of resilience in the American alt-right, Nicholas Michelsen and Pablo de Orellana show how the notion of truth becomes caught up in a larger project of resisting and fighting what is seen as dominant liberal thought and "cultural liberalism." The practice of resilience to the oppressive and manipulative presence of liberal values—values that are particularly evident and pernicious in claims to equality, racial integration, and gender—serves as a "unifying factor" among what is otherwise a considerable range and variation among alt-right movements (2019, 271). In fact, Michelsen and de Orellana argue, to the extent that there is "a clear and cohesive intellectual and political project present in these movements" or at least joint logics and sensibilities with "diagrammatic resonances," this can be located precisely in a resilience to "dominant liberal orthodoxy" (272). Such resilience becomes directly operational in the contemporary contest over the status of news and truth: "The subjectivity and believability of news is a key facet of alt-right resilience thinking" (282). It is tempting to parody this strategy as conspiracy theory, but, as Michelsen and de Orellana suggest, the "alt-right cleavage of fake/real is governed by a powerful conceptual structure predicated on believability according to speaker" (282). This cleavage posits "truth tellers" speaking on behalf of the real white American nation and identity as crucial counter-hegemonic forces against the discursive limitations and downright lies of liberal society. Developing resilience to mainstream news and liberal knowledge thus constitutes a crucial dimension of resistance that aims to salvage personal freedom and agency. This individual freedom and agency will be recovered by looking back—to a premodern mythic era—as well as forward—to a future free of liberal enslavement. The "purified subject" becomes possible by creating a "very real resilience to ideas, arguments and even information" (282).

Such discourse serves to widen the gap between realities. Truth is not about truth at all but about picking sides and pitting them against one another. Pushed to this extreme, resilience consolidates a very real paranoid chronotope that not only suggests that there are differences of opinions and interpretation of truth and reality, nor does it only confirm that there are disjunctive experiences of reality; it also, and much more detrimentally, insists that one of these realities is malevolent. With the step from acknowledging differing perspectives on reality to insisting on actual and opposing realities comes the fleshing out of this paranoid chronotope—the consolidation of two disjunctive spatiotemporal sides. Perhaps it is in this context that we can understand the success of Trump's "telling it like it is," not least when it comes to questions of race, ethnicity, and immigration, while leaving behind earlier Republican strategies of "dog whistling." Indeed, as Michelsen and de Orellana point out, Trump achieved "truth-teller validity" already during his election campaign (282). Outrageous comments and exaggerations and even overt lies function to unsettle, undermine, and implicitly criticize that malevolent "reality," as a way to stand against truths "peddled" by the media and establishment and that are, by virtue of their being such, out to deceive us. Trump is important, we can read on the white-nationalist website *VDare*, "because he represents the first figure with the financial, cultural, and economic resources to openly defy elite consensus" (Neiwert 2017, 173).

Truth Technologies

Contemporary configurations of truth in the public sphere are, of course, also technological. Technological mechanisms, as they have developed in recent decades, often serve not only to strengthen and radicalize existing biases but also to push them toward paranoia because trust is more clearly differentiated against what can or should not be trusted. As the truths or facts to be trusted are fortified by filters and algorithms, and as a public sphere in which they can be examined, deliberated upon, and debated thereby becomes one in which biases or "symbolic truths" are endorsed rather than critically analyzed, trust becomes acutely disproportionate. In fact, a curious configuration of trust surfaces in this context. On the one hand, trust dwindles as a dimension of society in general. On the other, people choose to rely on sources they should not trust. When healthy skepticism turns extreme, and when the "alternative" explanation is always better, skepticism, according to Neiwert, "flips into extreme gullibility" making the skeptics "suckers for conspiracy theories that confirm the narrative they want to believe" (32).

Contributing to such polarization and radicalization in the public sphere is what Bridle calls "overflow" and the way it undermines a sense of common reality. Historically, at least since the Enlightenment, we have had the idea that more information will lead to better decisions and thus to a better society. However, today, Bridle says, information darkens rather than enlightens the world. We are largely unable to navigate the overflow of information produced by and disseminated via ever advanced and advancing technologies. Access to data and advanced computation has resulted in an abundance of information so overwhelming that it disturbs our capacity to account for, much less process, it. Bridle describes a scenario in which experts as gatekeepers are outrun not just by economic forces but by technological ones. Gatekeepers come with "an expectation of specialism and expertise, a certain responsibility and, often, a position of authority" (92). While these still exist in, for example, various academic and journalistic contexts, Bridle explains how the overflow of information and the enormous potential of big data processing make such gatekeeping insufficient or even impossible. He describes a paradoxical situation where science cannot be produced without "messy" human cognition and empiricism but human cognition is too limited to be able to process all the available information that science produces.

What Bridle describes, in other words, is not just a question of access but a question of cognition and comprehension. In Lyotardian terms, knowledge is becoming circumscribed by information at the same time that information stands in the way of knowledge: "This is the magic of big data. You don't really need to know or understand anything about what you're studying; you can simply place all of your faith in the emergent truth of digital information" (84). Because we have access to more information than we can ever handle or process, a sense of common reality is undermined both by the overabundance itself and by the simplistic and often conspiratorial narratives we construct to negotiate it (10). Bridle calls this phenomenon a chasm that has opened between individuals because of their failure to accept the complexities of our "new dark age." Our radically different horizons, our conspiratorial narratives, and our "collapsing consensus" divide us and cause discord (15).

The information overflow is itself instrumentalized and politicized when what is communicated is sometimes less important than the overflow itself.

For example, a Russian activist says that the main point of his activity is not to try to convince Internet users of any one particular opinion—to "brainwash" them. Changing people's minds, he is convinced, is harder than that. A more fruitful tactic is to destroy democratic debate by flooding it with fake content and thereby inducing paranoia and polarization (Chen 2016, n.p.). This, then, is an agenda that is political not by virtue of its content but by its undermining of the very possibility of a democratic debate and the potential of the Internet as a public sphere. Such agendas are, of course, closely connected with our twenty-first century attention economy and the scuffle for the increasingly scarce but increasingly valuable commodity that is the attention of citizens. As many have noted, in an online ecology especially, attention has become a more valuable commodity than information. Whether for purely commercial interests, such as in advertising, or to pursue political agendas, it has become extremely valuable to capture people's attention, however fleetingly.

The pace and decentralized nature of information and communication further complicate their relationship to truth. Speed and decentralization, William Davies says, make knowledge and decision-making subject to availability as well as to intuition and emotion (2018, xvi). Expertise and the localization and verification of facts require time and patience, neither of which is a practicable quality today. Experts may produce facts, but Google and Twitter provide the trends that make the world go around. The "nervous states" that Davies sees as characteristic of the twenty-first century are such because our constant alertness incites the quick solution, the answer that seems intuitively correct, feeling rather than fact. It has become increasingly difficult to determine what is body and what is mind and what is war and what is peace, a situation that keeps both individuals and governments constantly on their toes (xi). Digital technologies have put speed before accuracy, and modern warfare generates "miasmas of emotion, information, misinformation, deception and secrecy" (xv) that create uncertainties and fears not easily abated. These feelings must not be dismissed as irrational, Davies argues, but must be taken seriously if paranoia is to be avoided.

Under the conditions just described, it is hard to grasp both our selves and a common world. We might, however, create a *sense* of our selves and a world common to *some* with the help of cognitive as well as technological filtering, an inevitable and necessary activity for everyone at all times that has been so for all time. It is simply not possible to take in all the information one is exposed to. In digital times, however, and when the range of available resources has become endless, filtering, Cass R. Sunstein warns, threatens to undermine democratic deliberation and freedom of expression, both of which are preconditions for "a well-functioning democracy" (2007, 6). If the preconditions for a democracy are to hold sway, he argues, people need to (1) be "exposed to materials that they would not have chosen in advance," including unplanned encounters, unanticipated topics, and unexpected points of view, and have at least some experiences in common (2). Without such preconditions, democratic deliberation is emptied of its meaning. When our social, economic, political, and geographical positions and preferences establish the grounds not just for our view of the world generally but for what we read and see and hear at every turn, we are increasingly folded into what Sunstein, following Nicholas Negroponte, calls "the Daily Me" (4).

When Negroponte, an MIT technology specialist, envisioned "The Daily Me" in 1995, he foresaw that technology would enable individuals to select news, information, debates, cultural expression, and so on, based on their interests. "The Daily Me," in other words, is "a communications package that is personally designed, with each component fully chosen in advance" (Sunstein, 4). Negroponte's prophesy only touches on a more contemporary reality, according to Sunstein. We do not need to create a daily me for ourselves anymore because others can do it for us (4). We can reinforce this and state that it is not just a matter of others being able to hand us our daily me but also a matter of it being done for us, regardless of our will and awareness of it. For every digital choice we make—that is, for every search we do, every article we open, every item we purchase, every song we play—our "me" appears more clearly. Thus for every such choice we produce a filter not only for what we access but also, and quite crucially, for what we do not access. Some of the latter we know—we might, for example, be quite purposeful in, or at least be happy, seeing the result of the filtering out of sports or popular music or whatever we are glad to live without. The severe and damaging effects of filtering emerge when it results in our separation from news and views that do not correspond to our preferences and worldview.

Again, there is nothing new in people choosing and/or getting certain kinds of information while ignoring/missing out on others. Neither is there anything new in citizens to a large extent making their own choices in these areas. However, Sunstein notes a more acute situation in a present characterized by an enormous increase in available communications combined with communication options, by the possibility of the individual controlling content, and by a decreasing role of what he calls "general-interest intermediaries." General-interest intermediaries are, for example, newspapers and broadcasters that cover a range of topics and thus expose us to a broader set of news and information (8). Sunstein insists on the fundamental importance of street corners and "commons,"—places virtual or actual where people are exposed to each other and each other's views in sometimes unexpected, arbitrary, and involuntary ways. This is central to democracy *tout court*. Sunstein is not implying that street corners and commons have disappeared; after all, many people are driven by curiosity and the Internet holds the potential for accessing facts, opinions, and topics in a revolutionary way. But he does suggest that what may be seen as perfectly reasonable and harmless choices on behalf of individuals can create serious individual as well as social harm: "I will emphasize the risk posed by any situation in which thousands or perhaps millions or even tens of millions of people are mainly listening to louder echoes of their own voices. A situation of this kind is likely to produce far worse than mere fragmentation" (13).

And it does. Algorithmic grooming happens not only on obscure and radical platforms such as Reddit, 4chan, and 8chan but also on the largest and most mainstream like Google. Looking into examples such as Dylann Roof, the white-supremacist killer of nine at the 2015 Emanuel AME Church in Charleston, South Carolina, Safiya Umoja Noble shows how such search engines support "racial identity development" by generating certain content. In the wake of the murder of Trayvon Martin, Roof is purported to have searched for "black on white crime" and been astounded to discover the "truth" on sites such as the white-supremacist "Council of Conservative Citizens." Performing such a search herself, making sure to cross-verify her results with another researcher on another computer, Noble's first hit was the overtly racist *NewNation.org*, followed by a whole set of conservative and white-nationalist sites geared toward racist hatred of African Americans and Jews (2018, 111). Those interested in facts about race relations, in other words, will not be led to FBI statistics on violence in the United States, which show that it is predominantly intraracial—that is, within racial groups—or to experts on race or histories of race or racist myths, such as "black on white crime," but to conservative, racist, white-supremacist sites (115).

Extremist beliefs are further strengthened by what Bridle calls "self-confirming groups" (211). Such groups may be purposefully constructed or unintentionally generated by online search filters but what they have in common is that they mainly describe the world that we want to see. As we will see in Chapter 4, such groups have the potential to create powerful paranoid identities. According to Bridle, a social media search on vaccines will get us to antivaccine beliefs, which will quickly lead us to "chemtrailers, flat-earthers, 9/11 truthers," and so on, and very quickly this will seem like a majority—an echo chamber of supportive opinion. In short, in these online marshes we find support for whatever we search for. To this we might add not just Noble's algorithmic grooming but also algorithmic radicalization. Algorithmic radicalization not only makes sure that we get confirmation of what we already imagine, whatever it might be, but also pushes us farther in that direction. We are "never 'hard core' enough for YouTube's recommendation algorithm," according to Zeynab Tufekci in a 2018 article in *The New York Times*. She describe the ways in which online Trump videos lead to recommended or "autoplay" videos featuring white supremacists, while Hilary Clinton and Bernie Sanders videos lead to leftist conspiracy videos on, for example, secret government agencies. Videos about joggers generate videos about ultramarathons (2018, n.p.).

Truth Economies

Contemporary configurations of truth depend not only on new media configurations and technological developments but also on the logic of neoliberalism. The battle for or around truth, as Foucault insists, cannot be a battle for discovering and accepting a pre-existing truth but for discovering the rules according to which true and false are currently separated and the "specific effects of power attached to the true." For Foucault, in other words, it is not about Truth in any disembodied sense or about ideology but about power. In this sense, "post-truth" may be an unfortunate coinage from a Foucauldian perspective in that the truth we have reached, if anything, is not "post" so much as a new regime of truth.

As a "regime," as an intelligible connection between laws, regulations, and rationalities, truth only emerged, argues Foucault, around the middle of the eighteenth century. Before then, there were, of course, laws, regulations, and rationalities—power structures and tax levies, codification of tax practices, and so on—but he suggests they were based on diverse principles and rationalities and subject to sovereign or feudal rights. As such, they did not necessarily form a coherent model of practices that could be judged as true or false. With the governmentality of early liberalism, however, appears a coordination of practices and their effects and, with this, the possibility of judging not according to moral or legal principles but according to a separation of the true and the untrue. What also materializes is a new set of practices that mark out and thus bring into being categories and orderings of society according to truth, such as sexuality, madness, delinquency, and so on. With this regime of truth is formed a *dispositif* of knowledge-power, effectively marking out "in reality that which does not exist and legitimately submit[ting] it to the division between true and false" (Foucault 2008, 18–9).

Approaching modern times, Foucault describes five central attributes in the production of truth in "societies like ours," in his case the West of the 1970s: (1) "the forms of scientific discourse and the institutions that produce it," (2) its modulations via economic and political "incitements," (3) its consumption and dissemination in society via "apparatuses of education and information," (4) the control of its communication by "political and economic apparatuses," and (5) ideological negotiations via political and social confrontation and debate (Foucault 2000, 131). These attributes have been evolving since then in the continued transition between discipline and control as discussed in the previous chapter but also as particularly adapted to the continued development of neoliberalism in America.

Foucault's conception of "contemporary" truth regimes is shaped by a disciplinary logic in a French context, characterized by relatively close connections between different institutions and apparatuses of truth. Later developments in France and certainly in America from the postwar period onward witness, as we also saw in Chapter 2, a dissolution of such coordinated apparatuses. There is, Jayson Harsin observes, a concomitant breakdown of the trust in "truth-telling and confirmation/judgment, and coordination of apparatuses" of such a regime. In its place has emerged a new regime in which both the spatiality and the temporality of news have changed quite radically (2015, 329). It is not enough to look to journalistic practices and new technologies to understand these shifts—they also need to be contextualized in terms of the shift between discipline and control that I previously outlined. Paying attention to these shifts is central to understanding current regimes of truth—what Harsin calls "regimes of post-truth."

Under this new regime, and in light of the dissemination of power as discussed in Chapter 2 and the "many-headed hydra" of the fragmented, segmented contemporary information landscape I have begun to describe here, we are in effect dealing less with institutional enclosures of truth and more with "truth markets" (329). Within such proliferating markets are enacted truth games appealing only in part to "convictions within ideological filter bubbles" because what is similarly important is the managing of participation according to the attention economy driven by big data and predictive analytics (331). In such truth games, the analysis and breakdown of audience and markets become essential, as does the breakdown of trust and encouragement of skepticism toward experts linked to cultural, journalistic, and academic disciplines (331). In other words, the truth regimes reigning today are not just progressing apace with the waning of the public sphere; they actually benefit from undermining it. Regimes of post-truth demobilize political subjects either by creating and encouraging acceptance of the impossibility of arriving at any truth or by mobilizing "a spectacle of claiming, sharing, liking, debunking, and refuting 'issues'" that ultimately blocks "the emergence of more inclusive social justice agendas or even the reorganization of the plane of political agency itself" (332).

Harsin's thesis is closely aligned with neoliberal governmentalities. As we saw in Chapter 2, neoliberal agendas have consistently regarded the public as a threat. Neoliberal governmentality has succeeded in demonizing the social and the political, in disintegrating society and the idea of a public good, and in undermining notions of equality and the public sphere. At the same time, it has strengthened and valorized traditional morality and markets. In a nutshell, argues Brown, this is how neoliberalism, quite against its own original intentions, has paved the way for the aggressive and increasingly effective antidemocratic forces of the twenty-first century (2019, 7). We have struggled to recognize and make sense of these developments, she suggests, not only because of their unfamiliar composite of elements and forces but also because hard-wearing assumptions about Western values and institutions such as Enlightenment, progress, and liberal democracy have blinded us to them (2). Yet we now witness a resurgence of right-wing identitarianism, of nationalism, of a perversion of identity politics, of the trumping of facts by affects. Truth, in other words, is put at risk not only via the onslaught of information and disinformation in contemporary media and communication or via the polarization of social life, but also more generally via an undermining of the belief and trust in the social and in the public sphere as marking sites of mutual interest and democratic deliberation. The demonization and undermining of democracy, Brown maintains, both positions democracy as a threat and undermines conditions key to its continued validity such as "modulation by informed deliberation, compromise, accountability, and legitimation by the will of the people." This results in a growing indifference to facts and truth, which in turn destabilizes and undermines conceptions of and trust in democracy in the first place (87).

To understand this development, Brown takes us back to Hayek and his quarrel with the social. For Hayek, the delegitimated force of the social is contrasted with the combination of freedom and tradition that he validates. Tradition—frequently in the shape of religion—builds a somewhat mutable scaffolding, one that must make space for individual freedom for its own survival but also keep it in check by binding it to common norms and practices. In this way, in Brown's explanation, the coercion of individual freedom by political power can be exchanged for a "voluntary conformity" emerging through habitual behavior (99). For this to be possible, deliberation, social justice claims, planning, and "nonorganic" strategies of the public sphere need to be minimized in favor of expansion of the "personal protected sphere" (104). This sphere guards what is seen as the more organic and spontaneous evolutions of traditional morality, private property, and markets. Expanding this personal sphere and making it a chief player in society is a way of protecting moralities, properties, and markets from the interference of the social. The "personal protected sphere" thus makes it possible to reject the political and the social in the name of tradition and liberty (105).

Crucial to our purposes are the effects of this demotion of the public sphere and concomitant expansion of the personal protected sphere on facts and truth, on the dialogue and deliberation required to understand and evaluate them, and on the political participation that enables action in accordance with their principles. Without such practices, and with what is ultimately the transference of authority from political life to individual freedom and tradition, truth is pulled in two directions—it becomes a matter of individual or market-based practicability, or it becomes a matter of religious or traditional authority and incontestability. In both cases, truth is severed from accountability (Brown 2019, 102). Brown provides examples of individuals and businesses relieved from accountability and discrimination charges. For example, the large chain of "crisis pregnancy centers" that deliberately obscured their antiabortion agenda fought and won in court against the State of California's demand that they openly declare their mission. The court's decision effectively made fraud protected speech. The state's recourse to fact was established as a state-sanctioned viewpoint forcefully imposed on and suppressing less popular viewpoints. Thus, Brown shows, truths, facts, and values are positioned not as democratically valuable in their own right and in need of transparency and accountability but precisely as viewpoints against which other viewpoints can be contrasted. And of course, in such a setting any "viewpoints" forwarded by the political become dangerous "state speech" (154).

In this scenario, truth, facts, and values become instrumentalized. Released from any foundations, they enter into contractual relations that are liberated not only from demands of the social but also from demands on conduct and consistency. As Brown says, the evangelical base ultimately does not care about assaults, affairs, or pussy grabbing as long as the "right" decisions are made on abortion, the military, and Jerusalem (172). In place of organic reproduction of conduct, morality, and tradition imagined by Hayek, we see an ever stronger nihilism and polarization. Traditional values become brands and weapons that protect privilege against equality rather than promote social integration (118). While Hayek's own belief in traditionalism benefited heteronormativity and white male supremacy, the spontaneous and organic freedom and tradition he had in mind is increasingly exchanged for an aggressive supremacist strategy working actively against egalitarianism and diversity (119). What Brown describes, then, is a neoliberalism in which truth really has become a viewpoint, where the social has become a threat, and freedom and tradition have become weapons. With this comes not only the demotion of the public sphere but also the "dethronement of truth in public life" (169). "It heralds," Brown says, "a world of 'fake news' all the way down" (160).

Truth, facts, and values become not only instrumentalized but also weaponized. Davies builds on Arendt's distinction between power and violence—essentially a distinction between organized, larger, visible structures and instant, instrumental force—and notes with Arendt that, while they are commonly associated, the power and security associated with democratic and civic institutions tend to be undermined by unpredictable violence, such as terrorist attacks (19). Violence, in other words, exacerbates the lack of trust in power. Importantly, Davies suggests that it has become increasingly difficult to identify violence (17). Daily life is weaponized not only by terrorists' use of everyday objects as weapons but also by social media and online trolls disrupting elections, spreading confusion, and unsettling exchanges between people (18). Davies especially stresses links between the mistrust of power and the mistrust of truth. As institutions associated with representative democracy are progressively discredited, their representatives—journalists, scientists, experts—are accused of weaponizing their status to pursue particular goals (26). In other words, they are no longer associated with securing basic facts and functions for society in general but with "elites" playing their own game. From this perspective, dismissals of expertise should perhaps not be seen as "an irrational rejection of truth itself" so much as "a rejection of the broader political edifice from which society is governed" (29). Truth and facts become polarizing political weapons rather than common starting points in a shared public sphere. The weaponization of truth and facts is, ironically, underlined by those working to protect them. Events such as the March for Science inadvertently strengthen the ways in which reason and fact become "political values like any others," values and phenomena that require justification and the very nature upon which different political players may have an opinion (24).

In an American context, the process by which truth and fact are turned into viewpoints is not only activated by alt-right news sources and online conspiracy theorists but also promoted by the Supreme Court. According to Brown, what made it possible for "crisis pregnancy centers," to circumvent the California FACT act—which requires all healthcare facilities to inform clients about the availability of family planning services—was the Court's ruling that they were covered by the First Amendment as well as by the principle of free exercise. Their refusal to abide by FACT and their continued misrepresentation of facts and fraudulent concealment of their own agenda were thus accepted on the basis of the rights of individuals rather than businesses, rights that FACT was seen to abrogate. Thus the rights of a corporation come to be equated with individual civil rights, the rights to free exercise are transferred from the private to the public realm, and public interest is reduced to the state's "viewpoint" (Brown 2019, 158). What is more, via FACT the state "viewpoint" was considered an authoritarian encroachment on the centers' viewpoint. One strategic move that made this possible, Brown argues, was the mobilization of such cases as a "controversy" by which facts and religiously held beliefs are considered equivalent. In the place of accountability to facts, science, and public interest, we find the free market and religious morality "in the name of freedom" (158).

If all conduct is economic conduct, then everything can be measured. Indeed, measurements and numbers seem to reintroduce some accountability in this otherwise fluid landscape of viewpoints and "symbolic truths." At first glance, and as I began to suggest at the beginning of this section, measurements and metrics do appear to counteract such fluidity. Numbers seem considerably more tangible and trustworthy than the cascades of emotion and polarized affect, alternative facts, fake news, and "symbolic truths" that characterize the contemporary public sphere. Numbers and metrics also seem to counteract what some contend is the theoretical undermining of truth associated with theories of the postmodern, which I will discuss further in Chapter 4. To preview that discussion just briefly, I claim that theoretical approaches to truth as embedded in social and economic power structures are typically, and quite symptomatically, rejected in this context because they are seen to promote rather than problematize the radical relativization of the present. Instead, facts and numbers are identified as the solution to this fluidity and to some extent they undoubtedly are.

At the same time, measurements and metrics are, of course, inherently economic and constitute a major component of an increasingly predominant neoliberal rationality. Accountability is referred to the market as "*the* rather than *a* site of veridiction"; what is more, it "becomes so for every arena and type of human activity." The market, Brown clarifies, "is generalized as a form of reason," a reason that rational actors are expected to accept as their truth and reality (2015, 67). Under such conditions, in other words, what is true and real and what is reason and rational are not something that is worked out by and among political subjects, as in the old liberal idea of the public sphere I described in Chapter 1, but are rather a matter of appeal to impersonalized metrics and numbers. As such, says Saltman, "data-driven accountability regimes" sweep across social institutions, facts are regarded as meaningful on their own—without context or interpretation, without theorization and argument. In other words, "facts are alienated from the conditions of their production and appear to speak for themselves." Via numbers and bodies, they offer "a false promise of certainty" (1). But of what does this certainty consist precisely? And for whom? Pointing in particular to education and to standardized testing, Saltman shows how such policies disregard "how learning and knowledge relate to the world and the capacity of subjects to use knowledge to shape it." Thus, they rely on a conception of agency that becomes such via the acquisition, consumption, and display of accepted knowledge rather than agency as emerging from "the use of knowledge to interpret, judge, act on, and shape the social world while reflecting on what one does" (3). Knowledge is thus disconnected from the subject as well as from the public sphere.

Without subjects or debates, without interpretation and contestation, without social, material, and political frameworks, Saltman points out, facts appear to come from nowhere (18). In such radical empiricism, knowledge is associated with authority but also with conspiracy (98). Where is this "nowhere" as the site for knowledge and facts? Who knows the truth? Who has access to this bigger picture? Who knows? Who knows what there is to know? Who knows how it all hangs together? Deprived of contextualization and historicization of a space and time for critical judgment and mutual interrogation, agency and action come to be especially reserved for "those with secret control over knowledge," for "superagents" with a virtually supernatural capacity to understand and act (99). Either these are stars and celebrities awarded the magical status of truth tellers regardless of their actual knowledge, or, and more conspiratorially, they are enemies, such as foreigners or scientists or elites, plotting against the American way (99). As we saw in Chapter 1, these conspiratorial ideas may be further encouraged via the "public secrecy" active since the establishment of the FBI and the concomitant "covert sphere." In short, unmoored from history, theory, evidence, argumentation, and individual and social realities, the recourse to numbers and facts under neoliberal empiricism does not abate but rather aggravate a conspiratorial approach.

Juggling a disregard for fact and evidence and a set of "hard" facts derived from metrics and numbers, one major response by individuals and groups in the public sphere is the production of paranoid identities, commonly by means of conspiracy theories. Conspiracy theories help "stabilize" truth and construct friends and enemies to fit. The paranoia described at the beginning of the chapter—targeting the public by specific social groups or society itself or the state—constructs and protects certain truths. Whether the problem is immigrants exploiting the system or Muslims needing to be banned to prevent terrorist attacks or the state itself colluding with liberals via the deep state or the New World Order, conspiracy theorists "speak truth to power," unveiling truths that society does not want us to see. In this case, the fluent status of truth generates strong formations of locally constructed "truths."

I have outlined the ways in which truth and our conceptions of it are undermined by a heady cocktail of a news media landscape encouraging blatant falsities and hate mongering; an online technological dynamics that breaks down a sense of common reality by isolating, polarizing, and radicalizing opinions; and an economic system that subjects truth to the market and metrics. These interlinked developments undermine conceptions of truth as grounded in political subjects and debates. Recourse neither to feelings and "symbolic truths" nor to numbers and alienated facts encourages such agents and such processes. They do, however, all contribute to a polarized and increasingly paranoid public sphere. Paranoid because we are suspicious of what statements and news out there might be untrue and because we have been given the leeway to adopt "truths" that correspond to already existing beliefs and convictions. Also, and crucially, paranoid because, without a striving toward truth anchored in a shared social world—however socially and political constructed this world inevitably is—we are left to our own devices.

Section 2: Truth, Self, and the System in Patrick Flanery's I am No One

Introduction

I read *I Am No One* (2016) to show how the separation of subject and shared platforms of thinking and reasoning that I have just traced through medial, technological, and economic configurations of truth in the contemporary public sphere produces an inaccessibility of truth—not just for society at large but for the individual subject. The paranoid chronotope brings out this key dilemma in society and fiction in two ways: it identifies disjunctive levels of reality and accentuates how paranoid subjects perceive themselves to have access to or at least insight into a level of reality other than the reality of their fellow characters. For the paranoid subject, the basis for judgment thus diverges not only because there is no sense of shared reality but also because the paranoid subject has recognized society's basis for judgment as defective. The rationality of the paranoid vision depends on the extent to which the supposedly more real basis of judgment—the truth to which only he, or the group, has access—can be made to constitute a coherent basis of its own.

We have seen how Bakhtin builds his conception of the chronotope around Kant's insistence on the imperative role of space and time in cognition via "elementary perceptions and representations," and how he differs from Kant in insisting on the formative importance of a concrete and immediate reality (1981, 85n). This is how the chronotopes of literature help shape the image of man: the spatiotemporal conditions constructed are concomitant with characters' conditions for cognition. But because the paranoid subject tends to be the only one on the everyday dimension of the chronotope who discerns another dimension—that secret and often malicious layer that truly regulates the world—he is estranged from a critical context. This subject cannot easily arrive at a truth or at least an identification of what is reasonable with the help of thinking and reasoning with others. In fact, others tend to be seen as ignorant of the true nature of things at best and part of that devious and manipulative other layer at worst.

As we will see, it does not matter that Jeremy O'Keefe, the protagonist of *I Am No One*, has a family and an academic job—he is still profoundly cut off from the type of social world that would help him ascertain what is true or even reasonable. Instead, he finds himself exposed to a large, indeterminable system that seems to be out to get him. The overwhelming facts and data about his past that mysteriously turn up at his doorstep (quite literally) seem to come from nowhere. As we will see, this data, which is intimately about Jeremy himself—printouts of his online activities, telephone calls, and so on—separates him from rather than brings him closer to the truth about himself. Having for the longest time refused to face or even acknowledge the dubious behavior to which the data speaks, Jeremy and the novel give up this truth and lay it in the hands of a conspiratorial external agency. This is, in effect, a concrete staging of the "radical empiricism" discussed previously, in which knowledge, as severed from subjects and debates, from social and political frameworks, from critical judgment and mutual interrogation, seems to come from nowhere. Under such conditions, knowledge comes to be associated with authority and conspiracy. Who knows the truth? Who knows what there is to know and how it all adds up? Conspiracy is nurtured when facts are "unmoored from argument, evidence, and history" not least because "conspiratorial thought presumes that agency is dominated by those with secret control over knowledge and hence secret action" (Saltman, 99). In *I Am No One*, this agency initially seems to take the shape of another character: Michael Ramsey. Intermittently, however, it also begins to appear as Jeremy's unconscious, as his society's "dirty secret," and, progressively, as the festering guilt of a white American man. *I Am No One*, as we will see, invokes a sense of guilt of Kafkaesque proportions as well as prevarication regarding the truth that is interlinked with an indeterminable system that nonetheless claims to determine them both.

I Am No One

The first of the series of unsettling events Jeremy O'Keefe experiences occurs as he is waiting in vain for a student in Caffè Paradiso, where cheap coffee and a variety of pastries are served, a place that Jeremy frequents to ease the blow of culture shock after returning from England to America. Jeremy is a university professor recently returned to New York City after working for some years at

Oxford. He left for England just after 9/11, having separated from his wife and having failed to get tenure at Columbia. He lived in Oxford for about a decade and has been back in America for less than a year. The unsettling event is the first encounter with Michael Ramsey, a character who will reappear throughout the novel and who will have a crucial but never quite established role in the plot's unfolding. The encounter with Ramsey serves a key architectonic purpose in the sense that Bakhtin defines such encounters. A particularly good place for the encounter is on the road, he says, but it can also take place at other intersections where characters from different walks of life and often kept apart can "accidentally meet." Chance is an important element here as distances may collapse and fates collide (Bakhtin 1981, 243). With such encounters, narratives take new turns. And a new turn this narrative will take, although neither Jeremy nor the reader knows it yet. Still, Jeremy seems to have a hunch. He walks away from Caffè Paradiso not realizing that this will have been one of many progressively unsettling confrontations with Ramsey, but he senses that this encounter—as well as the nonencounter with the student—has significance.

The encounter, Bakhtin notes, is characterized by intensity and emotion (243). A "saturation of experience occurs," according to Bart Keunen, as "everything seems interesting and the consciousness is confronted with the absence of repetition, losing itself in a world of difference, and, consequently, the spatial situation causes it to oscillate wildly" (2010, 44). Jeremy's encounter with Ramsey is both intense and disturbing, although its effects cannot yet be comprehended. In fact, it is the first to signal Jeremy's contradictory approach to his own truth. Or is it his contradictory telling of this truth? He claims that the meeting itself was not unsettling. But at the same time the young man Ramsey has left him looking over his shoulder on the way home. Once at home, he suddenly becomes aware of the visibility from the outside into his lighted apartment (8). That his disconcerted state is bound to be aggravated is indicated by Jeremy's increasing unease at catching himself having forgotten why he is troubled (9). His condition is further unsettled when he discovers that he himself appears to be the agent behind the missed encounter with the student. Checking his emails, he discovers that he sent an email to her canceling the meeting, but this is an initiative he has no memory of taking. At this point, then, truth and action seem already to have been surrendered to an external source.

Because perhaps, the novel seems to ask, thereby signaling its paranoid mode already in its opening pages, this encounter based on a missed encounter is not a chance one after all. That Jeremy arranges a meeting with a student in a café on a Saturday afternoon rather than in his office on a weekday he ascribes to the informality between students and teachers at Oxford (3). However, this sort of informality, as we later learn, caused him trouble in the past. But as is his first-person unreliable narrator's wont, and as I will return to shortly, he is either oblivious or in denial of his own history and his role in it, withholding, as he does, significant information not only from readers but also, it seems, from himself. So, is it a coincidence that he meets Ramsey in Caffè Paradiso? The novel would have us think not. Initiating a seemingly spontaneous conversation with Jeremy, Ramsey asks uncomfortable questions: whether Jeremy has been stood up, whether his student is male or female, whether she is pretty or ugly. These questions underscore a link to what we do not yet know to be Jeremy's rather complicated history of intimate relations with young female students. In fact, this early passage positions Ramsey as something of an externalized subconscious, an impersonation of a truth that Jeremy should but cannot seem to find it within himself to articulate or even recognize. Ramsey's potentially symbolic status is underlined by Jeremy's uncertainty whether Ramsey had been there before him or arrived after. Going to a café consciously and meticulously chosen to meet a student only to meet Ramsey instead reveals not only a confused sense of chance and intention; it is also a first sign that this Ramsey might be part of the intentionality and agency that Jeremy has externalized.

We never learn for sure whether Ramsey is the source of the anonymous parcels containing printouts of Jeremy's online history, including email exchanges, phone calls, bank transfers, and, later, "a photographic record" of his movements, extracted, seemingly, from CCTV cameras and enhanced by facial recognition software (287). Jeremy receives five parcels in total not realizing until after the second one precisely what he is looking at and what its implications are: "days or weeks or months or years" of his online history captured via "tens or hundreds of thousands of addresses" letting him know not only that someone is monitoring him but also, and more curiously, that someone wants him to know it (65). We also never know for sure whether it is Ramsey who is stalking him, but someone is frequently seen standing outside his building looking up at him and sometimes following him on the street. The first instance (38) is fraught with ambivalence: Jeremy thinks, just "for a moment," that someone is watching him and acknowledges that he is perhaps "already edging into unconsciousness," but although his mind "both registered and did not register" it, he is "certain" of "a reciprocal acknowledgment": that he and the man on the street are watching each other: "*Hello, hey you, my watcher, I can see you! I know what you're doing!*" (38).

After a few more indefinite encounters—"I felt a flutter of unease. Second encounter? Third?" (50)—Jeremy becomes convinced that a man with a ski mask is watching him through his window. This certainty, however, is still colored by the ambiguity that we learn to expect from him, expressed in equivocal formulations: Jeremy is convinced that they are looking at each other "as openly as two people can who are separated by glass and distance and the optical confusions of light and reflection" (85). The equivocality is also expressed in a vacillation between complete certainty and utter uncertainty: some pages on, the man is overtly standing still outside his window looking up at him. At the very end of a chapter (290), Ramsey stands outside Jeremy's window undisguised, but in the first sentence of the following chapter, Jeremy is again in doubt that it was Ramsey after all (292). But as Ramsey and Jeremy are invited to the same Thanksgiving party—it turns out that Ramsey is an old student acquaintance of Jeremy's son-in-law (105)—and as he rings the doorbell of Jeremy's upstate house one evening, having supposedly borrowed a house from a friend just down the road (164), the alternative that these encounters are by chance seems increasingly implausible.

The ambiguity of Ramsey's significance to these developments, and indeed the sources of the surveillance in general—Jeremy is at first convinced that it is the work of "some private entity" (65) and later that it is "the government, or some intelligence-gathering contractor affiliated with the government" (93)— are paralleled by the opacity of Jeremy's own role in the plot. Jeremy is unreliable both to himself and to the reader. As a first-person narrator, he avers that he has no idea why he might be surveilled. More than that, he insists that he is no one in particular, that he knows of "nothing that would or should make me a person of interest to the authorities on either side of whatever divisions now carve up our world" (59). He feels confident that he has "never done anything that would be judged, in the end, as intrinsically evil" (65), finding it "difficult to imagine why I might have become a person of interest to my own government, or to whatever intelligence division has seen fit to pay such close attention to my telecommunications" (93). And all this makes him wonder why "the NSA—for who else could it be?—[would] have any desire to keep me so closely in its sights" (95).

Analogous to this periodic insistence on his innocence are intimations of the opposite: that Jeremy is actually quite aware of the reason he is under surveillance. Most potent is when these conflicting assurances take place on the same page: just a few lines down from his question about the NSA, he mentions "the other matter" around which his mind dances "a great wide arc" (95). His mind and thus the narrative have in fact been dancing around the truth from quite early in the book, with references to "all that had happened so recently in Oxford" (39), to there being "without question secrets from the past decade" (65), to a face with a three-syllable name he tries to abolish from his mind (67, 120).

The ambivalence, or suppression, erupts when we finally begin to see how Jeremy becomes acquainted with a Stephen Jahn and through him is pressured into skirting the rules and admitting the Egyptian student Fadia to the university. Fadia comes from a powerful Egyptian family and has a brother Saif, who is involved in what US authorities would likely call terrorism. Saif used to work for the Egyptian government. He was a member of the Muslim Brotherhood before he disappeared. His sister thinks he is now fighting in Syria (270). As if these underhanded relations and actions were not enough, Jeremy ends up having a secret relationship with Fadia once she becomes his student, and he fathers her child. After he moves back to America, he sends Fadia money toward his son's support each month. Jeremy finally lists the possible charges against him, admitting, although continuing to resist the idea, that in theory he could have been pulled in to funding terrorism via Fadia as a front for a terrorist organization (252).

Jeremy withholds other significant information about himself. It seems quite a coincidence at first that, after having received the first parcel of his online history (not knowing at this point what it is), he turns on the television and happens upon Francis Ford Coppola's 1974 film *The Conversation*, followed by the film that is said to have inspired it, Antonioni's *Blowup* (1966). Also seemingly coincidental is that later on he is reading Timothy Garton Ash's *The File* (1998) and contemplating Simon Menner's photographs in *Top Secret* (2013). All of these films, books, and images famously center on the theme of surveillance. We learn at the beginning of *I Am No One* that Jeremy is an academic and fairly early on that he has an interest in twentieth-century Europe in general and East Germany and its informants in particular (17). But it is not until long after having received, and pondered the implications of, not one, not two, but three packages with material from his communications, that he lets the reader know that he actually has particular expertise in surveillance (163). At this point, we learn that Jeremy might actually be considered "not just as a surveillance neurotic but as one of the world's leading experts..." His preoccupation may encourage the reader to be suspicious of his suspicions, with, as he says, his being "obsessed by ideas of surveillance and privacy to more than an ordinary degree" (163). In this context, and especially because Jeremy has withheld this information, a reader may be tempted to ask if the constant sightings of the man watching him or even his own suspicion that he has somehow produced the boxes of material himself constitute a paranoid extension of his expertise in surveillance or his academic, historical, and fictional preoccupations with it.

Jeremy seems more prone to cast suspicion on his sanity than on his actions. His reluctance to recognize that the surveillance he is subjected to—the parcels, the man watching him—may be connected to his illicit entanglements with a student and possibly with her Egyptian family and, by extension, terrorist organizations, is repeatedly paralleled by his wondering if in fact he is the guilty party. This guilt is not applied to the relationship with Fadia or to potential terrorist activities, however, but to his possible involvement with the surveillance. He repeatedly tries out this idea. He is relieved when the third package listing his phone calls arrives because it seems to speak to his sanity—surely he could not have produced these records himself (93). Yet the doubt lingers. "This is not in my mind, surely, and yet, how easy it would be for me to order back statements, to pull up copies of my returns, to make the theater of my brain suspend its disbelief in the film projected on its internal screen, in the fiction—is it fiction?—that the projectionist has chosen from the reels at his disposal" (314).

In fact, Jeremy's protestations of innocence are haunted by a Kafkaesque sense of guilt. This becomes particularly apparent on the occasions when the narrative materializes most clearly as the record for posterity it gives itself out to be. Jeremy worries that someone will soon put an end to his freedom. The narrative is Jeremy's first-person account and is supposed to follow and mirror events as they unfold. The intended audience is future readers—sometimes a "someone" and sometimes a "you." Jeremy is uncertain about the status and ultimate purpose of his own writing—will it be "an eccentric legacy left to my heirs" or "entered into evidence" (21); will it be "a confession I cannot provide" (254) or "proof of [my] own life" scribbled by one of the city's many unhinged citizens (300)? He is also constantly anxious about the judgment his future readers might pass. Both before and after he starts revealing some of his past, he is convinced that his future readers are "undoubtedly already drawing conclusions about me, reading between the lines and making assumptions despite my protestations of innocence" (21). "I write and write," he writes, "and, I have no doubt, someone at some point will read these pages, reach a judgment, and perhaps, if they find against me, seek to impose some form of punishment—against my person if I am still alive, against my legacy if I am dead" (236). The Kafkaesque nature of this ambivalent recognition of an indeterminate culpability becomes acute when his protestations of innocence are directly coupled with his admission of guilt. His concern that his writing may be "brought forth one day in [his] defense in a court either open or clandestine," that his past is filled with "entirely innocent activities," is combined with "a ghost of suspicion, as fleeting as the face I continue to see in the assemblage of text on a page" and the conviction that the "enfolding of all these elements" generates "a kind of destiny" (120).

The similarities between Jeremy's haunting and Josef K's tribulations in Kafka's *The Trial* (1925) are clear and instructive. The difficulties locating the source of Josef K's tribulations—"Someone must have been telling lies about Josef K . . ." the initial protestations of innocence—"He knew he had done nothing wrong but... "—and the inevitability of the real but nonetheless inexplicable nature of power—"One morning, he was arrested" (2) speak directly to the affinities between *I Am No One* and Kafka's novel. Both novels portray a curious compliance with a process of judgment that is incomprehensible and a gradual equivocation or even acceptance of guilt even as it remains indeterminate. Similar is also the way in which this acquiescence is seen to imply guilt, which in both novels remains unspecified—indeed, neither protagonist learns precisely what the charges are—but appears to be connected to the logic of external structures that they cannot grasp. As one of the officers in *The Trial* point out in response to Josef K's protestations of innocence at his initial arrest, how can he know he is innocent if he does not know the law? (9).

In both novels, it is the potential guilt before the law rather than the protagonist's actions in the past or present that remains in focus. The truth is thus reduced to a background murmur. In Kafka, the supposedly illegitimate actions are simply left out and Josef K never tries to learn what his charge is. According to Ritchie Robertson, the contemporary Austrian legal system with which Kafka was familiar had two dimensions: one was a Kantian dimension that emphasized the individual's moral responsibility for his actions; thus it focused on the punishment directly related to the crime. The other was the Austrian legal code that included intentionality. According to the latter, the judgment of guilt included the intent and motivations of a defendant. By foregrounding the blatant disinterest in what crime Josef K might have committed,

Robertson suggests, *The Trial* becomes a caricature of the Austrian legal system more interested in the criminal than the crime, in the guilt more than the act. In this way, the concept of guilt "slides from 'responsibility for an act' to 'subjective feelings of guilt.' Being accused seems to mean being a special type of person, destined for humiliation, and ultimately execution" (2004, 76). And the concept continues to slide, says Robertson, progressively moving away from subjective feelings of guilt to "being in the wrong, not in a legal but rather in a moral, conceivably even in a theological, sense" (78). Here, the guilt is lifted from individual actions to their motivations and expands to potentially include everyone. When Josef K protests his innocence to the priest by arguing that he is one human being among others—"How is it even possible for someone to be guilty. We're all human beings here, one like the other"—the priest agrees but says, "That is how the guilty speak" (Kafka, 251). While it makes little sense to single out one person if everyone is guilty, the priest implies that "guilt may be universal and still deserve punishment" (Robertson, 78).

Perhaps this sense of collective guilt can help explain Jeremy's withholding of or even disowning the truth. Where the potential crimes are left out in *The Trial*, in *I Am No One* they are continually withheld. This suggests that another, more vague but more profound sense of guilt overshadows Jeremy's actions. It is as if the system had caught him out being "one like the other." In this instance, being one like the other is being an American white middle-class male who has, on the one hand, been endowed with interpretative prerogative and with a possibly oblivious but nonetheless operational position of power vis-à-vis students. On the other hand, he is increasingly haunted by the emasculation of this position by an impersonal, larger system that he cannot comprehend but that seems to gradually undermine both this prerogative and this power. Indeed, he might have called this upon himself. One of Josef K's guards tells him that the authorities do not actively search the public for guilt but "it's the guilt that draws them out" (Kafka, 8), implying that proof of guilt is at hand simply by virtue of their coming to him. Similarly, the packages with surveilled materials and Ramsey's visitations appear in themselves as indicative of Jeremy's guilt. Yet, and because the actual content of the packages or the causes for their delivery are suppressed, this guilt seems less related to Jeremy's individual actions or even to his motivations and more to a sense of collective failing. It is not Jeremy's actions themselves but actions *of this kind* that must appear before the law.

The negotiation between individual and collective responsibility finds further resonance in the famous Cathedral passage in *The Trial*. Waiting in vain for admittance to the law, the protagonist in this parable can never hear his charges read or have the court test his case. Wondering why nobody but he has been seeking entrance, he learns that this door was meant only for him and "now," the doorkeeper declares, "I'll go and close it" (256). So while everyone is potentially guilty, Josef K is forced to accept that there is a guilt that will not be reviewed or tested in court. This paranoid vision, in other words, elevates the subject to great importance while leaving him entirely alone in the determination of truth. At any time, he can be charged with guilt but at no time is he in a position to identify, ascertain, or dispute this guilt with others. Despite the fact that potentially everyone is guilty, he is completely secluded both from a lateral processing of his potential guilt with others and from the truth as established by the system to which he is subjected.

A major but no less instructive difference between Kafka's and Flanery's novels is their chronotopic dimensions of power and truth. In *The Trial*, Josef K stands before the law, quite literally, and although this law seems inexplicable and inexplicably dispersed in space—interrogation rooms in private homes, courts in the attics of apartment buildings, execution places in seemingly random spots—there is still the sense that the law has a location. The novel equivocates between the disciplinary and control mechanisms that I discussed in Chapter 2. *The Trial*, Gilles Deleuze suggests, vacillates between "the *apparent acquittal* of the disciplinary societies (between two incarcerations); and the *limitless postponements* of the societies of control (in continuous variation)" (1992a, 5). Josef K seems to have accepted that power is inscrutable and that there is no way of establishing the truth. As the priest tells him, "you don't need to accept everything as true, you only have to accept it as necessary" (Kafka, 263). In *I Am No One*, in contrast, the truth seems to be connected with the anonymous packages and the communication and surveillance technologies that have enabled them. There is no physical place, no establishment to which Jeremy can apply for adjudication—there is no institution in relation to which he can appear as a subject. Neither is there an institution, or position, to which he is subject. Rather, both power and truth seem to come from nowhere. In Jeremy's head, there seems to be little connection between his actions—instantiated, once he finally tells us about them, in clearly marked physical space—and the abstracted material that potentially reveals them. There is a gap, in other words, between his worldly actions and their documentation in the packages—a gap between his potential actual guilt and the surveillance capable of recording it. The truth struggles to find its way into his physical reality.

The gap is partly due to the developments in control discussed earlier and in the increasingly abstract modes of power and surveillance that come with it, and partly due to Jeremy's reluctance to recognize the actions that may very well constitute the underlying reason for his being singled out. As long as these essential dimensions of the narrative are withheld, the chronotope is split and flipped—the flesh and blood of Jeremy's everyday life, as he tells it, is being shadowed by that other reality that he refuses to acknowledge. Bakhtin explains how the chronotope organizes "the primary point from which 'scenes' in a novel unfold" (Bakhtin 1981, 250) The narrative's key developments are thus interwoven with the flesh and blood of spatiotemporal settings. The centrality of the chronotope to the meaning of the narrative cannot, he says, be underestimated; in it is provided the grounds for its representations; it is the place in which "the knots of narrative are tied and untied." The "density and concreteness" of time—human and historical—is connected with "well-delineated spatial areas." Events of less criticality to the narrative, he suggests, are bound to the chronotope but lack its lifeblood: they "appear as mere dry information and communicated facts" (1981, 250). *I Am No One* contains several layers and remains hesitant until the very end to reveal which of them may be the determining and authoritative one. In its early stages, Jeremy delineates the concrete spatial and temporal conditions of the reality he shares with his fellow characters, including the persecution he seems to be under while pushing central events aside. It is only later on that this "dry and communicated" information purportedly existing on the outskirts of the narrative gains relevance and becomes chronotopic, gaining, so to speak, flesh and blood. It is as if the two realities cannot be combined and it is only when the packages start coming through that a leakage between them is initiated.

The Paranoid Chronotope of the White Room

The increasing sense of guilt as it is or is not linked to the truth about Jeremy's past produces a paranoia that struggles to settle on a more clearly defined enemy. Indeed, who is this fleeting ghost haunting the assemblage of his narrative? Is it the ghost of surveillance in twenty-first century America—the fact that technology has made it perfectly possible to trace anybody's online activity and movements? Is it the ghost of paranoias past—reflected in the East German totalitarian surveillance Jeremy has studied for so long? Is it the ghost of the classic American conspiracy films he is watching—and thus of the "covert sphere," the sphere of the cultural imagination of state secrecy and deception discussed in Chapter 1? Or is it the ghost of the terrorist threat that supposedly hangs over the American nation? Is it the face of Stephen Jahn? Saif? Fadia? Is it that of Michael Ramsey and, if so, is this the ghost of the truth that Jeremy is so very reluctant to embody?

"Is that what you deserve, Jeremy?" asks Fadia in one of his recurring dreams of being detained in a white room that is a combination of his home office and "the black sites of secret detention which must exist in America": "We want only that you should reflect on what you have done" (274). In these dreams, he is "almost disappointed" at the mildness of his punishment, by the way he is detained and isolated rather than tortured in ways that match his expectations (274). When he wakes up, this dream room is conflated with his real room and he remains in this room for days. The white room is not only similar to his home office or a detention center but also compared to a school hall where a misbehaving student may be detained as well as to many other institutions of power: the church, law, courts, police, military, and intelligence services (277). In the corner of his mind, we also glimpse the geopolitical dimensions of such power via those "other detainees in the first years of our new millennium" as well as the subjection to elimination via drone war that he himself might quite easily be subjected to by his own "American family" should he be expelled from its borders (277).

Here in the white room, we can return to and develop the chronotope of the threshold in Eggers's *Your Fathers* discussed in Chapter 2. As I noted there, this is a chronotope of crisis and indecision that falls outside normal, biographical time. In the white room, it becomes apparent that this space of decision and indecision harbors "the breaking point of a life, the moment of crisis, the decision that changes a life (or the indecisiveness that fails to change a life, the fear to step over the threshold)" (Bakhtin 1981, 248). The subject of this chronotope is filled with doubt, it freezes, according to Keunen, "in the face of the new experiential data," paralyzed by an ability to attune it with older experiences (2010, 45). Here, we recognize how the chronotope of the threshold is typically also a tightly circumscribed but also transitional or liminal space in which time as forward motion is suspended (Collington 2010, 189). Where Eggers stacks thresholds in space, barrack by barrack, Flanery allegorically condenses these thresholds in the bounded but transitional space of the white room. The two novels have in common this multiplication of spaces associated with societal power and control, spaces that are excruciatingly concrete in their spatiotemporal setup but haunted by elusive and persecutory powers and truths.

Where the barracks in *Your Fathers* bring out the disjunction between a concrete level of reality and another less visible but more powerful level, it is in the white room that the thresholds are amassed in *I Am No One*. It brings out and together all the levels of reality that Jeremy had tried to keep apart. Jeremy's own analysis of how power "breaks us in" and models our behavior is academic, informed by Althusser's analysis of ideological and repressive state apparatuses, but it is in a passage that describes the passing of a period of time during which he stays in his room for days on end—"not in a state of detention" but at least "in a state of suspension"—that he realizes that his freedom might have been illusory all along (276). This room, surrounded by white skies and adjacent buildings, is doubled by the white room of the home office, the detention center in his dream, and the various halls of the institutions of society. Yet, in this room the spacetime of everyday life peels off and is increasingly put into question. Lingering in this room, ticking off the days on a laminated calendar (but why has the ink smeared? Is it his own trembling hands that have caused the smudging or is it perhaps the woman cleaning his apartment and who "might be working for those who watch me so closely" [279]), Jeremy begins to wonder if perhaps he has actually "been in a cool white room all [his] adult life" (280). According to the theories of power he has himself just referred to, there would be a sense in which he has actually been sluiced through one institution after another to fit "the laws we have ourselves allowed to be written to control and organize our lives" (277). In this pale light, his subjection to the power of institutions delimits him to working through a never-ending series of white spaces. Thus, and as in *Your Fathers*, the minor chronotope of the threshold is multiplied and stacked, ultimately building the novel's most central and clear-cut paranoid chronotope.

In fact, the process that Ramsey—if it is indeed Ramsey—initiates by sending Jeremy the packages and by shadowing him may be seen as a Matrixian waking up to reality. The modern cult film *The Matrix* (1999) has played a significant role in the construction of a narrative for the online manosphere of contemporary America, as I will discuss further in Chapter 4. Central to the film, and to its employment in this context, is a magnificent paranoid chronotope: a distinction between a grim reality, in which human beings function as batteries for aliens who have invaded Earth, and a simulation that is fed to them that makes them think they live and move around in the world as we know it. A key dilemma occurs when the protagonist, Neo, having gained access to the real, is offered a choice between a blue or red pill: the former will return him to the oblivion of the pleasant simulation he has lived in so far; the latter will fully introduce him to the harshness of the world as it really is. In *I Am No One*, we may wonder if Ramsey is like the film's Morpheus or perhaps its Agent Smith. Introducing himself in the beginning as just "another corporate shill," he might be a representative of "the system"—an Agent Smith activated to keep unruly subjects in check. He might also be one of the members of Philip K. Dick's "Adjustment Team," discussed in the Introduction—the ordinarily invisible agents who adjust reality to its correct parameters. On the other hand, if Ramsey is the one who alerts Jeremy to the control he is subjected to, he is rather like Morpheus, gradually easing Jeremy into swallowing the red pill and thus opening his eyes to the true reality. Indeed, as Jeremy himself points out, it "is one thing to imagine a faceless government entity somewhere logging my activity, quite another to have someone go to the trouble of printing out the record of such activity on white paper, placing it in a standard cardboard box, wrapping it in brown paper, and addressing it in permanent marker before having it delivered, or delivering it himself, in person, in disguise, to my home address" (66).

Jeremy's waking up to reality reaches its peak in the white room. He has been living in a reality where he perceives himself to be an unrestricted subject, able to "walk free in the world," but his suspension in the room makes him realize that this freedom has always been deceptive (276). Like Neo in *The Matrix*, he has taken the red pill and discovered that what he has considered reality is only a deceptive varnish and that his body has served a different function all along. In this light, the way he has been withholding information about himself may be seen as his remaining blindness to his own role as part of a social. The fact that it takes him so long to connect the surveillance with his own actions speaks to a repudiation of his agency as implicated in networks of power—be they gender hierarchies at universities, Egyptian terrorists, or US government control systems. The ambivalent guilt suggests that he is as unable to blame "the system" as he is to blame himself. The closest he gets to the latter is the periodic questioning of his own sanity, as if it is more likely that his rational self has failed than that his social interactions have had consequences not only for others but also for himself.

But the room—this perfect paranoid chronotope in which layer upon layer of rooms of power are piled—brings out his self-awareness with a vengeance.

The packages—or red pills—that Ramsey has been feeding him seem to have caused the equivalent of a bad acid trip as they open Jeremy's eyes to a reality in which he is not only a "predatory teacher" and an "ogre" unable to control his desires but also, centrally, someone "who has no apparatus for self-control" and "who needs Althusser's repressive state apparatuses to keep him in check, to prevent him from turning himself, however unwittingly, into a traitor not just to the state but to every individual around him" (279). In other words, at this moment Jeremy recognizes not only the truth but his own unreliability as a subject, his failing capacity for reason and self-mastery.

Jeremy's insight is unbearable, however, and he soon slides over into a conception of this exteriority that allows him to salvage his own conception of himself. Hearing voices from upstairs or downstairs or the hallway, he worries that they might all be in his head, and soon he begins to imagine that all that he associates with reality and his relations in it are simply figments of his imagination. It seems easier to imagine his family and his past as such figments than to recognize them—and himself—as emerging alongside institutions—as influenced and controlled but also as subjects in that way. Indeed, a direct citation from Thomas Hobbes's *Leviathan* is required to abjure this threat from the social. Hobbes, Jeremy says, understood the power of figments and their personification (280): "An Idol, or meer [sic] Figment of the brain, may be Personated,' which is to say, *represented*, or acted, even performed, 'as were the Gods of the Heathen; which by such Officers as the State appointed, were Personated, and held Possessions, and other Goods, and Rights, which men from time to time dedicated, and consecrated, unto them. But Idols cannot be Authors, for an Idol is nothing" (Hobbes, 2018, 152). Perhaps, Jeremy thinks, his family and his past are merely such "Hobbesian idols, figments of my brain, that I have been personating to myself"; perhaps his thoughts have turned passing strangers into these close relations, into "a slideshow of false memory."

The disjunctive layers of this paranoid chronotope, then, allow Jeremy to complement or overwrite the realization that he is implicated in a state apparatus that delimits individual agency—as the narrative has been trying to tell him with increasing intensity all along—to a conception of this externality as figments. As figments, externality is less threatening because, while they may speak to his insanity, they do not question his interiority. Combined with the paranoid novel's wont to isolate its characters in their "realizations" of external threats and thus prohibit a collective understanding or community, this renunciation of his social milieu furthers the sense in which the individual subject is salvaged at the expense of the social. Jeremy is unable to settle on either of these levels, however, and the whole thing breaks down. If his family are but figments of his imagination, then who will read his text? The text may disintegrate before he has finished it, as he himself seems to disintegrate (280).

If any of the characters are indeed a figment of Jeremy's imagination, it is most likely Ramsey, at least as the person Jeremy sees him. Ramsey, as we have observed, is a constant presence in the story, but he is simultaneously decisive and indeterminate. We perceive Jeremy's uncertainty about whether it is Ramsey who is stalking him and sending him the parcels and whether the supposed influence Ramsey has on his life is malicious or benign. None of the other characters that have anything to do with him—mainly Jeremy's daughter Meredith and her husband—see him as anything other than harmless (107). Ramsey's training is similar to Jeremy's, having majored in history with a minor in German literature and cultural history. When Jeremy asks him if he can call him Michael, he responds: "Call me whatever you like, Jeremy" (245). Such a statement points to the idea of Ramsey as a figment of Jeremy's imagination—a function of his subconscious rather than a character. In all, this gives Ramsey an allegorical dimension: a Hobbesian "Personation."

Indeed, Jeremy ultimately accepts the continuous presence of the function called Michael Ramsey in his life. As the narrative begins to draw to a close, he says, "Every day, either in the morning or evening, sometimes at lunch, I encounter Michael Ramsey. Occasionally we greet each other, but often he pretends not to see me and simply walks away once I begin approaching him and then I ask myself if it is really Michael I am seeing, or if my brain is playing tricks. Sometimes I call after him, shouting his name, but he never turns around" (304). As a figment of his imagination, Ramsey the stalker may well be the allegorical representation of truth, spooky but ultimately reassuring because he is a visible and tangible impersonation of that truth coming from nowhere. This is implied at the very end of the novel, when Jeremy again summons up in Ramsey a still tentative but more resolute intention of retaining or perhaps regaining a sense of individual agency; determined to "take what little power we have been granted by Michael Ramsey, if indeed he is the one responsible for all that has transpired, and turn that power back on the powerful" (335). Jeremy has become subject in Foucault's two senses of the word: subject to but also subject of power.

During their longest exchange—when Ramsey, purely by coincidence of course, borrows a friends' house close to Jeremy's upstate home—Ramsey absolutely denies having interfered in any way with Jeremy's life. He insists that he had once been one of Jeremy's students, a claim that Jeremy does not corroborate despite the fact that Ramsey says he was in several of his classes (244). Since that time, their meetings—at the café in the beginning, at Jeremy's daughter's Thanksgiving party, and now in the countryside—have been purely coincidental. At this point, Ramsey offers what from Jeremy's perspective seems to be the least likely explanation: that chance or the networks we design simply by virtue of having certain kinds of friends, or jobs, or partners make us likely to meet and know some people more than others. We "don't really have free will," Ramsey insists, but are "players in someone else's simulation, and the rules and teams and relations, the *real* relations between us are invisible to us." Or at least they used to be invisible. Now, thanks to technology, he says, they are finally becoming increasingly visible to us, making it possible to draw actual maps of these interconnections and the movements between them (249).

In theory, such materialization of implicit networks provides an antidote to the paranoid sense that Jeremy is being followed. A paranoid conception of reality as I conceive of it here is not simply, or at least not only, recognizing the influence of external forces on the self but having the sense in which such forces are specifically geared toward and interested in the individual subject. However, while being able to link the virtual maps that technology has made visible with the flesh-and-blood reality of an interconnected sociality of which one is a part potentially eases paranoia—I am not being pursued, it is just a matter of structure—it may also, by virtue of recognizing such structures, enforce a revision of conceptions of the individual subject as free and autonomous. And, as we have learned, such recognition, at least when half-hearted and reluctant, is precisely what initiates agency panic or paranoia. Ramsey provides his own paranoid take on this, constructing a paranoid chronotope in which sociality is haunted by larger determining forces. This someone else, he suggests, may be "something, someone, some entity, call it the universe or God or the players controlling the simulation we might want to suspect is our collective life on this earth" (249). If this is so, Ramsey is of course a prime instance of the implicit networks and dynamics of coincidence and patterns. Ramsey's paranoid vision is different from Jeremy's, however, in that it overtly disallows the existence of free will, and Jeremy reacts correspondingly: "I guess we have nothing else to say to each other for now" (250). Yet Jeremy is relieved after this encounter, convinced that if Ramsey has any role in his life, it is of the benign kind (257). But "Idols cannot be Authors" and where Ramsey's explanation of the lack of chance represents one option, this can be seen as the warm-up to the other options presented in the more concrete and spatiotemporally determined chronotope of the white room.

The idea of waking up to a truer reality remains with Jeremy, as does his anxiety about the implications of differing realities for his conception of himself. What layers are the determining ones? "What is it," he says, "that I think I might be?" (316). To the "theater of my brain" and the "film projected on its internal screen" (314) is added "the fiction I present to others as well as myself," which makes him grope after what he might be "beneath the conscious fiction" (316). Watching the classic paranoid fiction of Ridley Scott's film *Blade Runner* does not help. Unlike Scott's protagonist Deckard, whose status as a human being or android remains uncertain throughout the film, can Jeremy know what he is? And the question that this reference to Scott's classic paranoid film generates is, again, to what extent are Jeremy's adventures linked to the world around him and to what extent are they the fruits of his own preoccupation with American late twentieth-century paranoid culture in the first place? It is clear, at any rate, that placing Jeremy so securely in a tradition of paranoid culture and cultural expression in America situates his predicaments as particularly linked to the American subject and its troubled efforts to access the truth.

Section 3: Critique

Introduction

So who will know the truth? Who is the bearer of knowledge? Where does it reside? Early in the chapter, I noted the diminishing role and authority of the expert as a gatekeeper in favor of a contemporary public sphere governed by complex media technological, and economic mechanisms. I then interrogated the way in which a fictional character faced with information and facts that are detached from a sense of shared world seems to lose his grasp of the truth, even of and to himself. In previous chapters, I began to discuss the fate of critique and the wish to problematize it in contemporary discourses on postcritique. Arguably, all these developments are connected not only to the logic of a faltering public sphere but also to changing conceptions of expertise in it. Before I address the specific role that the university as a public sphere plays in these developments, I first make a brief but hopefully informative comparison between the paranoia emerging with expertise in modernity with what I see as the deepening uncertainties regarding humanist knowledge production and expertise in the present.

Critique/Experts/Universities

One explanation for the rise of paranoia in modernity is the advent of new types of knowledge and knowledge bearers. David Trotter discusses how literature as well as psychiatry in the late eighteenth century believed that the fairly new so-called professional classes were particularly prone to paranoia (2001, 5). With the rise of the professional classes came problems of shaping a new identity. The very nature and status of knowledge was at stake for professionals and the authoritative and independent expertise that was expected of them. This positioned knowledge in an intricate bind with society. Unlike workers, who had their laboring bodies, or the aristocracy who had land or wealth, the emerging professional middle- but noncapitalist classes had only their symbolic capital, their integrity, their "knowledge guaranteed by a certificate to sell" (6). Trotter notes a peculiar kind of precarity arising with the professional classes. The usefulness and use value of the knowledge they represented depended on recognition of the state and the public. What had to be recognized was not only the role of the expert as a source of this knowledge and the usefulness of this knowledge, but also the intentions of the expert to benefit the people (6). Symbolic capital, as Pierre Bourdieu showed, relies on the mutual recognition of its value, "a veritable *magical power*" credited to abstract values and beliefs, and, as Trotter points out, the professional classes did not automatically obtain this status (2001, 7). Suggesting that they sometimes constructed this status of magical power with the help of a paranoid delusion, Trotter also underlines the tension between knowledge and uncertainty (2001, 7). Tracing it through literary fiction, symptomatologies, and case histories, Trotter argues that paranoia arose with the increasing dissemination of professional methods and ideals on all levels and in all activities of society in the nineteenth and early twentieth centuries. At this point, then, knowledge was not only secularized but also increasingly associated with a particular kind of person—the expert—and the materialization of a new class—professionals. On the one hand, the handing over of knowledge to experts and professionals could be seen to secure it a secular place. On the other hand, the uncertain grounds and justifications for this new knowledge made it susceptible to individual as well as societal forces.

Today, as we have seen in this chapter, the status of the expert and the identity of the knower have changed again. The identity of the knower, to build on Trotter's analysis of modernity, can no longer be ascribed a transcendent source. Nor, however, is it satisfactorily attributed to the professional classes. Who, then, is this knower? While the period immediately after the Second World War saw much uncertainty among thinkers regarding the possibility of confidently ascertaining the status of information, knowledge, and truth, the following decades saw growing faith in the market—or rather The Market—as the ultimate processer of information and producer of truth, according to Philip Mirowski and Edward Nik-Khah. (2017, 7). But this confidence comes at the expense of individual knowledge. Indeed, Mirowski and Nik-Khah insist, "a seemingly technical neutral notion like 'information' has been slowly changing what it means to 'know something' and by the twenty-first century has undermined liberal secular notions of democracy and Kantian notions of the ethical self" (9).

Comparing this implicit undermining of beliefs in a humanist subject with changes in spy narratives, Mirowski and Nik-Khah note that superior detectives like Sherlock Holmes or spies like James Bond were always on top of the game, capable of assigning guilt and innocence and, centrally, of ascertaining truth. During the twentieth century, however, we increasingly encountered protagonists who find themselves in messy and seemingly unoverviewable and far-reaching plots and conspiracies without ever grasping the whole or its implications. Rob Horning sees these protagonists as becoming "intelligence agents against their will. . . . the unwitting conduit[s] of vital knowledge that can be transmitted through them without their being capable of understanding its broader importance" (Horning 2012, n.p.). This development mirrors key advances in the history of economics pertaining to information and politics. To begin with, it illustrates a sense in which information is elusive and that, while we might have some access to and possession of it, we are incapable of sufficiently understanding or overviewing it. Horning says that new technologies and social media intensify this condition as we become "not the subjects who know things or intentionally produce knowledge" but rather the "means of circulation—objects through which information passes with more or less noise in the signal" (12). The transcendent subject, in other words, capable of reading and interpreting signals in the noise of the world, has itself been degraded to noise in the signal. Like Jeremy in *I Am No One*.

The second development the spy narrative is more directly political. Horning, like Mirowski and Nik-Khah, draws direct parallels to Hayek's recognition of the limited rationality of the political subject and its consequent susceptibility to manipulations by actors such as The Market, Government, and other large, shady organizations (13). Democracy is faltering because citizens cannot be relied upon to act in a rational manner. Only the processing of information by The Market can produce reliable knowledge. In this increasingly neoliberal context, human rationality becomes less relevant. Indeed, Mirowski and Nik-Khah argue that even conceptions of human rationality become less relevant: "The ultimate inversion of conventional narratives is to realize that knee-jerk humanist concerns about what human beings are *really* like and how humans *really* think have become all but inconsequential in modern economics" (29). Conceptions of knowledge are curiously vague or absent from this paradigm, as Mirowski and Nik-Khah point out: "Who or what is supposedly doing the thinking?" (43).

In the first section of this chapter, I discussed the accumulative discrediting of what used to be seen as critical players in representative democracy such as journalists, scientists, and experts. These players are not only less important to contemporary discussions of truth; they are also, as we saw, accused with increasing frequency of weaponizing their status to pursue specific political agendas. Such accusations are frequently directed at academics, not least those in the humanities. Under pressure from neoliberal reform as well as authoritarian aggression, research in the humanities is particularly and persistently embattled, either for being superfluous and elitist or for being dangerous and, well, elitist. Forced into the instrumental measures of neoliberal economics and attacked by right-wingers for being leftist, it is unsurprising that academics in the humanities have started interrogating their role in society.

The University as a Public Sphere

More than a space for the exercise of critical thinking, the university is also, ideally, a crucial space for the honing of critical thinking in the first place. In America, while other spheres have been less obviously public, the university is frequently seen as a significant component of the public sphere. As I touched on earlier, the public sphere does not translate equally well to all social, political, and national contexts. American sociality is not directly comparable with that in a European context, in which it has been most directly theorized. But universities have been recognized as enabling critical thinking and discussion as well as promoting public values and democratic ideals. Public education, McClennen says, and in particular the university, has been a key place in which a vital public sphere has been fostered (31). Higher education, Henry Giroux says, is one of increasingly few public spheres where knowledge and learning promote "public values" and "critical hope" (2016, 9). What has been recognized in the twenty-first century, however, is the growing threat to this space—this university-as-public sphere—by the intrusion of market principles, as well as by overt and direct attacks on research and education in the humanities, in political discourse. While both McClennen and Giroux recognize the university as harboring a lingering possibility of critique, they also note that this public sphere is in danger. Traditionally, Giroux says, universities have been crucial spaces for producing critical citizens and the public spheres essential to the democratic ideals of civic society, but these ideals are becoming increasingly difficult to uphold. Universities are progressively forced into the instrumental, measurable, and market paradigms characteristic of neoliberal principles (5).

We have seen how neoliberal and technological developments complicate divisions between public and private. If we add to this the neoliberal university's increasing specialization and the proliferation of polarized and opinion- and emotion-based discourse in the public sphere more generally, we recognize that exchange between these spheres is shaped by great difficulties. According to Jeffrey Di Leo and Peter Hitchcock, "a wedge has been driven between the interests of academe and the interests of public-private sectors" and while new media requires the participation of many (2016, xiv), it has become difficult to keep American public discourse on "a distinctly critical level" (xvii). Thus, and more than a little ironically, an exponential expansion of knowledge production as well as venues for disseminating it have resulted in a reduction in relevant critical reflection (xi).

Let us begin by reminding ourselves of the role of the university as a public sphere in the first place. The university as a modern institution emerged from the Enlightenment. Bill Readings calls it essentially a "historical project for humanity" that was also "the historical project of culture" (1996, 5). Given its role to affirm and teach culture and critical judgment, the modern university is connected to the advent of a particular notion of culture and liberal subjectivity. The culture is essentially a national one pertaining to the emergence, consolidation, and maintenance of the nation-state. In this sense, it gives the subjects of the nation-state a sense of identity and the nation-state itself legitimization.

The liberal subject is a reasoning one trained in and capable of critique and thus of being a modern citizen. Thus, the modern university is envisioned as "a microcosm of the pure form of the public sphere" (20). In the nineteenth and twentieth centuries, Readings says, this task, which had been largely one of philosophy, gradually became entrusted to the discipline of literature (70).

The university in general, then, and the humanities in particular have played a critical role in building on and reflecting cultural identity. Its mission, says Readings, has been "the production of national subjects under the guise of research into and inculcation of culture, culture that has been thought, since Humboldt, in terms inseparable from national identity" (89). The modern university, in other words, has served an important ideological function. We might also want to emphasize that cultural learning, along with critical thinking, ideally produces Kantian subjects capable of critique as a way of interrogating and thus legitimizing power. With the gradual decline in the importance of the nation-state, however, this function, too, declined. Readings points out that, toward the end of the twentieth century, the very idea and importance of culture was in decline. The underlying reason for this, he argues, was the rise and intensification of global corporate capitalism. When the nation-state is no longer the main site for the reproduction of capital, the ideological function of national culture loses relevance. With this comes what Readings calls "Americanization"—importantly, not to be confused with old-school national imperialism, which obviously has strong ties to national culture. Rather, Americanization, in America as well as elsewhere, is about "the generalized imposition of the rule of the cash-nexus in place of the notion of national identity as determinant of all aspects of investment in social life" (3). In an American context, Readings observes, this emasculation of the political importance of a national culture became particularly evident after the Cold War (14).

In place of the modern university evolved what Readings calls the "posthistorical University." Having lost much of its function as a safeguard of national culture as well as an ideal public sphere, the posthistorical university becomes increasingly governed by economic imperatives. As such, the new way for this university to justify itself is by appealing not to culture but to "excellence" (12). Unlike culture, but like the cash nexus, "excellence" has no inherent content, meaning, orientation, or referent (13). In the process, culture too becomes "dereferentialized"—that is, like excellence, it can come to mean or refer to anything (17). Excellence becomes a currency that can be traded and a unit of comparison without anyone necessarily knowing what it is or what it means

(27). Rankings and accountings abound and universities and departments are caught up in a race linked directly to the market without recourse via culture. The posthistorical university gradually becomes one bureaucratic corporation among others. Invoking excellence rather than culture becomes a way of forcing the university, previously "a prime model for the community of the public sphere in the nation-state" to operate according to economic rather than political principles (144).

When the university no longer performs an ideological function, Readings says, it is undermined not only as a locus of culture but also as a locus of critique (13). On the one hand, we might think that a university freed from its role as part of an ideological state apparatus is free to improve its critical approach, and Readings does detect an upsurge in ideological critique concomitant with the waning of the university's ideological function (166). On the other hand, critical activities are inevitably caught up in dereferentialization. In fact, according to Readings, what is gained in critical freedom stands "in direct proportion to the reduction in [such activities'] general social significance" (168). Put simply, the less it matters what we do, the more freedom we have to do it. In accordance with the principles of the university of excellence, critique, like culture, becomes relevant only insofar as it shows as a successful performance.

So, then, what is a successful critical performance today? Justifications in terms of use value and profitability increasingly push thinking into a marketized metrics and measurable modules. Gregg Lambert describes a gradual shift in American universities from a more industrial—we might also call it disciplinary—model, where students pass through programs, classrooms, and offices and come out as a finished project to what he, via Readings, calls the cafeteria model. In place of preestablished "class assumptions concerning what it means to be 'educated,' 'cultured,' or 'a citizen'" emerges rather a set of "ad hoc criteria" (2001, 184). This model implies that students pick and choose, that they are customers, and that they are, in a sense, placed "to the side" of the production process. The model places students in a position where they are not only to choose but also to know for themselves the criteria for what makes a good choice. Lambert says that, put together, these developments have transformed the university from a place somehow separate from society and hosting a particular expertise not always translatable directly into its logic, into an increasingly integrated part of a general buffet of neoliberal self-realization. It also places theorists in a tighter bind with the political and economic conditions of the surrounding world.

Brown speaks to this same situation when describing how neoliberalism progressively undermines not just knowledge but the very conception of it. As universities are drawn into the neoliberal reconfiguration of everything, everywhere, and everyone as capital, knowledge becomes little more than a capital investment (2015, 176). To the extent that knowledge of the humanities is still desirable—although the dire fate of many such departments and institutions seems to question that—scholars in the humanities and the liberal arts find it more and more difficult to defend their work because the vocabulary of capital investment and market metrics rhymes ill with that of the kind of knowledge that these scholars stimulate. According to Brown, "it renders what scholars do increasingly illegible and irrelevant to those outside the profession and even outside individual disciplines, making it difficult to establish the value of this work to students or a public" (196). Becoming accountable for one's work—less in terms of humanistic inquiry and independent knowledge and more in terms of neoliberal strategies and discourses of use or economic value—not only pushes scholars to defend themselves via vocabularies and practices that are not applicable to their work but also blurs the relationships between theory and its objects.

American middle-brow media in the mid-1990s was intensifying its attacks on the university, arguing that university research was out of touch with the "the demands of the real world" and out of bounds for common readers. Readings suggests that this was primarily because of an "uncertainty as to the role of the University and the very nature of the standards by which it should be judged as an institution" (1). The uncertainty speaks directly to economic as well as political interests. Today, there is decreased funding and reduced faculty influence and, indeed, the diminishing of tenured faculty in the first place. There is the intrusion of both market mechanisms and the national security state. And there is also, as Giroux points out, the unprecedented scope and strength of the attacks on higher education "by religious fundamentalists, corporate power, and the apostles of neoliberal capitalism" (6). Providing numerous examples of the ways in which critical education is confused with or exchanged for the pragmatics of training and economic instrumentalism, Giroux argues that academic culture becomes infested with "a kind of stupidity receptive to what Hannah Arendt once called totalitarianism" (8).

This stupidity can also be understood as emerging from two key trends that, according to Saltman, have shaped the development of public education from the 1980s onward. The first is the already mentioned neoliberalization, including the defunding of the public sector, privatization, and a focus on commercial, managerial, and corporate culture. The second is accountability via a heavy reinforcement and standardization of testing and curricula (7). Together, these have contributed to what Saltman calls the "alienation of fact" in contemporary society. As I touched on in earlier sections of the chapter, the limited requirements for contextualization or understanding result in students learning, effectively, that facts appear from nowhere and knowledge "appears disconnected from its conditions of production" (67). Together, commercialization and the increasing emphasis on standardized testing also generate pedagogical tools and modes that depersonalize learning—ironically, perhaps, since learning is typically marketed as "personalized." While personalized learning may alleviate the pressure of larger, single exams, it builds a pedagogy of constant testing, a procedure that generates a monologic mode of learning. Passive absorption becomes a main mode in the place of "dialogue, curiosity, investigation, interpretation, judgment, and debate" (67).

This development has been called the "Netflixing of education" by Heather Roberts-Mahoney, Alexander Means, and Mark Garrison, who say that it stems from a felt need to adjust education to the contemporary "global 'knowledge economy,'" "information society," and "global economic competition," and it is promoted by policy makers as well as education technology companies and venture philanthropists. Personalized learning technologies, inspired by and mirroring Netflix, Facebook, and other digital platforms, are promoted as working toward efficacy as well as meeting the specific needs of individual students. Personalized learning constitutes a crucial component of corporate school reform, which Roberts-Mahoney, Means, and Garrison identify as emerging from free-market think tanks, Wall Street hedge funds, transnational corporations (including Rupert Murdoch's News Corporation), educational entrepreneurs, and politicians. It departs from and breaks down the earlier disciplinary, industrial model of learning in the twentieth century. What is perceived as hierarchal and public mass education is replaced by personalized learning enabled by effective control systems such as data mining and algorithms (2016, 407). Students produce data that algorithms use to track their behavior and preferences and to generate "new knowledge products" as well as, of course, targeted advertising (407). Furthermore, and with the help of algorithms that test skill development as well as modify behavior, the increased importance of standardized testing can be built into learning activities themselves. The result, Roberts-Mahoney, Means, and Garrison argue, is essentially a "perpetual behavioral modification and examination" (416).

The aggressively promoted and progressively pervasive new model effectively reworks education, knowledge, and expertise. "What emerges," say Roberts-Mahoney, Means, and Garrison, suggests "that social context and human interaction are largely irrelevant and that 'learning' can be reduced to a set of prescriptive skills and behavioral attributes removed from questions and debate over meaning and values" (415). At the same time, algorithmic loops of information and testing not only generate capital but also efficiently render algorithm developers as well as the algorithms themselves more influential and, according to their proponents, more credible than teachers (413). Professional and specialized knowledge and independent expertise are de-emphasized as teachers become facilitators of technology to curricula and pedagogical decision-making that takes place elsewhere (413). That this "expanded" notion of the expert potentially and effectively includes various nonspecialists is reflected in society as a whole and relates to the crisis in knowledge, fact, and truth. Apart from the absence of context discussed by Saltman, there is an unmoored sense of who will know, as noted throughout this chapter, not least in the analysis of *I Am No One*.

More than the expert and knowledge is at stake. What risks disappearing, say Roberts-Mahoney, Means, and Garrison, is the very notion of the individual as citizen: "Personalized learning transforms persons, reconstructs the personal characteristics of students into the assets—private property—of database creators and education technology vendors" (417). Under such conditions, higher education fails to perform the function of a public sphere. It fails to train critical citizens who will enable it. On a university level, the enormity of student debt effectively keeps students from thinking and critically engaging with society. "Debt bondage," as Giroux puts it rather bluntly, "is the ultimate disciplinary technique of casino capitalism in that it robs students of the time to think, dissuades them from entering public service, and reinforces the debased assumption that they should simply be efficient cogs serving a consumer economy and a punishing society" (8). In other words, the university not only fails to provide a public sphere in which critique can be taught and practiced; it also effectively precludes the formation and sustenance of such spheres and activities in society as a whole.

The neoliberalization of the university is also creating a pedagogy that effectively trains students to see the public sphere as a market. According to McClennen, "key to understanding the social influence of neoliberalism is appreciation of its pedagogical function, of the precise ways in which it teaches individuals to live, to understand their place in the world, and to imagine the future" (32). Both McClennen and Giroux draw a direct link between neoliberal economic policy and its detrimental effects on public education and the demise of the public sphere in America. Under contemporary neoliberalism, says Giroux, market principles are confused with democracy and mass-mediated ideas are confused with free thinking (9). Not only is critical reflection missing from such societies; also missing are public spheres, whether in public and higher education or in mainstream media, in which "people can develop what might be called the civic imagination" (4).

Critical pedagogy seems enormously important in this context. According to Saltman, it is crucial in dealing with the contemporary malaise as it provides the means to identify and contextualize theoretical and ideological assumptions and underpinnings as well as material, social, and symbolic interests, forces, and contests "that are imbricated with claims to truth" (23). Critical pedagogy represents what he calls "a good alienation of fact" in that it "reinvests claims to truth with the conditions of their production" (23). Good alienation is enabled by theory. Theory is necessary to correct naïve beliefs or lies about disinterested objectivity. Theory offers the possibility of recognizing "how the interpretive scaffold of the subject is formed by the social." It also makes it possible to examine more concretely "the values, assumptions, and ideologies that undergird claims to truth" and more generally an interpretation of facts as "situated in terms of broader structural and systemic patterns, history, and context" (17).

As we have begun to see, however, theory is attacked or undermined from all directions, not least from those who used to be its proponents in academia. In light of the multiple challenges to truth in contemporary America, the temptation to retrace the steps of a tradition of critique associated with always questioning it is understandable. The longing for a "new empiricism" that Latour expresses, and updating or "crafting new rationales," as Anker and Felski propose, in different ways strive toward a constructive approach to dealing with the present. In light of the crisis in knowledge in general and the crisis in the university as a public sphere in particular, postcritique appears as part of a larger political, technical, and economic, but also distinctly epistemological, crisis that is instantiated in society on a larger scale. A critique of critique could interrogate precisely these contexts and conditions. As I noted in Chapter 2, however, postcritique does not to take into account developments in the public sphere but rather turns inward. In the Critique section in Chapter 4, I will suggest that this results in a paranoid chronotope of postcritique.

4

IDENTITY AND PARANOIA / PARANOID IDENTITIES

Introduction

The crisis of truth, argues Kenneth J. Saltman, steers people not only in the direction of "decontextualized numbers" but also, and more dangerously, toward "essentialized identitarian forms of politics that seek to ground truth in allegedly good and bad bodies." In this way, the crisis of truth, fact, evidence, and theory must be recognized as deeply interlinked with the renaissance of white supremacist, anti-Semitic, xenophobic, sexist, authoritarian, and frequently conspiracy theory–driven movements in recent years (2018, 1). As we saw in Chapter 3, neoliberal rationalities contribute to the undermining of knowledge, critical thinking, and grounded contextualized fact. Believing in "symbolic truths" even in the face of their blatant falsity is also profoundly interdependent with a polarized public sphere, a sphere in which another, or another's, "truth" is perceived as a personalized threat. The fortification and consolidation of aggressive, identitarian opinions and groups via mechanisms ranging from a suspension of belief to a radicalized conspiratorial view would not have been possible without the polarization it feeds on and encourages.

A key question for this chapter is how people enact identity in a polarized public sphere in the twenty-first century. A democratic people, Seyla Benhabib suggests, "needs to reenact its identity in the public sphere" in order to "recognize and come to grips with the implications of its own diversity" (1997, 19). Influential accounts of public space—such as those of Arendt, Habermas, and

John Rawls—see it, according to Benhabib, as "a space in which a collectivity becomes present to itself and recognises itself through a shared interpretative repertoire" (5). Public space—whether theorized as a space of appearance enabling the debating of reason in public with a view of a common goal; as a public sphere of communication, information, and deliberation with the goal of democratic legitimacy; or as a restricted and regulative principle governed by the state and its institutions with the aim to justify its practices—has a central normative requirement to "think and reason from the standpoint of concerned others" (14–5). The ambition to arrive at principles acceptable to all involved may be idealistic and ultimately impossible to realize, but this does not make the objective any less relevant. The view that democracy requires recognizing ourselves as different and differing parts of a larger whole still seems painfully real, not least because of the increasing absence of such recognition.

In earlier chapters, we observed some ways in which identities are affected by and affect configurations of power and truth. In this chapter, I focus on the question of identity formation specifically as it emerges from what I identify as the paranoid chronotope of the public sphere today. In Chapter 1, this paranoid chronotope was addressed in terms of a public sphere that methodically fuels certain types of suspicion and conspiratorial logics while systematically denying others. As we saw, such configurations reach back at least to the Cold War and continually invite citizens to ponder threats posed by more or less specified external enemies. A central configuration of the paranoid chronotope in this chapter pertains to the disjunctive relation between a broader sense of commonality—a public space in which we are constituted as part of the social—and the narrow and aggressive dimensions of commonality evolving with contemporary configurations of the public sphere. What we see is a multiplicity of shared but severely demarcated interpretative repertoires—repertoires that function precisely as the opposite of the public sphere theorized by its proponents (as outlined in Chapter 1) in that they are delimited to and promote perspectives already agreed on rather than subjecting such perspectives to others. In a control society where power is disseminated beyond visibility (as discussed in Chapter 2) and in a neoliberal world of fluid truths (as outlined in Chapter 3), the collectivities "present to themselves" in such groups encourage and strengthen paranoid identity formations.

This final chapter analyzes how fraught relations between individuals and the public sphere, particularly when it comes to power and truth as they have been discussed in earlier chapters, give rise to paranoid projections that seem to stabilize and give shape to conceptions of the self and of others. The first section of the chapter sees these fraught relations of power and truth as closely connected with, if not giving rise to, the transmogrification of identity politics from the radical solidarity projects of the sixties and seventies to an identity politics encouraging, rather, individualization and right-wing movements. Here, the role of a fraught white masculinity becomes central to the analysis, which thus builds and expands on earlier, briefer discussions of such masculinity. The second section analyzes Ben Lerner's novel *10:04* and shows how the identity crisis of white American masculinity, largely and popularly associated with midwestern unemployed men, Internet trolls, and right-wing extremist organizations, is articulated in a more cultured and literary context. My reading of the novel in the context of what has been called "new sincerity" highlights an anxiety regarding the hitherto normative and formative role of the white male literary author at a time when his influence seems under threat both by a growing disinterest in literary culture and by the attention given to other literary traditions. Such anxiety about the status of its own field becomes evident also in the discussion of postcritique in the final section. Building on the critique sections in Chapters 2 and 3, and noting literary criticism's preoccupation with its own role and relevance today, this section suggests that there is an uneasy, if not disjunctive, doubling in discourses on critique. It underlines what it recognizes as a general ambivalence regarding how, and if, we should be suspicious in a contemporaneity that is itself infused by paranoid dispositions.

Section 1: Identity, Paranoia, Society

Identity Politics 1950–2020

Of incalculable importance during the second half of the twentieth century were the powerful political activities associated with the civil rights movement, with the counterculture, with the new social movements, and, via these, with identity politics. In America, an earlier and more homogeneous "counterculture" phase, including, famously, the Beat generation and its reaction to the social norms of the fifties, was succeeded by Students for a Democratic Society, or SDS, in the sixties and the organizations of the New Left and international countercultural movements of the sixties and the early seventies. The ambitions of these various movements, most of which were actively resisting the idea of unitary and hierarchal organization, ran from rebellion against traditional rules and conventions, insofar as they obstructed individual freedom in general, to social equality and justice, political civil rights, and international solidarity. None of these movements would have been the same without the civil rights movements and the Black Panthers. According to Marianne DeKoven, the "grounding in concrete activism and organizing" and "the emotional and intellectual frames of reference" for these movements paved the way for political radicalism, whether second-wave feminism, gay liberation, or other issues, in the sixties and seventies. They were also a major starting point and instantiation of a radical and progressive identity politics informing ensuing decades (2004, 228–9).

That the race-based identity politics of civil rights activists and Black Panthers developed in America has obvious historical motivations. There are two major reasons for this, the first, of course, being the particular history of slavery and racial oppression and discrimination in this country. The sense in which race is seen as more dominant than other inequalities and discriminations, such as class, gender, or sexuality, can be situated in a long history of systemic racial oppression. The second reason that identity politics—in terms not just of race but of other categories—became a major mode of political organization in America was the country's weaker traditions of Marxist and class-based opposition and organization. Indeed, working-class movements grounded in overarching ideological frameworks have historically been stronger in Europe than in the United States. Distinctly critical of the attention paid to identity before class, Walter Benn Michaels tartly explains it this way:

> We like a vision of America organized around the concept of identity, especially (but not exclusively) racial or cultural identity, and we like thinking that the great problems that confront us are essentially problems of prejudice, both personal and structural. Which means that we like the difference between black people and white people or between whites and Asians much more than we like the difference between the rich kids and the poor ones. (2011, 1923)

It is easier, put simply, to fit movements based on identity into American society and politics than those based on class.

Working to specify and delineate the particularity of the new social movements, Hank Johnston, Enrique Laraña, and Joseph R. Gusfield suggest a set of key characteristics: common ground is established in structural roots other than class—such as race or gender—or in specific topics such as nuclear proliferation or animal rights. Such movements are sharply contrasted with working-class movements and Marxist conceptions of ideology and totality, relying more on pluralist ideas and pragmatic orientations geared toward improving the democratic participation of the group in question. Such groups materialize via a focus on cultural and symbolic (and I want to add economic and political) issues linked with the identity around which they form and serve to strengthen. The issues are frequently related to the personal and private, for example, to abortion rights and sexual freedom. These groups tend to be nonviolent and decentralized, emerging from a crisis in credibility of the channels of participation offered. Worth emphasizing here is their belief that individual and collective identities are blurred: "The movement becomes the focus for the individual's definition of himself or herself, and action within the movement is a complex mix of the collective and individual confirmations of identity" (1994, 7).

In general, then, central to the new social movements are questions of identity and equality. The "new" can and has been questioned as many, if not all, of the movements, whether initiated by students or related to gender, race, ethnicity, or issues such as ecology or peace, obviously have historical precedents that they build on to a varying degree. Those who nonetheless insist on their novelty often accentuate aspects such as their postmaterialist, postideological, posthistorical, and pragmatic approach, their constitutive link to modernity in a society in which cultural orientation can be challenged, and their consistent repudiation of established political parties and politics (Buechler 1995, 448). The new social movements are thus seen to deemphasize class- and economy-based conflict and resistance as theorized in Marxist contexts and instead to turn up on the battlefields of the social and culture. In short, equality and resistance are not viewed in the first instance as a question of class but as a question of identity and social structures.

At the same time, and as I keep noting, America has a complicated relationship with the social. Suspicion of society and the social itself is deeply ingrained in American culture. Over time, such suspicions are reconfigured to fit political and economic developments. Although with some variation, the ordo- and later neoliberal agendas developing after the Second World War and with the Chicago school in the 1980s have, as we have seen, consistently undermined, attacked, and delegitimized the social and society. Because if one denies the concept and existence of society, which some, like Ronald Reagan and Margaret Thatcher, famously and quite explicitly, have, conceptions and attempted enforcements of the social become limitations or even threats to the free individuals imagined as existing beyond it (Brown 2019, 29). As Wendy Brown sees it, "If there is no such thing as society, but only individuals and families oriented by markets and morals, then there is no such thing as social power generating hierarchies, exclusion, and violence, let alone subjectivity at the sites of class, gender, or race" (40). In this light, the social as promoted by the new social movements and social justice warriors from the middle decades of the twentieth century and the first decades of the twenty-first is regarded as an illicit encroachment on the liberty and choices individuals themselves can and should make. Indeed, in such a scenario any attempts at negotiating or ameliorating inequalities and working toward social justice become illegitimate—they become, according to Brown, either "the baseless whining of 'snowflakes'" (41) or "tyrannical norms and rules imposed by left-wing mobs" (45).

What we see in America during this period then, is an intensification of a historically and culturally determined suspicion directed not only at other ideologies and peoples or only at surveillance and control mechanisms, but also, and perhaps quite centrally, toward the country's own social fabric. In fact, Peter Knight suggests that the new social movements from the sixties onward reconfigured the formerly so-common sense of a foreign threat to the American way of life in order to emphasize instead the threat of "idealized and ideologized normality" to black power, radical feminism, and gay liberation among others (2000, 144). And while it is certainly true that there are elements of conspiratorial thinking within these groups, this internalized threat is arguably more conspicuously posited today as one that the groups themselves pose to the liberty beyond the social so precious to America. Because does not the struggle toward equality for women, minorities, and homosexuals associated with these movements look suspiciously like a strengthening of and insistence on the social? This makes it acutely relevant to ask at what point such movements became associated with oversensitive snowflakes or dictatorial left-wingers at best or, at worst, as insistent threats to the paranoid white masculinities that are now mobilizing against them. And when did identity politics—while typically derided or even attacked precisely by such white masculinities—become a major (if predictably unacknowledged) force in contemporary white alt-right and nationalist movements?

A fundamental dimension of identity politics is the emphasis on the fact that the abstract, universal subject upon whom democratic societies rely for their justification has not been universal at all. In this light, identity politics constitutes a crucial means of asserting the particularity and rights of the identities that the supposedly universal fails to include. Work toward equality in this field is inestimable, but many have noted potential problems, including the reinstatement of otherness as well as suppression of internal and individual differences. In 1996, Jodi Dean urged that the way forward—building on while avoiding the pitfalls of identity politics—was to work toward a solidarity that would stretch beyond the "we" of groups. The 1990s was supposed to be the we decade—replacing the me decade just before it—but "no one really knew who 'we' were" (1996, 1). For her the final decade of the twentieth century was the struggle to find the correct labels for the right identities in America at the same time that Europe was seeing the reemergence of nationalist forces. Dean proposed working instead toward "a 'we' without labels," made possible by a "reflective solidarity as the bridge between identity and universality." Building and expanding a Habermasian approach, she suggested "a communicative understanding of 'we' [that would] enable us to think of difference differently, to overcome the competing dualisms of us/them, male/female, white/black, straight/gay, public/private, general/particular" (3). With hindsight, we know that this was not to be the fate of identity politics in the twenty-first century. Instead of reflective solidarity—"as the mutual expectation of a responsible orientation to relationship" (3)—the first decades of the century have been characterized by a continued perversion of identity politics alongside increasing polarization and paranoia. If anything, as polarization, hate, fear, and paranoia overrun the public sphere, what we see is the direct opposite of reflective solidarity. Two major developments that have moved us away from what Dean called "the solidarity of strangers" can be discerned.

One development is the increasing role of identity and recognition as a matter of self-realization and border policing. Continuing to develop alongside neoliberalism, identity politics has gradually become less about social justice and solidarity and more about what is in effect an undercutting of such projects via mutual hostility and morality. A public sphere that centers on neoliberal logics and on a new regime of truth, which I discussed in previous chapters, pushes identity politics into an individualist and recurrently paranoid mode. Over the years, platforms such as Tumblr, deriving originally from activist and academic culture, have honed a progressively extreme political and aesthetic sensibility of inclusion and diversity. While the identity politics of the new social movements of the sixties and seventies, which worked on the premise of group solidarity to effect structural political difference, contemporary online identity politics has gradually and partly been transformed into a liberal and self-oriented morality. Preoccupied, as Angela Nagle puts it, with "the minutia and gradations of rapidly proliferating identities" (2017, 69), the style and vocabulary developed in such spaces have transformed aspects of recognition, inclusion, and vulnerability into an increasingly hostile politics of "identitarian privilege-checking" (75). Nagle exemplifies this change with the case of Mark Fisher, one of many left-wing materialist critics to take issue with identity politics (Benn Michaels, she notes, is another one), who—although actually afraid of doing so—spoke out against the "witch-hunting moralism" of this online dynamic and as a result suffered a "deluge of personal and vindictive mass abuse" (75).

The other dominant development in identity politics in the twenty-first century is the white male identitarianism that has grown increasingly ostentatious in both Europe and America. In this version—or versions, because of course there are many—the link between identity and paranoia is both more visible and more constitutive. Essentially, a white male identity needs to be protected from terrorizations coming from independent women, from those of other ethnic or racial backgrounds or sexual orientations, from immigrants, and, of course, from the social more generally as a sphere that gives space and voice to these groups while threatening to unravel white male identity. Frequently, this paranoia is geared to an "elite," supposedly left-wing, that viciously contributes to the undermining of white masculinity, for example, by allowing immigrants to invade and ultimately take over the population or by giving women power enough to become independent of men and destroy family values. Building on Barbara Ehrenreich's conception of white middle-class "fear of falling," Liam Kennedy suggests that this fear—of losing control over oneself as well as society—comes with a particular anxiety for white men "who must confront their diminishing ability to assume normative roles of power and authority and transcend the politics of identity formation" (1996, 89). Interestingly, such identity politics is typically articulated—and aggressively asserted—in opposition to the very groups associated with identity politics in the middle decades of the twentieth century in the first place. In other words, one of the most effective identity politics practiced in the 2000s and 2010s runs on its very opposition to identity politics as we used to know it.

White Male Identity Politics in the Twenty-First Century

I begin my narrative with the white male victimization in the 1960s that has led us to the consolidation of aggressive white masculinity in the present, and with the various transformations that the movements of that time generated. Summarizing a fairly common, left-wing narrative of these developments, Brown claims that neoliberal economic policy destroyed suburban and rural regions, not least by moving jobs to cheaper locations in the Global South, dispossessing and disenfranchising whites, Christians, and males. At the same time, and at a growing distance and estrangement from the American heartland, there materialized an educated, multicultural, globetrotting urban population emerging from a "different moral and cultural universe." While being continually sacrificed for economic gain, dispossessed midlanders were fed a "political symphony" of Christianity, family values, racism, and patriotism in a strategy that, after the financial crisis of 2008, intensified to keep its hold over this population—"serious displacement was now required"—centrally by blaming on undocumented immigrants, affirmative action, and the social state. Enthused by the right-wing commentary of Fox News and other outlets, increasingly brought together by the Internet, and ultimately strengthened by the "siloization" of modern media consumption, hitherto isolated movements—"white nationalist, libertarian, antigovernment, and fascist"—paved the way for "the political earthquake of November 2016" (2019, 3). Brown adds to this story an emphasis on the demonization of the social and political and the concomitant promotion of markets and traditional morality to replace them. The fragmentation of society and of the idea of the public good, she observes, facilitates the undermining of sexual, gender, and racial equality and the emasculation of the mechanisms of a nonviolent public sphere, which in turn lays the ground for "'tribalisms' emerging as identities" and "ferocious antidemocratic forces" (7).

The development of a white male identity politics has, in other words, been heavily promoted by economic inflation, globalization, and neoliberalization. Referring to a long list of previous scholarship, Casey Ryan Kelly observes that the historical emergence of this contemporary victimization of white American men can be found in a combination of social changes inaugurated and increasingly implemented during the latter half of the twentieth century and an inflationary, progressively global, and, in America, deindustrialized economy (2020, 11). To this we add the radical rise in income inequality and impoverishment across the globalized West in the twenty-first century, which has hit Americans particularly hard. Its exponential growth has opened up "an outright social chasm," according to Marco Revelli, as millions and millions of people in advanced economies "feel themselves being pushed to the margins or losing their class position" (2019, 198). As such observations suggest, we may come a long way toward understanding contemporary working-class white male xenophobia and paranoia by means of a Marxist analysis of class and economy. If we "follow the money," we see that declining prospects and snowballing inequalities have underwritten and intensified populist sentiment.

Bearing in mind the history of identity politics and the particular configurations of the social in an American context, however, and considering the predominance of white men in these movements as well as the fact that much of this frustration has taken shape not as left-oriented or socialist political struggle but as populist discontent, we need to pay attention to the dynamics by which such frustration has taken the gendered and colored shape it has. "It's not 'Americans' who are angry," as Michael Kimmel notes, "it's American *men*. And it's not all American men—it's *white* American men" (2017, 6). One result of the combination of social changes and escalating inequalities in America is an aggrieved white masculinity that feels that it has been violently stripped of its identity, giving birth to an ever more violent and paranoid white male identity politics.

The aggrieved white male identity is, as we have already seen, reinforced by progressively established discourses of fear and hate in the public sphere, which Sara Ahmed shows to be circulated between objects and signs, becoming more affective in the case of accumulated circulation. Making use of Marxist as well as psychoanalytic theory while eschewing depth, Ahmed argues that hate and fear do not emerge from subjects and are geared to given objects but rather become "nodal points" in an affective economy (2014, 45). In other words, rather than preconstituted subjects exercising hate toward specified others, identities are forged by affective economies that determine the borders between them. Hate thus shapes bodies and worlds by generating both a subject "endangered by imaginary others" and an object as the source of the (potential) injury. In this fashion, negative as well as positive attachments are formed—the former to those seen as a threat to the subject and the latter to a community of "imagined subjects" under threat. Such discourse, Ahmed notes, is characteristic among racist and nationalist groups. Normative white subjects are aligned and animated as such via the fantasy that they are, precisely, ordinary or even "pure" and that this ordinariness or purity is under threat from "imagined others whose proximity becomes a crime against person as well as place" (42). These imagined others are typically immigrants or regarded as racial others, but they are also typically nonspecified. To the extent that the hatred is aimed at specific body, this body is taken as a stand-in for the general imagined entity of these others (49). Part of the discourse is also the sense in which anybody can be this body of the enemy. Taking as an example the "bogus asylum seeker" that might be a terrorist, all asylum seekers, indeed all people of certain colors or ethnicities, are constructed as "bogeymen," stalking the nation and its subjects, haunting their "capacity to secure its borders" (47). The affective value of such figures, Ahmed suggests, is increased by its lack of fixed referent (47). Constructed as constant and devious threats to the ordinary and normative aligns and animates a community of aggrieved and I would emphasize, paranoid white masculinity.

Online networks contribute to actualizing and consolidating such communities and masculinities. Of varying degree of extremism, they shape a manosphere of connectivity. *Manosphere* is a term sometimes used to describe progressive men's rights activists but more frequently describes a variety of more or less loosely connected sites and message boards that associate and consolidate an alt-right, antifeminist, and conspiratorial online culture. Online misogyny is not reducible to individuals or frustrated trolls but must be recognized as the result of a combination of systemic misogyny and sexism in culture and technological platforms and subcultures that augment and polarize gender politics (see, for example Ging and Siapera 2018, 522). The Internet and the manosphere are in fact central tools not only to consolidate but also to popularize male activism in various and diverse forms. Members of these communities come from diverse socioeconomic backgrounds—blue collar workers who feel threatened and replaced by immigrants taking their jobs and women and private school graduates who are "furious," as Laura Bates puts it, "that their 'rightful' place at the top of the political food chain is being challenged" (2020, 17). What they have in common, however, is being white: "It really is white, western men—and in terms of the education: it is very much the developed countries, very much the US, Canada, Australia and the UK" and it "links back to the altright; it's about white supremacy, and there's very disparaging rhetoric coming out towards black and Asian men as well, which is where you get the suggestion that this is a predominantly white space" (Lisa Sugiura, quoted in Bates, 20).

Both the manosphere and the alt-right consist of different and overlapping groups and communities, many of which have consolidated and grown stronger under their respective umbrella term. In both instances, consolidation occurs via a strong narrative that insists that white men are facing discrimination and prejudice. *Misandry*, say Alice Marwick and Robyn Caplan, is a term used increasingly and extensively in online forums. While it "is as old as feminism itself" (2018, 550), it serves to create a shared sense of identity and community among the diverse groups of the manosphere (553). This is a shared identity and community built on conspiratorial thinking that feminists are malicious and devious man haters spreading outrageous lies in order to vilify and oppress men while denying that this is their project (554). The concept of misandry serves as a "boundary object" consolidating otherwise diverse groups around a joint arrangement (548) and as "a call-to-action" for all who regard feminism as the equivalent of man hating (551). According to Marwick and Caplan, it "encapsulates the perceived persecution of men by feminists, which is used throughout the manosphere to justify networked harassment" (554).

The connectivity of the manosphere brings together previously isolated individuals and communities— bringing, as Casey Ryan Kelly puts it, "men's rights proponents, misogynists, white supremacists, and far-right extremists" out of "the forgotten silos and distant outposts that once constrained [their] scope and intensity," thus enabling "new expressions of white masculinity" (2020, 59). The interconnectivity and speed of online networks—quite distinct from the medial and communicative conditions of social movements of the past—facilitate cross-pollination and assimilation and repeatedly steps toward increasing radicalization as well as toward the mainstreaming of reactionary views (59–60). It is "an interconnected spectrum of different but related groups" making up "a kind of living, breathing ecosystem in close, symbiotic relationships with other online communities like white supremacists and trolls" (Bates, 5). This sphere includes sites such as Reddit and 4chan as well as subreddits such as "r/TheRedPill," "r/ForeverAlone," "r/incel," and other platforms like *MGTOW*, or *Men Going Their Own Way*, and *love-shy.com*. This sphere, Kelly observes, unites men eager to vent their frustration over women's cruelty and take help from pseudoscientific "laws" to justify inequality with those wanting to actively subjugate women and those ready to adopt violent and lethal means to reinstate their power. The outcome is a "larger overarching structure: a network that intones, repeats, and synthesizes different and sometimes contradictory discourse into a cohesive yet neurotic [and I would add paranoid] project in which everything is connected" (64).

It has been suggested that we need to look beyond the human or at least beyond human agency to understand the development of paranoia under these technological conditions. Jessica Johnson maintains that we fail to properly understand radicalization via digital technologies unless we recognize the nonhuman agentiality of online networking. Investigating specifically the links between white male radicalization and digital technologies, Johnson argues that many studies of this phenomenon place too much emphasis on individual pathologies and motives and too little on networks that include nonhuman actors (2018, 103). Engaging actor network theory, she suggests that these networks mobilize and radicalize white nationalists by producing paranoia "without a subject or object" (110). Referring to Melley's agency panic, she proposes that it is "built into the social process of human and nonhuman communication" enabling the proliferation of conspiracy theories (113).

Efforts to conceptualize the role of technology in the engendering of paranoia are clearly important. Johnson's project of lifting paranoia from notions of individual pathology and recognizing it as a larger, societal, and political problem corresponds with mine in this book. Her specific observation about the ways in which networks themselves produce a paranoid mode is also fruitful. Perhaps the ANT theory she proposes also helps us move away from a paranoia that is itself engendered by polarization between human subjects and the technologies that control them. Yet Johnson's conceptualization of "social relations and political action in terms of networking processes that involve human and nonhuman actors" (103) risks obscuring the very concrete political agendas that promote and gain from the proliferation of white male paranoia and conspiracy in contemporary society. I am not trying to push paranoia into the lap of individual subject and pathologies, but I insist on recognizing the ascendancy of economic and political forces that have clearly learned how to work network culture and that are themselves quite agential. Johnson's—or rather Bruno Latour's—networks include both human and nonhuman actors, but suggesting that white radicalization and extremism are generated in this "ecology" blurs not only the structural and economic background of these developments but also the quite purposeful and politically motivated activation of conspiracy sites and fake news strategies. As Johnson herself remarks, Infowars, Breitbart, 4chan, Reddit, Facebook, and Twitter have all played an important part in "the affective networking of paranoia" (105). She also says that fake news and conspiracy have an "affective value" that "inflames and networks paranoia without belief" (111). It is precisely "the affective networking of white masculinist paranoia" and the way it has mobilized Trump voters, alt-right supporters, and neo-Nazis that she is interested in (102).

Johnson's proposition that terrorist acts by individual white men occur through affective networking processes with no coordination does make us acutely aware of the need to rethink political coordination and organization under current conditions. Such rethinking clearly constitutes a significant dimension in understanding the political success of the alt-right—not structural political organization in the sense historically associated with growing political developments so much as an engagement of affect facilitated by networks. But although it is impossible, of course, to completely establish cause and effect, it is hardly the networks themselves that have produced and pushed this specific agenda. Indeed, as the discussion of truth in Chapter 3 began to indicate, the undermining of truth and the engagement and proliferation of affective economies that give scant interest to it are clearly promoted by a very powerful and dishearteningly human political agenda. While Fox News and sites such as Infowars and Breitbart may very well have contributed to creating the monster of the paranoid affective networks Johnson identifies, their role in getting Trump elected make them, and the people who run them, political agents in the more traditional sense. An ANT theory that suggests that "there is no social or real space outside of associations" can still apply to this situation, but if we insist that there is "no a priori relation of scale or order according to binaries of macro/micro, local/global, individual/mass, or subject/society" (102), we severely downplay the political and economic forces that have steered the ship in this direction.

Denying a priori scale or order, we also, I would argue, downplay the dynamics underscored throughout this book—that is, the collision, or disjunction, between a particular conception of the individual subject and the senses in which it is undermined. The resilience that many of the otherwise diverse alt-right communities and convictions have in common, Nicholas Michelsen and Pablo De Orellana observe, emerges from a strong sense of a political agency that is nonetheless under threat. This is an agency, they say, with as divergent origins as the autonomous neoliberal subject that underpins Hayekian neoliberalism as well as traditions that are vehemently opposed to liberal and market ideologies (2019, 276). For founders of Alternativeright.com Richard Spencer, Breitbart's Steven Bannon, and Jared Taylor of the online platform American Renaissance, this, in many instances, is also a subject position inspired by the antimodernity and radical racism of Italian fascist theorist Giulio Evola (275). Central to the contemporary versions is the desire to protect white male agency—and thus humanity—from the insidious threats of miscegenation, gender ideology, and liberal mind control.

A Paranoid Chronotope of White Male Identity

In Chapter 3, we saw that contemporary configurations of truth as fueled by a paranoid resilience against liberal mind control are a shared strategy among otherwise disparate alt-right groups. The range of the various groups, sites, and movements is large and consists of numerous and sometimes clashing factions, but, according to Kelly, they do have one narrative in common characterized by a mixture of victimhood, melancholia, radical vanguardism, and apocalyptic thinking (2020, 60). At the core of this narrative sits a conviction that men have been duped by other narratives, that is, by narratives that are now prevailing in society, primarily those offered by feminists and progressives and that are allowed to influence and shape society and its relations and institutions (62). The "overarching forms and genres" of men's narratives help unite and organize their otherwise divergent projects (66). In fact, what holds these communities together is "a kind of rhythmic repetition of the same narrative form" (66). Looking more closely at this form, it becomes quite clear that paranoia is a central ingredient. Indeed, as we will see, there is a distinct paranoid chronotope materializing through this narrative.

The narrative Kelly identifies consists of four major and chronologically related components: The white male has been duped and doped into unthinkingly accepting the simulated reality created by progressive feminist narratives; this false reality makes it impossible for white men to recognize their estrangement from each other and their victimhood; by shocking and raising the consciousness of white men, the manosphere helps them see the bleak but true reality of their existence; together in cyberspace, and eventually in real life, white men will be a liberated multitude that will "overthrow the evil autocratic rule of feminism" (67). Of course, as many have discerned and as the name and influence of "r/TheRedPill" signals, this is a narrative transposed from the film *The Matrix* that I addressed in my reading of Flanery's *I Am No One* in Chapter 3. As I stated there, key to the story is the protagonist Neo's choice between the blue pill, which will deliver him back to the obliviousness of the simulated reality he has hitherto lived in, and the red pill, which will open his eyes to the ugly reality which this simulation has concealed. The red pill is a recurrent trope in most major manosphere communities. The manosphere offers its participants the red pill; that is, it allows them to wake up from "the blissful mind prison of liberalism" to "the unplugged reality of social misandry" (Nagle, 88). As Kelly points out, this is a metaphor that builds on a theory of consciousness resembling Lacan's conception of the Real but with one noteworthy difference. Lacan, as I also noted in the Introduction, sees no way of accessing the Real without mediation. Red Pill proponents, on the other hand, tend to think it possible "to pierce the veil between the simulation of reality and the Real" (70).

The aggressive and toxic environment of much of the manosphere is in itself regarded as instrumental in reaching behind the veil. This environment is not just an outcome but also a requirement because it will help men reenact the trauma they have had to keep at bay. At the same time, this aggression and toxicity will serve to scare off skeptics and insufficiently motivated visitors and affirm and reinforce an "in-group's experience." Once behind the veil, in the "desert of the Real," Red pillers will discover that the system is rigged against men, that the real motive of feminism is to exploit and dominate men, that men have been programmed to accept equality, that men have been socially conditioned to remain docile, that men have been made to suffer from a false consciousness making them identify with their oppressors (Kelly 2020: 70–4). But the mythic structures of this narrative will also ultimately endow men—as individuals as well as a group—with the agency not just to see through this system but to overthrow it.

The paranoid chronotope could hardly be more clearly illustrated and, indeed, instantiated than this. Just as in *The Matrix*, there are two "realities:" one that seems real to people who are oblivious to its true, or rather false, nature and one that only the "initiated" subject is capable of seeing. The two realities are not just disjunctive or allegorical but the one is orchestrated to dupe the subjects of the other into compliance. Unlike the film, the simulated reality is produced not by evil aliens using humans as living batteries in an apocalyptic future but by what most of us would call everyday social reality. From the perspective of the aggressive segments of the manosphere, however, this reality is one generated by liberals and feminists, by the new social movements, and by the government and the institutions and media supporting them. Unlike the film also, the two spacetimes of this real-life paranoid chronotope are not quite as spatiotemporally separated. Where *The Matrix* portrays pods containing the human bodies that are components of gigantic batteries on the one hand and a simulated reality that looks like everyday life on the other, the paranoid chronotope of the twenty-first century manosphere locates these two layers as covering the same ground. In other words, the two realities are virtually identical when it comes to their construction of space and time. As in David Neiwert's account of "Alt-America" discussed earlier, the second layer "has a powerful resemblance to our own, except that it's a completely different America" (2017, 27). We recognize this disjunctive duality from the paranoid chronotopes in the literary narratives discussed in the Introduction: in the short story by Philip K. Dick analyzed there, of course, but also in Thomas Pynchon's *Crying of Lot 49* and Don DeLillo's *Point Omega*.

Significantly, the key distinction between the two layers of the real-life paranoid chronotope lies in their differing distribution of agency. Where everyday reality has emasculated and undermined the agency and authority of white men, the unveiling of the devious forces of society as it really is—the activation and mobilization of this paranoid chronotope—helps these men recognize their true identity as well as the identities of their joint enemies. The paranoid chronotope that the manosphere enables and encourages thus not only restores to individual men a sense of agency of which they have been robbed, but also, and quite crucially in order to begin to follow these relatively marginal trends into the bigger picture, this chronotope is politically activated and put to work beyond such individual subjects. I noted in the Introduction how paranoid novels typically position the paranoid protagonist as secluded in and by his identification of a truer reality. I also highlighted this mechanism in the readings of Eggers's *Your Fathers* and Flanery's *I Am No One* in Chapters 2 and 3. A crucial difference between literary paranoid chronotopes and the real-life paranoid chronotype of the manosphere is that in the latter, the identification of a truer reality is not exclusive to individual subjects. Instead, the connectivity of the manosphere mobilizes a collectivity around this disjunction.

The paranoid chronotope, as I have shown, radically separates the reality of the paranoid subject or group from a common reality shared by others. Just as paranoia functions to separate the individual subject from a shared critical context, it also effectively and efficiently welds together a group. In particular when gaining force and momentum from shared conspiracy theories, paranoia helps create a powerful sense of joint identity among those "in the know." Thus, this paranoid chronotope generates a powerful white masculinist collectivity and agency precisely by consistently dismissing the reality and truth of the social as a devious and counterfeit narrative. According to Patrik Hermansson, David Lawrence, Joe Mulhall, and Simon Murdoch, sections of the manosphere have gradually come together, developing "from anger to ideology" and "becoming both increasingly politicised and conspiratorial" (2020, 164). With enough support, as we will see, not only from members of individual networks or even the manosphere in general but also from major news networks and sites such as Fox News and Infowars and by Donald Trump during his presidency, this essentially paranoid white male agency contributes to very real developments in society in the twenty-first century.

Paranoia Top-Down and Bottom-Up

The paranoid masculinity we see today stretches, as I stated in the Introduction, from lonely incels to the highest office. In between, we see smaller or larger nationalist and white-supremacist groupings as well influential media personalities. Let us start at the top. The Trump presidency was quite overtly characterized by conspiratorial discourse. When he was not himself actively promoting conspiracy theories, such as in the "birther" theory back in 2011 (insisting that Barack Obama's birth certificate was fake), or deep state theories (suggesting that there is a deeper and hidden level of power beneath the elected government), or that climate change is a hoax (invented by leftist elites to rob ordinary Americans of their jobs), Trump was retweeting messages from anti-Muslim, white-nationalist, and online conspiracy-theory sites. In this manner, he lent credibility to groups and accounts that had previously been seen by the general public as too extreme. He also gained enormous support from the far right, from fractious but interrelated groups of conspiracy theorists, white nationalists, white supremacists, neo-Nazis, and Klansmen. Rather than condemn such movements, Trump encouraged them and even, in some instances, provided them with new mottos, as when asking the all-male far-right extremist and violent Proud Boys to "Stand back and stand by" in the presidential debate with Joe Biden in October 2020 (Obeidallah 2020, n.p.).

Crucially, Trump has also aggravated the lack of trust and fueled a general atmosphere of suspicion in American social and political life. Continually serving a heady cocktail of mistrust not only toward immigrants and leftists but also toward what was then his own government and mainstream (or as he calls it, "lamestream") media, he managed to forge a politics that has made nuance, deliberation, and trust virtually impossible. The less than new way in which political opposition works to question the other party's narrative was thus radically upscaled so that all divergent perspectives could be framed as rigged or conspiratorial or, quite simply "fake," or even "FAKE." Repeatedly accusing mainstream media of fake news, Trump identified fake news as the enemy of the people. And this is an enlarged Enemy—with a capital *E* imposing upon the People with a capital *P*: "The Failing @nytimes, &amp, ratings challenged @CNN, will do anything possible to see our Country fail! They are truly The Enemy of the People!" (@PresidentTrump, June 9, 2019), "Lamestream media, which is the Enemy of the People" (November 7, 2019), "Lamestream Media is totally CORRUPT, the Enemy of the People!" (May 3, 2020).

In this way, an antagonistic rift in the public sphere has been actively encouraged. The goal is not to reach a common understanding or way ahead, and political debate is not about discussion and deliberation. Rather, political discourse has increasingly been characterized by the identification and ousting of or even attack on a malevolent enemy. In the context of the concrete political system over which he was President, this became apparent also in Trump's assaults on congressional hearings and debates and the media (the system is "rigged," the rules are "rigged," the election is "rigged," the media is "rigged"). In the general political climate that he has helped feed, the habit of conceiving the other as an antagonist and other experiences or perspectives as invalid at best and as malicious threats at worst undermines reality as a space in which experiences and perspectives are shared or negotiated. Instead emerges a splitting and splintering reality—one in which one layer is real and the other one is false and, quite frequently, malevolent and personally persecutory. "I watch and listen to the Fake News, CNN, MSDNC [sic], ABC, NBC, CBS, some of FOX (desperately & foolishly pleading to be politically correct), the @nytimes, & the @washingtonpost, and all I see is hatred of me at any cost" (Trump March 22, 2020). Trump, then, and as has become apparent to many, has helped normalize paranoia and conspiracy theories in general and among those who identify members or dimensions of the social as the enemies in particular.

The paranoid public sphere that has benefited Trump and that he has subsidized must also, as we began to see in Chapter 3, be recognized as encompassing sites and networks such as Fox News, Breitbart, and Infowars, and numerous smaller and even more extreme sites and Twitter accounts as well as the various dimensions of the manosphere. All of these are keen to feed fear and mistrust and thus contribute to conspiratorial thinking. Online attention economy dynamics, says William Davies, favor emotion and conflict, making fear a more productive weapon than trust in engaging crowds (21). This development produces a generalized fear upon which authoritarian and nationalist groups thrive while also undermining trust in society and its institutions. According to Davies "Weaponisation of everyday things weakens the distinction between war and peace, injecting fear into politics as it does so. It casts fresh uncertainty upon the possible sources and nature of violence, divorcing them from recognised institutions and groups" (2018, 19). When power seems inaccessible or insufficient—associated with "elites" or with a society incapable or unwilling to protect its members from threats from the outside—violence becomes more attractive. The "reframing of public debate along the lines of 'war'"—encouraged, perhaps, by the attention economy more generally but also actively galvanized by far-right organizations such as Breitbart—escalate the destructive spiraling of fear and suspicion (22).

Against a contemporary reality full of rapist Mexicans, terrorist Muslims, deep state infiltrators, leftist subversives, and baby-killing feminists, then, is summoned another reality, a reality that needs to be recuperated, a reality beyond the corruption of the social. This other reality is frequently located in the past. Both during the presidential election in 2016 and when in office, Trump spoke directly to such concerns. As Casey Ryan Kelly puts it, the call to "Make America Great Again" ostensibly "hailed a melancholic subject beseeched by an intoxicating fantasy of return to an imagined past before feminism, the Black freedom struggle, and queer activism fundamentally questioned cisgender heterosexual white men's primacy in all aspects of public and private life" (2020, 2). This nostalgia repeatedly points back to the fifties, a decade frequently identified and celebrated as that time in history when America was "great." Or as Philip Roth's narrator in *American Pastoral* (1998) muses, "The Swede was giving in to the ordinary human wish to live once again in the past—to spend a self-deluding, harmless few moments back in the wholesome striving of the past, when the family endured by a truth in no way grounded in abetting destruction but rather in eluding and outlasting destruction, overcoming its mysterious inroads by creating the utopia of rational existence" (Roth 1998, 122).

But the angry white men of the twenty-first century spend more than a harmless few moments thinking about the past. As this feeling is popularized and politicized, it confers a sense of agency and commonality on these otherwise lonely souls. Encouraged, as I began to note in Chapter 3, by radio hosts such as Limbaugh, Savage, and Hannity, and other virtual presences and forums, collective and sometimes legitimate complaints are consolidated into what becomes "angry white male clubs" and directed at specified enemies, typically women, immigrants, and gay people. These men, Kimmel says, recurrently speak of a manhood or identity in general as "something they have to 'preserve,' or 'retrieve,' or 'restore.'": "To them something has truly been lost—and it is their job to restore men to their 'rightful' place" (18). While there is great variety between different groups, what brings them together is a sense of aggrieved entitlement, the "sense that those benefits to which you believed yourself entitled have been snatched away from you by unseen forces larger and more powerful" (18). Kimmel gives this nostalgia an historical perspective suggesting that where earlier masculinities—epitomized in the self-made man of the American Dream—had space to pursue this dream via America's continuous expansion to an "ever-receding frontier," be it in the West or overseas or in space, such frontiers are closed to the white American men of the twenty-first century—as we saw in the reading of Eggers's *Your Fathers* in Chapter 2—leaving them to "look to the past for their imagined and desired future" (21).

Nostalgia also constitutes a decisive element in the melodramatic style in which Trump excelled and which, Melley says, characterizes the paranoid style in American politics more broadly. Underlining the centrality of melodrama to American paranoid discourses, he emphasizes a formal correspondence between these two modes. A nostalgic view of a better past, a clear and "morally legible" division of good and evil, type characters such as the villain, the victim, and the hero, and a temporal urgency that pushes the moral question into precarious and polarized conflict are all key to melodrama and the paranoid style alike. Both melodrama and paranoia rely on the central importance of the individual in two ways: the centrality of the strong and heroic individual in defeating the evil villain is underscored, and the conception of social processes as not that but rather as the consequences of individual will is accentuated. Thus, Melley shows, the paranoid style is not just, or perhaps even primarily, a matter of interpretation but also a matter of narrative structures. These narratives structures do not allow time for structural change but demand "the transformative intervention of a hero." Thus, they help conserve that most American "fantasy of sovereign agency" (2021).

In this light, the attraction to an authoritarian discourse and practices that reassert the sense of a lost—but ostensibly recuperable—reality make sense. It also makes sense to be attracted to an authoritarian-sounding leader who personifies the strong white male power, truth, and identity that has, or risks being, misappropriated. One of the absolutely fundamental functions of paranoia, as we saw in previous chapters, is to ward off threats to the subject and instead construct a very strong subject position. Richard Hofstadter, regarding the paranoid subject, states that, because he "is capable of perceiving the conspiracy before it is fully obvious to an as yet unaroused public, the paranoid is a militant leader" (2008, 31). In contemporary American culture, as we can see, such warding off has meant positioning social and political challenges and problems not in the context of a general social public sphere in which our lives and fates are inevitably but also meaningfully linked to each other, but on a separate level and as an identifiable and malicious force with an ill will directed toward an individual subject or a group identity. "Decisive events," Hofstadter says, "are not taken as part of the stream of history, but as the consequences of someone's will" (32). In our case, the social itself, exemplified or even personified by groups insisting on it, such as women or liberals, becomes a willful, evil force. In such a setting, as Brown puts it, individuals become units of "extreme and uncompromised positioning, and liberty becomes a right of appropriation, disruption, and even destruction of the social—its named enemy" (2019, 29).

Popular academics in the new public sphere contribute to this polarization of the social. Globally admired Jordan B. Peterson, for example, indicts efforts toward equality for disturbing what he insists are natural gender roles and hierarchies. Equality, in other words, is not just something that is undesirable: in the Peterson scenario, masculinity and agency are effectively put at risk, or, more accurately and aggressively, are under threat from liberals, feminists, and "postmodernists." Peterson's rise to fame along with a considerable following and support among the online alt-right was largely caused by his loud refusal to follow the new Canadian ruling (Bill C-16) protecting gender expression and identity (for example, by allowing everyone to be addressed with their preferred gender pronoun). The federal expansion of the Canadian Human Rights Act to protect gender identity and expression from discrimination and Peterson's university plan to initiate obligatory antibias training established a starting point for his attacks on "Marxism, human rights organisations, HR departments and 'an underground apparatus of radical left political motivations'" (Dorian Lynskey 2018, n.p.). Peterson not only refused to follow this ruling in his work life as a professor at the University of Toronto; he also, in a series of YouTube lectures in 2016, uncompromisingly positioned himself as a "Professor against Political Correctness." Peterson builds on arguments from the so-called political correctness debate in the 1990s and its resurgence today in right wing and nationalist discourses, not least in the manosphere and, quite overtly, via Trump.

One of the central arenas for the struggle for the alt-right resilience against "liberal mind control" is, as I began to note in Chapter 3, free speech and freedom of expression. These are frequently posited as in opposition to liberal conceptions of gender and equality norms, which are seen to constitute oppressive ideologies. While much of what Peterson says is familiar—political correctness is threatening free speech, individual responsibility is undermined by ideological orthodoxy, marginalized groups are infantilized by discourses of victimization—Peterson takes such observations "into its most paranoid territory" (n.p.). Giving legitimacy and academic flair to such discourses, Peterson weaves a whole set of disciplines into a "grand theory" to prove these convictions (n.p.). While reluctant to speculate about his motives, Peterson has garnered spectacular and sometimes quite fanatical fame and following. He has become a major proponent for conspiracy theories on racism ("Islamophobia is 'a word created by fascists and used by cowards to manipulate morons'; White privilege is 'a Marxist lie'" n.p.); on gender (denying the existence of patriarchy, the pay gap "can be attributed to male/female personality differences" [see Peterson "The Gender Scandal," n.d.], comparing neutral gender pronouns to authoritarianism (Jessica Murphy 2016, n.p.); and, quite centrally for our purposes, on academia—not having succeeded with their economical argument, Marxists have decided to infiltrate and manipulate the education system (Lynskey, n.p.).

Peterson's public project thus plays straight into discourses on the university as a public sphere as well as its precarious position as it has developed during the past few decades and as examined in Chapter 3. A political agenda—right-wing conservatism, old-fashioned views on gender equality not to mention LGBTQ+ issues, attacks on political correctness and on intellectuals—is pursued by polarized, aggressive, pseudofactual, if not downright nonsensical or false, but also theatrical and charismatic means. Peterson's academic status as a university professor combined with his expressed hatred of attempts to pursue or maintain the university as a liberal and intellectual environment has endowed him with credibility for people wary of, if not in opposition to, what they—and he—see as the left-wing intellectualism of the universities.

Centrally—and we begin to recognize argument now—Peterson promotes a masculinity that is seen as endangered. Gender hierarchy is natural, he insists, because men are naturally more competent. Masculinity is order and chaos is feminine and the cure for the deplorable state of the world is, as Nellie Bowles observes (2018), clearly stated in the subtitle of his 2018 book *12 Rules for Life: An Antidote to Chaos*. Cultural Marxism and liberal ideas of equality have upset this natural order. By now, we recognize the nostalgic recuperation of a masculinity past—in Peterson's case this reaches all the way back to ancient times but he reiterates the conception of a better time before the new social movements of the late twentieth century: we need to look back to the fifties at least, he insists. We have not talked about living "an honorable life" "in any compelling way in three generations," he says, "probably since the beginning of the '60s" (cited in Bowles n.p).

Despite Peterson's stately appearance and appeal to large audiences of costume-clad middle-class men, the step from this supposedly house-trained white masculinity to the aggressive and sometimes homicidal underground of incels is not a large one. In fact, Peterson attracts supremacists and trolls and has a massive following in online communities like Reddit and r/TheRedPill.

Like incels, Peterson claims that the problem is that women who are allowed to exercise their free will choose only high-status men, and Peterson reaches the same conclusion and solution: enforced monogamy. Thus, tracing paranoid white male identity further down, we descend into the online underground. An atmosphere of fear and suspicion and a rhetoric that targets whole groups of people—women and racial others—as enemies, sometimes even as enemies of war—has become increasingly acceptable and corresponds well to rhetoric common among incels.

Incels—self-identifying as such—represent an online subculture for men who identify as involuntary celibates who have been wronged by a society that has allowed women to become independent. As a post in one such forum suggests: "Women are the ultimate cause of our suffering. Women have "UNJUSTLY made our lives a living hell" (Tolentino 2018, n.p.). Researching by infiltrating incel communities via her alter ego Alex, Bates shows how these communities make it easier over time for participants to see women as the true enemy: "When [Alex] had doubts, messages he read reminded him that he had been deliberately blinded by the female-centric conspiracy designed to keep men docile and passive. He had been tricked into allowing himself to be downtrodden and discriminated against." And perhaps best of all, he was not alone—he had "compatriots," "brothers-in-arms," he was one of thousands of men "with a cause to believe in and an enemy to fight" (Bates, 13). In other words, Alex has been redpilled—he can now see the world as it really is.

Elliot Rodger, who killed seven (including himself) and injured fourteen in California in 2014, has become something of an icon to incels. "What happened," argues a blogger on the incel website *loveshy*, is "punishment for evil and violence of feminists and liberals" (quoted in Kelly 2000, 83). Rodger has been summoned as an inspiration for later fatal deeds such as that perpetrated by Alek Minasian, who killed ten and injured fourteen in Toronto in April 2018 and who hailed the "Incel Rebellion" he considered Rodger to have started—"All hail the Supreme Gentleman Elliot Rodger!" The manifesto Rodger left behind—a 141-page document—may be more paranoid, conspiratorial, and violent than most manosphere discourses in general, but it is not different in kind. Women and immigrants are enemies. There is a war. Rodger himself was able to see this more clearly than anyone else. Thus, women "are like a plague. They don't deserve to have any rights," they are "vicious, evil, barbaric animals, and they need to be treated as such" (*New York Times* 2014, n.p.); women's "rejection of me is a declaration of war, and if it's war they want, then war they shall have"

(131); "I have been able to see the world much clearer than others. I have a vision that other people lack" (135).

Rodger's manifesto speaks to a fantasy of the regeneration of white masculinity and virility through violence, and to the junction between such masculinities and fascist ideologies. While violence is commonly attributed to hegemonic masculinity in general, the violence of aggrieved white men in the twenty-first century is increasingly characterized by "a *thanatopolitics*, a politics of death, that seeks to extinguish that in society that threatens the white male ego—not just women and people of color but institutions that represent the threat of emasculation, including government and the mass media" (Kelly 2020, 4). But Rodger's manifesto, and incel discourse more generally speaks directly to a paranoid imaginary: delirious systematicity, perceived persecution, delusionary grandeur. Apart from speaking to paranoia, it is also eerily similar to the discourses, not just of the manosphere, to which Rodger was a frequent visitor and contributor, but also, and as this section has shown, to twenty-first century American society and politics.

Section 2: Totaled White Male Identity in Ben Lerner's 10:04

Introduction

Unsurprisingly, as we will see, the paranoid protection of white male identity is much more polite among middle-class literary authors than it is in the obscure online communities and conspiratorial think tanks discussed so far. Literary paranoia in the tradition of William Burroughs, Pynchon, DeLillo, and others, also, as Melley points out, tends to shun the grand gestures of the more melodramatic narratives of American politics. It is also typically more humble in its characteristic awareness of its own uncertainties (Melley, 2021). Yet, and without meaning to ascribe any of the authors I will discuss here such attitudes or convictions, there are similarities and concurrences between the increasingly aggressive defense of what is felt to be a beleaguered white masculinity in American society and politics more generally and the literary context that I address in this section. I suggest that, while writers may not explicitly see attempted expansions of literature beyond its traditional entrenchments and canonizations as attacks—indeed, they may even sympathize, if not with neoliberal infringements then at least with the promotion of literatures other than their own—they do more or less implicitly express paranoid anxieties regarding a perceived precariousness of a certain kind of authorial position and identity. The literary writing I discuss helps us see something of the struggles for salvaging or reinventing white, male identity beyond its deconstruction and felt devaluation in the face of attention to other groups and the overwhelming force of political and economic dynamics. This writing also makes it possible to better understand something of the literary gambits of a white paranoid masculinity today.

My reading centers on Lerner's novel *10:04* as associated with what some have come to call "New Sincerity." The term is contested and it remains unclear if and what writers actually associate themselves with it. In the critical literature, however, it has been submitted that the writings and writers discussed in terms of New Sincerity constitute the most coherent and explicit attempt in American fiction to move on from the skepticism and irony associated with postmodernity. Foster Wallace's fictional as well as nonfictional writing at the end of the twentieth century and the early days of the twenty-first and his suggestion that "fiction should be about sincerely communicating what it means to be a 'fucking *human being*" is frequently seen as a starting point for this supposed turn and many well-established but also rather diverse contemporary writers have come to be associated with it, including Eggers and Lerner but also Colson Whitehead, Junot Diaz, Jennifer Egan, and Michael Chabon. One thing such writers have in common, Adam Kelly proposes, is that they grew up as the radical politics and social hope of the sixties seemed increasingly distant and the postmodern neoliberal era all the more pressing (2016, 197). In other words, the postmodernism they wish to move on from is not the more radical and creative versions of its earlier instantiations but rather the engulfment of its various strategies, such as irony and pastiche, into a heavily televised and progressively neoliberal landscape. In the face of this, and what this otherwise rather disparate set of writers are seen to have in common, is a desire for more sincere modes of communication and working toward trust and faith, to express empathy and compassion, to search for a space for literature and life beyond a cynical market logic. But they are also recognized as speaking to a post-postmodern tendency in that they are fully aware of and entangled in the challenges that shaped and still shape literary expression under the logic of late or perhaps just-in-time capitalism, even as they struggle to find a way beyond it.

New Sincerity—as a concept that highlights certain tendencies in particular authors more than actually delineates an organically emerging movement—speaks in interesting ways both to the questions of identity—white, male, aggrieved, as discussed earlier—and to the tendencies of postcritique, to which I will return in the final section of this chapter. Adam Kelly has already made the link to the latter in noting how Foster Wallace and Derrida both work to produce critical alternatives to the hermeneutics of suspicion (2010, 138) as well as how a fruitful comparison can be made between Kosofsky Sedgwick's argument about paranoid and reparative reading and New Sincerity (2017, 9). In Foster Wallace's fiction, says Kelly, both paranoid and reparative reading are dramatized and problematized as the negative consequences of the former are staged at the same time that the latter is seen to be exploited by white males (2017, 9). I will develop this comparison between these similar tendencies toward sincerity and affect in literature and literary theory later. The turn away from the critical to the affirmation of affect and emotion exists in an uneasy tension with contemporary affective politics and the play on emotions in post-truth society. Equally uneasy is the thought that both New Sincerity and postcritique inadvertently speak to neoliberal objectives of innovation and resilience, of individual responsibility and positive thinking.

But first I will address the former issue: the particular ways in which New Sincerity—regardless of whether we recognize it as a literary turn or regard the critical coinage and conception itself as the interesting part—can be read as being in dialogue with a fraught white male identity in contemporary America. Although a few female and nonwhite authors tend to be included in discussions of the genre, New Sincerity is largely associated with white male American writers and is in fact premised on a problem specifically associated with the thematization of such identities in the literature itself. My reading of *10:04* will show how the difficulties in discovering a (new sincere) self are associated not only with the contemporary market principles that this literature and period overtly juggles, nor only with attempts to get beyond the cynicism and irony of postmodernism, but also, and more specifically, with the American literary history of paranoid fiction from the fifties to the present. Positioning discussions of New Sincerity in relation to my central argument about paranoia enables a discussion of the exposed position of certain conceptions of literary and literary writing in relation to the mechanisms of paranoid identity in the twenty-first century.

At first glance, Lerner's more recent novel *The Topeka School* (2019) may seem like a more obvious choice for a reading as it deals directly and explicitly with the struggles of young, white, middle-class masculinity in the new millennium. The novel is quite unambiguously about young men who are "individuals, rugged even, but in fact ... are emptied out, isolate, mass men without a mass, although they're not men, obviously, but boys, perpetual boys" (60). Titles such as Foster Wallace's *Infinite Jest* (1996) or *Brief Interviews with Hideous Men* (1999) would have spoken more directly to New Sincerity preoccupations. However, Lerner's *10:04* shows in particularly intricate ways how questions of white male identity are linked to the current anxieties about the functions of literature and identity. In Chapter two, I suggested that Eggers's *Your Fathers, Where Are They? And the Prophets, Do They Live Forever?* invites us to inquire into the relation between the individual subject, the novel form, and disciplinary society. By comparison, we will see how *10:04* bids us ask what happens with literature and certain conceptions of literary authorship alongside the rise of neoliberal capital. Like much other writing associated with New Sincerity, *10:04* raises questions about the usefulness of literature when deeply imbricated in neoliberal structures. But it also, as I will show, raises questions about the fate of a specifically white male tradition of writing. Positioning this novel in the tension between a paranoid fiction tradition and ambitions toward New Sincerity will illuminate the problematic of white male subjectivity as it struggles to find its feet in the twenty-first century. In *10:04*, we recognize the thematic concern with the volatile nature of reality and temporality from the paranoid traditions analyzed so far. As the novel also thematizes the challenges of writing fiction in neoliberal times, it provokes questions about the white male liberal subject's grasp on power and truth as well as its ability to express itself—its author(ity) so to speak.

In the Introduction, I defined the paranoid chronotope as centrally about how characters see themselves positioned in relation to space time. Lerner's *10:04* is intensely and quite self-consciously preoccupied with this question. Its protagonist, Ben, recurrently fails to feel grounded in a spatiotemporal presence. This is one of the many features that the novel has in common with paranoid fiction as I outlined it in the Introduction, but it is also different from it, which becomes more apparent when reading it in the context of New Sincerity. Whereas many "classic" paranoid novels construct a more coherent other layer of society that serves as the comprehensible explanation that everyday life cannot give them—an adjustment bureau, a system, a matrix, a Valis, a clandestine cult, a conspiracy—the uncertainty and suspicion in Lerner's novel emerges rather from an intense sense of everyday reality never becoming completely real or graspable. In other words, the protagonist senses but is simultaneously haunted by his constant inability to grasp an explanatory framework for and more coherent layer of his everyday reality. To the extent that there is an intelligible other layer, it seems to consist in a neoliberal fluidity that, by its very nature, escapes fixed meanings. As all phenomena are caught up in this fluidity, they are given purpose without narrative meaning. A larger narrative framework is thus undermined by what seems to be an all-encompassing agenda without a stable narrative or identity. Could it be that neoliberalism has taken over the role of explaining and making sense of the world?

The confusion and contention surrounding neoliberalism can at least in part be cleared, according to Mitchum Huehls and Rachel Greenwald Smith, by looking at its different stages: an economic phase emerging in the first decades after World War II and especially after the deregulation of the dollar in 1971; a political, phase that integrated economy into overt political rationalities and agendas in the Reagan and Thatcher 1980s; a sociocultural phase in the 1990s as literature and all forms of art increasingly became saturated and neoliberalism gradually shifted from "from political ideology to normative common sense" (2017, 8); and an ontological, phase in which neoliberalism simply "becomes what we are" (9). In this latest phase, it no longer matters what we are and what we believe in terms of personal identity or political convictions—as long as we are—and we inevitably are—present (5). Huehls and Greenwald Smith also see a thematization of neoliberalism in 1980s literature that in the 1990s began to affect literary form—a more acute awareness of the overpowering role of the market model influencing the formal innovations of writers such as Foster Wallace, Franzen, and Eggers (8).

In *10:04*, the undermining of recognizable narrative frameworks and the identities they enable specifically destabilizes the sense of identity that Lerner's protagonist associates with being a literary author. The novel thus positions itself in general and novel writing in particular as increasingly inadequate and impotent instruments for articulating and making sense of contemporary life. In this way, it problematizes authorship as linked to certain predominantly white male conception of the subject as one not just subject to but subject of his own destiny. More than that, he is subject not only of his own destiny but of the destiny of the world. What seems to be at stake, in the face of the dwindling role of literature, is not just the possibility of literary fiction shaping the way we see the world in general, but also, and more specifically, Lerner and several of his contemporaries seem to suggest, a cultural tradition in which literature of a certain kind has had a considerable and authoritative influence over this shaping. This strong link between literary authorship and the everyday shaping of reality becomes evident in the way Ben's wrestling with his role, purpose, and ability as a literary author is paralleled by his increasingly impotent mastery of spacetime in everyday life. Thus, a paranoid chronotope emerges at the heart of which we, as we so often do, find a white American man losing his sense of agency and control.

10:04

The thematics of an unsettled spacetime is with us from the novel's epigraph. In it, a quote from Giorgio Agamben attributed to Walter Benjamin relates a Hassidic story "about a world to come" in which everything "will be just as it is here" and "as it is now, just a little different." This idea recurs throughout the novel in different guises: "*Everything will be as it is now, just a little different*" (19), "Everything in the photograph was as it had been, only different" (21), "What if everything at the end of the book is the same, only a little different?" (156). It not only points to a world to come, in which everything will be the same but different, but also simultaneously and inevitably infuses the present with this difference. The present is thus no longer the same as itself since it is always already carrying that future difference within it.

This difference in itself has often been seen as enabling postmodern fiction and poststructuralist theorizations that strive for interaction and engagement with the world beyond identity and identities. With this difference appears the possibility of exploding the stratifications of life reinforced by tradition, convention, and capitalism and the delimited and delimiting subject positions that they construct. With this difference, not different from anything but precisely difference in itself, as Gilles Deleuze teaches us, emerge possibilities of becoming—of developing in directions that are not reactive in that they need not differentiate themselves from something else in particular and thus their becoming is shaped in relation to already determined identities. In this sense, conceiving of the world as infused with difference is in some ways the very opposite of paranoia: there is neither an identity to protect nor one to confront.

As Deleuze and Félix Guattari show, however, difference in itself is also a characteristic of the schizophrenic flow of capitalism. They identify three historical forms of *socius*: an early "Primitive Territorial Machine" that organized people mainly through kinship and territory, a "Barbarian Despotic Machine" which saw "a new system of alliance and a new form of filiation" relying on states, institutions, and property, and, the "Civilized Capitalist Machine," which is profoundly dissimilar to the previous two in that it relies on a generalized "decoding of flows"; that is, it does not fall back on anything other than itself. As pure flow, and pushed far enough, this *socius* becomes the very dissolution of the *socius*, a complete deterritorialization, pure desire, a body without organs. While capitalism thus produces "an awesome schizophrenic accumulation of energy or charge," it also protects itself from complete deterritorialization by restoring residual territorialities of previous systems. "Everything returns or recurs," they say, "states, nations, families" (1983, 34). In other words, capitalism positively requires paranoid recuperations of identities to remain relatively stable. As fixed meanings, established belief systems, and stable filiations are outrivaled by the unlimited semiosis of the market, the paranoid tendency ensures the continuous reinscription of meaning as a delimitation of this otherwise unlimited flow. The emergence and gradual but steadfast exacerbation of neoliberalism in the decades following Deleuze and Guattari's observations speak to the further escalation of such deterritorializations and perhaps can explain the analogous intensification of paranoid identities during these decades.

Lerner's novel is clearly troubled by the deterritorializations of neoliberal capital, and we will return to this shortly, but it is also framed by unsettled spacetime and human agency in the face of climate change. Two historical storms frame the novel—Irene and Sandy—and in both instances Ben and his best friend Alex do what everybody else who has the resources seem to be doing—bunker up and hide away at home. Symptomatically, then, the two friends "fail" to experience either storm properly (232), being too safe and secure in their New York middle-class location to be truly exposed. I would suggest, however, that Ben's continuous feelings of unreality and unsettled chronotopes can also be understood in relation to the sense in which human time—in particular the kind that has been constructed culturally in literature—appears as quite brutally insufficient to our understanding of the contemporary world. In this sense, it can perhaps also be related to a more general feeling of unreality in the age of the anthropocene—the way we all struggle to match our regular everyday time with a planetary temporality that we vainly try to grasp. Even so, being too much at the center, too privileged to experience the storms, exposes the periphery and minuteness of human subjects who have not been accustomed to such marginalization. And indeed, the exposedness here lies less in the brutal suffering of those directly and physically unprotected from climate change and more in the sense of being incapable of grasping and authoritatively narrativizing it.

Ben not only has a sense of the world being infused with difference; he also has the recurring sense of the world "rearranging itself" around him. This sense of a present that is not identical to itself reappears in the novel in a number of ways pertaining to what he perceives as the increasingly blurry limits of his own identity. A first recounted instance, one that speaks to what he describes as having become "a familiar sensation," occurs as the result of receiving an important message via cellphone while on New York's Upper East Side: "So much of the most important personal news I'd received in the last several years had come to me by smartphone while I was abroad in the city that I could plot on a map, could represent spatially, the major events, such as they were, of my early thirties" (32). The chronotopic dimensions are quite interesting here, especially as they are symptomatic for our age. Personal events or, rather, the personal emotion associated with learning about them, are spatialized and splayed out across the city. Events from elsewhere are associated with specific places:

> Drop a flag on Google Maps at Lincoln Center, where, beside the fountain, I took a call from Jon informing me that, for whatever complex of reasons, a friend had shot himself; mark the Noguchi Museum in Long Island City, where I read the message ('Apologies for the mass e-mail ...') a close cousin sent out describing the dire condition of her newborn; waiting in line at the post office on Atlantic, the *adhan* issuing from the crackling speakers of the adjacent mosque, I received your wedding announcement and was shocked to be shocked. (33)

The list continues. These events also remain in their place—"in situ" as he puts it—their "attendant affect" always waiting for him there, "like a curtain of beads" (33). There is nothing necessarily paranoid about what has become a recurring feature of twenty-first century everyday Western life. The instantaneous spatialization of memory and affect is perhaps a generic chronotope for contemporaneity. In this more general chronotope, however, there is not one more coherent and malignant layer of reality that doubles on a more messy everyday level, as in the paranoid chronotope. Nevertheless, this spatiotemporal thickness has made it more and more difficult to navigate and determine the role and impact of different layers of reality. "IRL"—once such a useful differentiation between virtual reality and real life—seems, as we began to see in the previous section, increasingly ineffectual in accounting for the intricate and intermingled affective and subject-shaping dynamics of twenty-first century encounters and communication.

A subject position attuned to the constitutive affectivity of reality may not struggle quite as much with the inevitable entanglements of embodied subjectivities. However, a subject position built on the premise that it can transcend its environment easily becomes susceptible to a paranoid determination of coherency. Indeed, a key distinction can be discerned here, between a subject position that recognizes itself as linked with or even emerging from situated and thus specified chronotopic conditions, and one that has traditionally seen itself as transcending such embodied conditions. That the latter are particularly susceptible to the construction of a paranoid chronotope becomes acutely apparent in Ben's case. The idea emphasized here is not that he changes with the personal news he receives or even that his perception of the world around him changes, but that the world *itself* changes and changes itself around *him*. This points to that simultaneous uncertainty and grandeur typical of paranoia that we have seen numerous times: on the one hand, the borders of the individual subject threaten to disintegrate, and on the other, this subject position is so important that the world—or the veils that hide its true nature—is constructed specifically around it.

Ben not only senses the spatiotemporal disjunctions resolving themselves by arranging themselves around him; he is frustrated by his inability to actually *make* the world rearrange itself around him. This speaks both to a strong sense of a subject position and to such a subject position slipping through his fingers. He tries to take charge of these world-rearranging moments in a later passage in the novel when he is on a writing retreat in Marfa, Texas. Finding himself in curious company and doing what he perceives to be out-of-character things, he wonders "how many out-of-character things did I need to do ... before the world rearranged itself around me?" (182). In this instance, Ben seems stuck in a reality that does not belong to him or appear quite real and he begins to long for some synchronization, a rearrangement of the world to fit around his own identity. Where the first dimension of the paranoid chronotope at stake here is seen in the grandeur of the world arranging itself around the subject, this is the other dimension: an ambivalent sense of agency that on the one hand believes that the subject's actions can willfully bring about such rearrangements and that on the other recognizes the inability to judge what it takes to make this happen. Like Thomas in *Your Fathers* and Jeremy in *I Am No One*, Ben is trapped at a threshold; he is intensely caught up in the world but acutely uncertain about how to attune himself to it and move forward. A conventional sense of being a subject in control of himself and his own narratives is contrasted with a world in which this control is challenged. As we will see, this threshold becomes paranoid for Ben because he simultaneously recognizes his impotence while also being preoccupied with a lingering conception of subjecthood. In the following section, I show how this paranoid threshold seems to obstruct Ben's creative capacity; in the final section I show how his affirmation of this disjunctive chronotope ultimately proves productive for Ben as a literary author.

Paranoid Authorship

Ben can make the world rearrange itself around him, however, but only by means of writing such an event into being, that is, by mobilizing his own subject position as a literary author. The middle section of the novel consists of the short story that he published in *The New Yorker*, the story that he has been paid to develop into a book (supposedly the book we are reading but not quite). Unlike the sections before and after, this one is written in the third person and in it we recognize many of its characters and events as fictionalized by Ben. Ben also allows his alter ego to yearn for and achieve a more harmonious relation between subject and world. Here is a passage in which the protagonist reaches a critical decision with the help of a moment in which he and the environment strike a perfect balance: "Everything suddenly complied, corresponded: the pink paper streamer in a girl's hand echoing the rose streak of cloud that was echoed in the water. He felt the world rearrange itself around him" (65). On the one hand, then, this fictional account allows for the harmony and coherence that Ben the fictional author's life will not yield. In his literary writing, the threshold of uncertainty and indecision can be overcome. On the other hand, the account is haunted by self-awareness. His friend Liza teases him about this romanticized moment—"'The sublimity of the view has lent the young man courage,' Liza said, deepening her voice" (65). That the novel needs to counter a longing for a world in which everything "complies" and "corresponds" not with irony so much as with the recognition of such longing's susceptibility to irony makes even this literary attempt at synchronicity and harmony flawed. As this event takes place in the story that Ben writes within the story, it is the fictional author's negotiation of his own longing in the rest of the book. It also is also placed squarely in negotiations between irony and sincerity and elucidates the paranoid tendencies of such negotiations.

Building on Lionel Trilling, Adam Kelly observes that sincerity, as a conception influenced by, for example, Rousseau and Hegel, takes off from a congruity between declaration and feeling: "Truth to the self is conceived of as a means of ensuring truth to the other." During the twentieth century, however, authenticity becomes more important and truth to the self becomes an end in itself. And "whereas sincerity places emphasis on intersubjective truth and communication with others, on what Trilling calls the 'public end in view,' authenticity conceives truth as something inward, personal, and hidden" (2010, 131). Both sincerity and authenticity, however, rely on a surface-depth relation and, as Trilling defines them, both rely on an inner wholeness: "a lack of internal division regardless of what shows on the outside" (136). The irony of the postmodern and poststructuralist influences later in the twentieth century, however, downplayed the model or surface and depth upon which both sincerity and authenticity rely. This entails, suggests Kelly, following on Foster Wallace's writing, that any new sincerity cannot simply return to "older and more naive forms of communication" (134). One of the problems that newer attempts at sincerity have to struggle with is the realization not only that communication is full of uncertainties but also that the surface cannot be rejected in a post-television era. As Foster Wallace puts it, what is at stake is "not just what's true for me as a person, but what's gonna sound true" (quoted in Kelly 2010, 134). Thus, Kelly argues that Foster Wallace's fiction addresses the dynamics whereby anticipation of others' perception of the self overrides the autonomy of the self. It asks, according to Kelly, "what happens when the anticipation of others' reception of one's outward behavior begins to take priority for the acting self, so that inner states lose their originating causal status and instead become effects of that anticipatory logic" (136).

Sincerity under the influence of such fraught self-awareness is open to its own kind of paranoia. Indeed, intense self-awareness is seen to constitute a key trait of paranoia in a post- and possibly post-postmodern setting. First on Patrick O'Donnell's list of "speculations" on the prevalence or "epidemic" of paranoia in contemporary cultural expression is that paranoia becomes "the last refuge of identity so aware of itself as a construct and as constructed by desires assembled for it that it becomes a parody of itself" (2000, 9). The self-awareness that Kelly ascribes "New Sincerity" authors clearly points to paranoia erecting a sanctuary to protect an identity incessantly aware of itself as a construct. Also, and more specifically, this self-awareness evinces a paranoia that Kelly suggests in addressing the fiction of Foster Wallace, is born from the recursive cycle of anticipation of how sincerity will come across to others, acutely visible also in Lerner's novel. It would be quite characteristic of Ben's friend Alex, upon whom Liza is modeled, to tease him should he express his longing for the world to correlate with his sense of self in his real life, but the point here is exactly that she does not have to because Ben employs his own writing to both express and negate it. "The 'fiction writer,'" says Iain Williams about Foster Wallace's work, "simply *must* systematically work through each stage of irony (and the attendant awareness of it) to pre-empt the knowing wink of readers," he must also preclude "theoretical critiques of authorship" by "asserting that he is acutely aware of their premises," and he must differentiate "his own avowal of sincerity from other purported attempts to circumvent the hermeneutics of suspicion by claiming that these are themselves insincere" (2015, 305).

The ambivalent combination of a constant insistence on sincerity and a continual alertness to its constraints resembles the agency panic Melley recognizes in paranoid fiction. More precisely, it resembles the way such panic emerges from a disjunction between an enduring belief in the autonomy of the individual subject and the reluctant and anxious awareness of the ways in which this subject is regulated and controlled. The insistence on sincerity and meaning, while recognizing and admitting both the irony and the constant unsettling of meaning in postmodern fiction and the neoliberal undermining of its value, in itself produces a similar disjunction. This disjunction differs from the agency panic Melley describes, however, insofar as it is typically not a reluctant but a quite overt acceptance of the perils of the contemporary subject. We can see this, for example, in Adam Kelly's comparison of Foster Wallace and Derrida and their common recognition of Western culture's preoccupation with univocal meaning and belief that a more useful strategy may be finding a way to account for the impure and the impossible (2010, 137). And to some extent, perhaps such open admission diffuses the paranoia born from a more suppressed and possibly misdirected manipulation threatening a formerly autonomous self. Yet in *10:04*, Ben's preemptive inclusion of irony in order precisely to diffuse it may reflect an acceptance of the impossible but it may also reflect a paranoid warding off of threats to his competence as a literary author. In this particular instance, at least, Ben cannot be said to belong to the "new rebels" that Foster Wallace hopes will emerge, authors who will be "willing to risk the yawn, the rolled eyes, the cool smile, the nudged ribs, the parody of gifted ironists, the 'How banal'" (Foster Wallace 1993, 193).

Ben's anxiety arguably concerns not only or even primarily the wish to be taken seriously and sincerely as a person but also and more predominantly his own (in)ability to produce serious and sincere literature. Although the novel also thematizes what borders on his superfluousness as a male generally—his services, whether sexual, parental, or societal are all in question—what really seems to speak to his emasculation is his loss of authority in and over the literary text. The most concrete and playful example of this is a character who insubordinately appears in the author's story despite Ben's insistence that she is not in it (78). On a more general level, what haunts the text is the specter of a capitalism grown out of control. More specifically, the text is haunted by the neoliberalism that Brown describes, in which a more classic liberal idea that the free market is there for individuals is replaced with a reality in which individuals are there for the market. Constantly aware of our complicity in a neoliberal profit machine but also our ultimate irrelevance to the machine, how do we push through without irony? And, more pressingly, where exactly do we begin to localize our own intentions? The sincerity of our own intentions is inevitably and radically called into question when "one cannot help but take one's interpellation into various structures (whether economic, institutional, or linguistic) as causal to both inner feeling and outward avowal" (Kelly 2016, 205). As we are slowly beginning to see with the help of my reading of Lerner, placing this tension between sincerity and irony in literature and literary tradition generally and in authorship particularly suggests that at stake for these writers is not just, or perhaps even primarily, their own subject position but their sense of individual as well as collective authorship of and control over the narratives that shape reality.

In Chapter 2, I began to describe the role of the novel as a disciplinary form shaping the modern subject as they both emerged alongside industrialization. I suggested that on a very general level the modern novel tends toward chronotopic conditions specific to the period in that it becomes "flat"—it reflects and shapes a secular modernity in which man must use his own capacities and moralities and rely on his own agency to navigate space and time. This means that modern man must mobilize his own, secular, narratives to construct and account for his own transcendent relation to his surroundings. Thus, for example, the liberal subject evolving with and alongside the modern novel is fortified with and alongside it, as I proposed via Nancy Armstrong (2011), by constructing borders against the potentially "engulfing otherness" of growing masses of poor people, against colonial subjects, against the nonhuman, against mass media. Armstrong's description of the subject of the early European novel can, as we saw, be compared with the paradoxical subjectivity of American individualism described by Melley because it is simultaneously inscribed as strong and as constantly at risk. As I noted in the Introduction, the possessive individualism theorized by C. B. Macpherson (1962) is intent on warding off outside influences on a self that owns, if nothing else, this self. The individual thus needs constructing with but also against collectivity and the social.

The novel has played an important role in the cultural construction of Western conceptions of selfhood in general and of a certain liberal subject position in particular. This literary construction became particularly apparent via the increasingly desperate attempts to protect it in the post-war period in America. We have seen this in the brief account of the paranoid chronotope emerging in fiction of this period in general as well as in the more detailed readings of *Your Fathers* and *I Am No One*. As Melley has shown us, the progressively paranoid position materializing in post-fifties paranoid literature is such exactly because it clings to these long-standing conceptions of the individual subject even as it more or less consciously recognizes its limitations in the face of social, technological, and political apparatuses. We have begun to see via Deleuze and Guattari, that the consolidation of paranoid identities may also be an effect of the more fluid and schizophrenic nature of capitalism in its neoliberal shape. This conception of the liberal subject has also become more blatantly white and male and appears not exclusively but quite acutely as American in what Emily Apter, cited in Chapter 1, calls oneworldedness—the grandeur of its own globalist and monoculturalist projections combined with its fear but also its articulation and aestheticization of precisely such delirious systematicity (2006, 366).

In American paranoid fiction of the postwar period, this ambivalent position emerges more overtly as nurtured by a white male tradition of writing. Apart from the fact that the paranoid genre discussed here is so overwhelmingly male, and that its preoccupation is so insistently the threats to a conception of liberal individuality that has been distinctly masculine, the preoccupation with the role of the writer himself as under siege speaks further to the sense of losing a grip on reality and its productions. Paul Auster's novels, for example, as I touched on in the Introduction, are populated by novelists struggling to work out the relation between the reality they live and the reality they write. And in DeLillo's novels, the job of creating narratives has been appropriated by terrorists: as he famously put it in *Mao II*, "I used to think it was possible for a novelist to alter the inner life of the culture. Now bomb-makers and gunmen have taken that territory. They make raids on human consciousness. What writers used to do before we were all incorporated" (1992, 41). Whereas much of DeLillo's fiction, particularly after 9/11, is preoccupied with the role of terrorism narratives in our constructions of identity, it is important to recognize and expand on this general sense that the literary author is losing authoritative influence on a culture's perception of itself more broadly. Like Mr. Blank in Auster's *Travels in the Scriptorium* (2006), the author risks forgetting what the relation between writing and reality might be and, more detrimentally, what his function might be in negotiating this relation. "Who is he? What is he doing here? When did he arrive and how long will he remain?" (1).

All of these examples in different ways point to a crisis among literary authors who previously perceived their role in cultural production and formation as significant and influential. Confronted with a disturbing sense of their own powerlessness and redundancy, the once prevailing authors of the era are reduced, as in Auster's *Travels*, to amnesiac old men barely able to ascertain their own identity no matter that of others. Frequently, these uncertainties force them to retreat to, or be contained in, clearly delineated or confined spaces—the compulsive wanderings of the streets of New York and locked rooms in Auster's *New York Trilogy* (1987), the single locked room in his *Travels*, the secluded house that hides the literary author in DeLillo's *Mao II*. Thus, we find these fictional writers repeatedly caught at a chronotopic threshold, stuck writing about their felt inability to write. As we saw in previous chapters, the minor chronotope of the threshold is typically a delimited space in which characters are paralyzed by the new and by the decisions and indecisions that it provokes and requires. Historical forces push the subject of these chronotopes beyond their biographical time and force them toward resolutions and futures that they may not be ready to face. Frequently, irony is at play at these thresholds and enables characters to negotiate the liminal spaces. The irony exists, of course, on a metaliterary level as well, as prominent postmodern fiction writers write about not being able to write and write influential novels about no longer being able to write influential novels.

The authors discussed under the rubric of New Sincerity are seen as such because they supposedly want to break out of these self-referential boxes, or thresholds, and move beyond irony. At the same time, they inherit and perhaps reinforce their predecessors' anxieties regarding the decreasing influence of literature in society. We have already noted some of the concerns: with the infringements on or downright superseding of literature by other media (and here, of course, Foster Wallace's concern about television appears quaint in the face of the constant online connections of the twenty-first century); with the infractions or downright engulfment of neoliberalism of the possibility of making art or resistance; with the increasing attention and place yielded to writers of other genders, sexes, and colors during this period. As "would-be inheritors of high literature culture," Huehls and Greenwald Smith say, these largely white male American writers "saw their time as a moment of scarcity" (8).

The anxiety regarding the role of literature and literary writing in the twenty-first century, then, which is something that concerns anyone who believes in the importance of literature to life, can also be situated in relation to a more specific diminution of the dominant role of a particular literary tradition. Ehrenreich's "fear of falling" that describes the affectivity of white middle-class men points not only to a sense of losing control of the self and of society but also to an increasing inability to claim and maintain a normative and authoritative position (Kennedy 1996, 89). In other words, it is the position of the white male subject as supposedly universal that is at stake. Significantly, it is also this position from which normative conceptions of reality are shaped that is at peril. Critically addressing Foster Wallace as a prime mover for New Sincerity, especially as identified and theorized by Adam Kelly, Edward Jackson and Joel Nicholson-Roberts argue that Foster Wallace's fiction—and, by implication, New Sincerity as theorized by Kelly—performs precisely such codification of the universal as white and male. Thus, this fiction does not move beyond the white male liberal subject at all, but rather prioritizes the affectivity of such a subject at the expense of black and female characters (2017, 2). They maintain that novels of this kind, such as *Infinite Jest*, function as a "therapeutic intervention" of white male experience (4).

The most obvious example of therapeutic intervention in Lerner's novel is its virtually eponymous preoccupation with the 1980s film *Back to the Future* (1985). The film is set in the 1980s when it was made but its major plot centers on its main character Marty McFly traveling back to 1955. The title of Lerner's novel, *10:04*, is the time of day when the lightning hits the courthouse clock in the film, enabling Marty to escape from the fifties in which he has become stuck and fly back to the future. *Back to the Future* is Ben's favorite film, and he and Alex watch it at least twice during the course of the novel, in both instances while barricading themselves against the two hurricanes that frame it: "It could be," Ben proposes in yet another (ironic!) example of the temporal disjunctions of the novel, "our tradition for once-in-a-generation weather" (230). Here, then, we have another closed room, a moment of crisis, a liminal and transitional space—a chronotopic threshold.

This is a threshold for the anthropocene—a call from a future that is already here and that is more portentous than the subjects involved can grasp. We have seen that a key element of the Bakhtinian chronotope of the threshold is that it falls outside biographical time, that it escapes the duration of private life and speaks to forces beyond it. The temporalities of climate change and the anthropocene clearly do that, knocking with increasing force on the small boxes not only of human shelter but also of human-sized perception and culture. As we have noted, Ben and Alex symptomatically fail to experience the storm and devote their time to a nostalgic moment. Watching *Back to the Future* while sheltering from the enormity of the storms and the climate change the storms imply in fact appears as an active retreat from this terrifying threshold. Against the immense forces of the anthropocene is weighted human-sized and man-made spacetimes. If this threshold cannot be transcended, let us at least integrate it into a narrative that salvages agency for the human subject. More than that, the film is not only therapeutic in the positing of human control over temporality; it is also curative in its quite explicit portrayal of the white male subject's mastery of time and history. In fact, the film signals this same subject's capacity to claim and rewrite history—as Ben (self-aware as always) points out to Alex that in the film Marty introduces rock and roll to Chuck Berry and thus allows a white man to invent rather than appropriate it (230). Marty also interferes just a little with the self-confidence of his then very young father-to-be, which endows his father with a much more successful masculinity in the film's present.

Here, rather awkward parallels can be drawn to the contemporary political celebration and mobilization of a pre-postmodern America that were discussed in the previous section. The nostalgia for the past seems a recurring feature in New Sincerity writing—for example, Ben's recourse to the restoration of white masculinity in *Back to the Future* can be compared with Foster Wallace's *Pale King* (2011), which, notes Clare Hayes-Brady, invokes "a nostalgia for the lost coherence of identity displayed by the narrator's fictional father, which marks an earlier instance of the yearning after 1950s masculinity" (2016, 148). As we have seen, attacks on political correctness and social equality in the present are frequently inspired by Donald Trump's quite overt hailing of a melancholy white male heterosexual subject with fantasies of a more felicitous time, before feminist, African American, and queer movements of the mid- to late- twentieth century and before the globalized capitalism that America may have been the first to promote but is associated with mass unemployment and increased immigration. The decade or so after the Second World War has been portrayed as a golden age, and in recent years this idea of the fifties as a time when men could still be men and America could still be great has been converted into an important political weapon. In this light, the wish to reach beyond postmodernism associated with New Sincerity fiction risks pushing such efforts, too, toward an idealized past. What is worse, they supposedly face it without critical weapons.

It is a rather common feature of postmodern fiction to trouble the idealized American culture of the fifties and early sixties. A general problematization of the idealized consumerist vision of a post-war America stretches across the second half of the twentieth century and from literature from the early sixties, such as John Updike's *Rabbit* novels, to Roth's *American Pastoral* in the late nineties. Perhaps nothing captures this troubling more exquisitely than the opening images of David Lynch's film *Blue Velvet* (1986), in which the idyllic imagery of suburban white picket fences, green lawns, and smiling firemen is disturbed by an amputated fly-infested ear that, of course, begins to signal the darkness lurking behind the idyllic surfaces. Indeed, as Robert L. McLaughlin suggests, one of the factors that made such fiction rebellious was the way it deflated the myth of the loving, just, tolerant and "unambiguously moral" America of fifties and sixties television (2004, 63).

Irony was a main tool in such postmodern debunking of nostalgic ideals. But recognizing irony as co-opted by television, it is one of the modes from which writers with New Sincerity ambitions supposedly aim to escape. Irony, Foster Wallace says, was soon co-opted by television itself, as it is "ingeniously absorbing, homogenizing, and re-presenting the very cynical postmodern aesthetic that was once the best alternative to the appeal of low, over-easy, mass-marketed narrative" (1993, 173) and television, according to McLaughlin, was increasingly making irony its "dominant mode of operation" (64). Irony as a subversive tool to illuminate insincerity is thus reshaped to incessantly undermine the possibility of sincerity. Here, we must recall that the writers associated with New Sincerity were too young to have directly experienced the radical politics, social hope, and artistic experimentation of the time in which they were born. Instead, they are all the more steeped in the "postmodern, posthistorical, neoliberal, age of fracture" of the final decades of the twentieth century (Kelly 2016, 197). Importantly, then, it is not postmodern fiction as such that they react against; the co-opting of its "bag of tricks," as McLaughlin puts it (65), and a co-emergent neoliberal context are the problem.

Still, such negotiations of postmodern culture risk dismissing the cultural tools for negotiating the economic and political postmodernity that postmodern fiction too critiques. In this instance, uncomfortable parallels can be drawn between this effort and critical conceptions of postmodernism such as Jordan B. Peterson's. In addition, a generation of young writers voicing their disenchantment with postmodernism coincides, Jon Doyle points out, with conservative politics and populism (2018, 259, 263). Actually, he says, Foster Wallace's "compassionate vision" of a renewed focus on empathy and sincerity "faces a growing rival in intolerant, potentially extremist forms of sincerity" (259). It is therefore dangerous to dismiss skepticism and renounce cynicism and irony as subversive tactics in a time when we risk falling victim to naïve and reductive conceptions of the complexities of reality and to manipulative, even fascistic, dynamisms (263). In fact, Doyle argues, in the twenty-first century, sincerity and affect are productively co-opted by populist, nationalist, and conservative forces (259) that can be directly related to the discussion of truth in the previous chapter and the blatant disinterest in truth when compared with the force of allowing people to say and hear what they want and believe beyond both truth and political correctness.

New Sincerity, Williams observes, has been seen either as "a reactionary turn to or nostalgia for a 'pre-ironic' sincerity, or a 'post-postmodern' hybrid or synthesis of irony and sincerity (or, indeed, an amalgamation of these two positions)" (301). It has also been suggested that the impulse toward sincerity drives authors to return to historical settings. I have noted Lerner's travels to the fifties via the eighties, and Sam Sacks notes how Michael Chabon, Colson Whitehead, and George Saunders among others, authors of a generation in which it is not the homogenizing of television but the divisive effects of social media that are the threat, frequently return to "a safer, more myth-friendly past" and "the hopeful feelings of a simpler time." They are, Sacks says, "the last escapists: If their books still resonate, it is not because they reflect the zeitgeist, but because they run so profoundly against it" (2017 Sacks, n.p.). It is important to recognize, however, that although those imagined historical settings might run against the contemporary zeitgeist, the nostalgic return to the past is in itself very much part of the zeitgeist in twenty-first century America. As we have seen, part of making "America Great Again" is precisely the mobilization of an idealized vision of pre-sixties America. Comparing writers coming of age in the 1990s with the paranoid fiction of writers such as Pynchon and DeLillo, Sacks observes that, while the latter's conspiratorial worldview "spoofed or subverted the country's origin myths," the former "enlarge them," creating a "feel-good vibe" about America's past (Sacks 2017, n.p.). Interestingly, then, paranoia appears in this context as a tool for criticizing national romanticism rather than for endorsing and protecting it, the latter of which seems to have become a more common function of paranoia today.

The struggles of literary authors among this generation with recovering identity and expression are obviously not as aggressive as the masculinity discussed in the previous section of this chapter; nor is it politicized in the way of Trumpian slogans about making America great again. Rather, it is an example of what Kennedy calls "liberal forms of white male crisis management," which acknowledges cultural diversity while also working—and, at least as it pertains to my discussion of these authors I add more or less subconsciously—"to reinvent and reassert the authority of white male identity" (90). Despite its ambitions toward ethics, empathy, and sincerity, this reassertion, Williams says writing about Foster Wallace in particular, "encapsulates both the universalism of the New Right and the individualism of the Old Right." Ultimately, he says, Foster Wallace's project as well as that of New Sincerity writers more generally reveals its "underlying conservative, elitist, individualistic nature" (311). Similarly, Jackson and Nicholson-Roberts suggest that "the premise of a universal affectless in need of curing—the premise from which New Sincerity proceeds—is in fact coded as white and male" (11).

Although *Back to the Future* was made in the eighties, its therapeutic attention to and intervention in the fifties is an issue in *10:04*, which signals its (ironic?) awareness but also irresistible preoccupation with a nostalgic conception of masculinity. This is a conception that matches the yearning for a masculinity associated with the mastery of space, time, and history. This yearning is, as becomes increasingly clear, also doubled by Lerner's excruciating awareness of it. Because Ben's therapeutic obsession with the masculinity and mastery in *Back to the Future* is, of course, accompanied by his mindfulness, as we have seen, of the "ideological mechanism" of, most blatantly, allowing a white man to invent rock and roll. I noted earlier how writing associated with New Sincerity speaks to the first item on O'Donnell's list of "speculations" on the pervasiveness of paranoia in contemporary culture, that is, paranoia as a refuge of an identity that has become acutely aware of itself as a construct. Now we discover how this literary trend corresponds to additional items on the list: how the commodification of time forces us to search for depth in contemporaneity by turning back toward a nostalgic past and how paranoia gives us a pleasurable sense of depth as well as personal history and destiny (9).

As the highly self-conscious writers they are, the predominance of white men among those with explicit New Sincerity ambitions is an observation that has not escaped them either. Foster Wallace acknowledged in an interview that he was writing about "a real American type of sadness," he is "white, upper-middle-class, obscenely well-educated" and his colleagues are "the whole 'great white male' deal" (Laura Miller 1996, n.p.). Symptomatically, this self-awareness is also reflected in what Hayes-Brady describes as a "paralyzing consciousness of alterity" reflected in a nearly compulsive engagement in preempting this diagnosis. She demonstrates how this points to a more general dilemma in identity politics: how to speak or not to speak for someone else. Foster Wallace, she suggests, refuses to speak for someone else but implicitly assumes and privileges "the identity he *does* speak for—White, American, male" (168). This self-awareness may be useful, but because it rarely results in moving beyond but rather in a constant turning back on itself, it also delimits the perspectives and possibilities of writing and literature to a narrow but historically dominant and supposedly universal set of positions. Says Williams, rather cuttingly, about the sincerity problem so central to Foster Wallace and other writers associated with New Sincerity: It comes across as "very real problems for an economically secure, culturally and intellectually understimulated swathe of 'postmodern' U.S. society" (311). In this light, New Sincerity emerges as a sanctuary constructed by the need of "relatively empowered, educated, financially comfortable individuals seeking a lost sense of community" (311). In this way, Williams argues, the striving toward ethics, empathy, and community comes to rely not only on a proffered universalism but also on a conservative, elitist individualism (311). Ultimately, according to Hayes-Brady, it functions "to entrench and defend the privileged position of white American masculinity" (35n.35).

Lerner is not only highly aware of the damage done to literary and artistic autonomy and integrity under neoliberalism; he anticipates it by building it into *10:04*. This corresponds to yet another point on O'Donnell's list of speculations on the prevalence of paranoia in contemporary culture, which is how paranoia besieges us because we desperately and hopelessly try to find a way out of late capitalism (9). *10:04*, Jennifer Ashton says, willingly subsumes such damage within itself and is thus "totaled in advance" (2017, 135). "Totaled" recurs within the novel and it has its most explicit articulation in Ben's lover Alena's "Institute for Totaled Art." Having discovered that insurance companies save art that has been damaged and for which they have paid out, Alena and her friend build the institute's collection from such objects. The artworks are "totaled" not necessarily because they have been completely destroyed—quite the contrary, many of them appear completely unspoiled—but because their value has been reduced to zero. Or, as Ben puts it, "the twenty-one grams of the market's soul had fled; it was no longer a commodity fetish; it was art before or after capital" (134). Alena also "strategically damages" her own paintings, whether to preempt their subsumption under commodity fetishism or the potential damage made by the hurricanes and the climate change that haunt New York as well as the novel. Ashton suggests that Lerner's novel presents itself as preemptively damaged in the same way—an "ingenious form of aesthetic resistance" based on "Alena's ingenious form of risk management" (134).

Ironically, of course, "risk management" does not sit at all well with ideas of artistic or literary autonomy, but plays rather directly into the neoliberal discourses that the novel works to escape. But it does sit well, as Ashton observes, with a sense of the totaled as related to notions of a total work in the first place and to questions of totality. Using an example from the novel, where Alena presents Ben first with a set of porcelain-like balls that turn out to be pieces of a damaged Jeff Koon's sculpture—a fact that only becomes visible once Ben learns about their former Balloon dog shape—and then a Cartier-Bresson print which is clearly identifiable as such but in which the damage is hard to detect, Ashton argues that the works are conceivable as totaled specifically because of a conception of a lost wholeness. "Without the concept of the work as a whole, without the concept of the *total* work, there can be no 'totaled work'" (132). The idea that the integrity of a work is violated even by seemingly imperceptible damage intimates that the integrity of Lerner's novel is similarly interfered with even, or perhaps especially, when he pre-empts such totaling. Ashton maintains, however, that Lerner incorporates this damage and builds a new "total" novel (135).

I suggest that the relation between the total and the totaled can also be applied to conceptions of white masculinity that color the novel's wrestling with literature. If it is correct that a totaled work can only be seen as such from a perspective from which the total can be imagined, then presumably a damaged or even totaled writing position and literature similarly depends on a conception of such a position and literature as having been autonomous in the first place. It is precisely such conceptions of autonomy that, as I have argued with the help of Melley's agency panic, produces paranoia. The ambivalence that Melley underscores arises from an insistence on an autonomous subject position combined with a reluctant recognition of encroachments of the outside, be it social, political, economic, technological, or all of them. In this light, we see the kind of literature discussed here as striving to preempt the damage to a tradition of a (male) liberal autonomous subject. The position at stake is less like the Koons statue, the wholeness of which can only be grasped once the parts have been identified, and more like the Cartier-Bresson print, which seems self-identical but is still changed simply because we know it has been damaged and we know so because it has been professed to have lost its value. But the difference remains hard to identify—it is almost the same, just a little different. Ben's fascination with Alena's institute seems almost Freudian: the objects that are and are not the same move him, both because their fetish value has been "converted back into cash" and because they convey "a messianic sense of being saved from something, saved for something" (134).

Ben's interest in Christian Marclay's work *The Clock* (2010) speaks to this troubled sense of the total, totality, and the totaled. *The Clock* is, precisely, a clock: "it's a twenty-four-hour montage of thousands of scenes from movies and a few from TV edited together so as to be shown in real time; each scene indicates the time with a shot of a timepiece or its mention in dialogue; time in and outside of the film is synchronized" (52). The work's gesture toward a striving for totality and control is particularly interesting in the context of the novel's preoccupation with disjunctive chronotopes. The artist captures every minute of the day, both in the fictional material from which it is assembled and in its 24-hour screening time. This seems comforting—if not therapeutic—to Ben, both as compared with his constant exposure to the unsettled chronotopes of his everyday life and in light of his uncertainties regarding a sense of losing authorial agency and control. Like the prominent role played by Douglas Gordon's art installation *24 Hour Psycho* (1993)—Alfred Hitchcock's famous film slowed down to last across so many hours—in DeLillo's novel *Point Omega*, this attention to graspable temporalities becomes particularly acute when contrasted with both protagonists' and, indeed, both *10:04*'s and *Point Omega*'s, preoccupations with a sense of losing control of the narrative. In *10:04*, the mention of the 10:04 moment when lightning strikes the courthouse in *Back to the Future* not only serves as an explicit key to readers who may not have caught the reference in the title, but also aligns the novel with the artwork that accomplishes the synchronization and mastery of spacetime that the novel itself fails to achieve. Where Ben helplessly feels the world rearranging itself around him, he sees *The Clock* as successful in its ambitions toward totality in that it manages to synchronize fictional time with nonfictional duration: "the beating of a compound heart," he says admiringly, the creation of a "supragenre that made visible our collective, unconscious sense of the rhythms of the day" (53).

Ben seems keen to maintain and reinforce the borders of fiction. He resists descriptions of *The Clock* as "the ultimate collapse of fictional time into real time" and an obliteration of "the distance between art and life" (54). Catching himself repeatedly looking at his own watch, despite the clocks the film incessantly shows, he sees that, although time becomes indistinguishable mathematically, it still belongs to "different worlds." This realization helps Ben recognize "how many different days could be built out of a day," which speaks to a democratization of time, to "possibility [more] than determinism," to moments belonging not only to different characters and storylines but also to different directors, to "the utopian glimmer of fiction" (54). Ben's ruminations inspire him to write more fiction, and he begins to describe the story within the novel discussed previously.

The attempted entrenchment of and insistence on a subject position associated with a privileged identity—especially to the extent that it is underwritten by a subscription to "the myth of masculinity in crisis" and attempts "to narrate and occupy instead of converse and understand," according to Hayes-Brady(177)—is shaped by an intense awareness of the increasing inadequacy of such a position, specifically its role in the shaping of conceptions of the self and the world via literary writing. Ben's sense of the world rearranging itself around him occurs, as we have seen, as a momentary spatiotemporal disjunction amended by adjusting itself around him. These moments are triggered by momentous and personal events and news. Notable, though, is how these rearrangements are recurrently associated with writing or literature. This is visible already in our earlier example, where the benevolent and fruitful congruence between the protagonist and the world is finally made possible, if forever put into question, by fictional writing.

There are several additional examples of Ben's struggle with questions about dimensions larger than himself that point to a certain history and tradition of authorship. One is Ben's graduate student's realization that he has misconceived and severely overestimated the relationship between Ben's friend Bernard and the poet William Bronk, about whom the student is writing. At this point, Ben imagines Bernard seeing the world rearranging itself around this student. Ben's projection of what Bernard might see that the student might feel reflects, of course, Ben's own anxieties. The occasion, centrally, is one pertaining to authorship, identities, and tradition and, more specifically, the strong sense of authorship, identity, and tradition passed between poet, author, professor, and literature student—all of whom, in this case, are white males in a classic intellectual and academic setting. The crack in such tradition, perhaps detectible in the graduate student's disappointment but explicitly so in Ben's conception of this as a world-rearranging moment, simultaneously points toward the significance of tradition and community of male authorship and authority and to the fragility of such authorship and authority beyond this tradition. The crack may always have been there, but has now become evident.

To reach the heart of this anxiety, we go back to the message Ben receives in the first recounted instance of world rearrangement discussed earlier. This message, from Natali, "a mentor and literary hero," concerns the sudden and rather grave illness of her husband, the aforementioned Bernard, who is an "equally important figure" (32). For Ben, Natali and Bernard stand for the literary in a fashion that is extremely desirable but also radically out of sync with the present. In fact, he says that Bernard and Natali had never "seemed to exist in time, at least not in the same temporal medium I occupied" (33). Bernard has a "wizardly beard and otherworldly learnedness" (33) and Natali "always seemed the same age to me" (34). They are both marked by a "condition of temporal exception" in their aging, in their working ("always working and never working"), in their overwhelming and therefore anachronistic literary accomplishments, and even in their everyday life, their house being "not subject to quotidian rhythms but to the strange duration of the literary" (34).

This idolization of a literary project and a life grown out of sync with the present is an essential key to Ben's anxieties about the waning role of the literary author and literature. The paranoid dimensions of these anxieties become observable when we connect his struggles and preoccupation with the threatened role of writing and the literary throughout the novel with his personal sense of losing his grip on the spatiotemporal construction of reality altogether, as discussed at the beginning of the reading. Bakhtin's conception of the chronotope as pointing to "the intrinsic interconnectedness of space and time" in literature can help us see this better. I noted in previous chapters that Bakhtin sees the chronotope as that which gives literary narrative flesh and blood and thereby its meaning. "Time becomes, in effect, palpable and visible, the chronotope makes narrative events concrete, makes them take on flesh, causes blood to flow in their veins." The chronotope concretizes representation with the help of the "density and concreteness of time markers—the time of human life, of historical time" (1981, 250). But in *10:04*, Ben consistently fails to concretize time and space as it pertains to his own self. Scissors in his hand become alien as does the hand that holds them in an "intuition of spatial and temporal collapse, or, paradoxically, an overwhelming sense of its sudden integration" (14). What "normally felt like the only possible world [becomes] one among many, its meaning everywhere up for grabs" (19). Moments are "enabled by a future that had never arrived" and therefore cannot be remembered from the future that does (24). Remembering events may mean they "never happened" (81), and he feels "equidistant from all [his] memories as [his] sense of time collapse[s]" (236).

As we know, Bakhtin's account of differing chronotopes of different periods and genres elucidates distinct conceptions of the human self—of how the relation between the individual and its surroundings is conceived at various times. Where time and place seem to have no impact on characters in adventure time, space is abstract and interchangeable in Greek romance literature. In Renaissance literature, an emerging humanist conception of the interrelation of space and time generates a proportionality between characters and their actions. I noted all this in the Introduction and described how paranoid fiction is typically characterized by a lack of synchronization between characters and their surroundings. This is certainly true in *10:04*, as I have begun to show, but it is also worth noting the particular way in which the literary itself is seen to play, or rather to have played, a role in the construction of a chronotope that corresponds to the subject position of the likes of Ben.

This authorial chronotope allows the subject a sense of control over his spatiotemporal conditions via his co-construction of their narrativization. It becomes apparent precisely because it seems to be disintegrating. Lerner's novel thus not only presents a reality in which the chronotope of everyday life is unsettled and hard to grasp; it also specifically associates this unsettling and increasing ungraspability with the falling away of the literary. Bernhard and Natali still inhabit an intellectual, authorial, confident, and seemingly self-evident subject position associated with literary authority, but, as we have begun to see, they seem to belong to a spatiotemporal realm that is not of this world. Especially, it does not belong to the same world as Ben. Even as he is invited to become a close friend and also, eventually, their literary executor, the spatiotemporal existence of Natali and Bernard's literary project remains out of reach. In fact, Ben's intense preoccupation with temporality is suggestive of an intrinsic connection between the more general unsettled chronotope of his everyday life and his (in)ability to write.

The association between disjunctive chronotopes and the ability or inability to write becomes obvious in the very beginning of the novel, as Ben is having an outrageously expensive dinner with his editor to celebrate the contract for a new book based on his *The New Yorker* story. In response to the editor's question about how he plans to expand the story, he says, but does not say, that he will "project [himself] into several futures simultaneously" with "a minor tremor in my hand; I'll work my way from irony to sincerity in the sinking city, a would-be Whitman of the vulnerable grid" (4). Several temporalities are at play here. First, we have the one in which Ben imagines that this is what he says (which he immediately qualifies as what he "should have said"). Second, we have the one in which this ambition is nonetheless conveyed to us (we are, after all, reading these words on the page). In addition, we have the second iteration of this event much later in the novel, which tells us that he neither says, nor says he thinks, anything of the kind. In this latter account of the scenario, his response to the same question is that he will expand the story: "Like the princess in *Sans Soleil*, I'll make a long list of things that quicken the heart," and will "write a novel that dissolves into a poem about how the small-scale transformations of the erotic must be harnessed by the political" (158). Finally, we have the temporality from which the (non)statement comes: a past that did not in fact happen and a future, or several futures, toward which it points—the several futures that will make sincerity possible, in which one of America's most famous poets will inspire new literature that makes a difference in a fragile world.

That Ben's ambition toward sincerity and reparation is explained as something that should have occurred but did not speaks to the reluctance or perhaps anxiety of it not being realized. In the face of what Ben actually says, such an authorial ambition appears too grand, too aspiring, too confident about the role of literature in the contemporary world. This corresponds to what Adam Kelly sees as a common awareness in New Sincerity fiction: a foreknowledge that telling the truth cannot "be separated from the ends that truth will be put to," that "necessarily contaminates the telling with manipulative overtones" (2016, 204). In *10:04*, the statement Ben does make fits more neatly with the physical location of this episode—an exclusive restaurant full of investment bankers, market analysts, and generally rich and beautiful people. The location itself encourages one statement rather than another; indeed, it rewards and enables one type of literary authorship before another. This is underlined by the editor's explanation in the face of Ben's incredulity—because surely the size of his book advance might have made sense "in the eighties or nineties, when the novel was more or less still a viable commodity form" (154)—that it is the idea of the novel rather than the novel itself that the publishers are paying for. The book proposal, or his "virtual novel," as he puts it himself, may be "worth more than my actual novel," with the book as symbolic capital for publishers that make most of their money "by teen vampire sagas" (154). After wriggling like a fish on a hook—"What happens if I give them a totally different book than the one described in the proposal?" (157)—Ben seems to give in to "the majesty and murderous stupidity" of every thing around him being "coordinated" by money: "One big joke cycle. One big totaled prosody" (156).

Ben's desire to write a book that makes a difference, that moves on from irony to sincerity, as in the nonstatement of the first account of this dinner, parallels the ambitions of New Sincerity, as does the second account in that it overtly acknowledges the "economic and emotional fraudulence underpinning literary production" and its influence on all kinds of writing, be it sincere or not, as Jacqueline O'Dell puts it (2019, 451). In *10:04*, this struggle repeatedly verges on the paranoid as it is not just a matter of being able to write sincerely but of actually being a writer at all. The undermining of literature and sincerity threatens to undo Ben's sense of self. Because it is not just a matter of selling one's work or even selling oneself—there is absolutely nothing new about that. Rather, it is one of being emptied of value as well as meaning in the present, of sensing that your worth is always contingent and always in the future and never ever again to be located in yourself or in your own work. Ben and the editor's discussions about Ben's novel within the novel reveals, according to Arne De Boever, "a keen sensibility, a heightened awareness, of its own value not so much as a capitalist commodity but in particular as a financial instrument, a tool for speculative value generation—a novel bubble" (2018, 154). De Boever stresses the distinction between commodity and investment and thus explains the development of the novel from its "viable commodity form" in the late twentieth century to its economic inscriptions in the present. As Ben himself is only beginning to grasp, his future novel is not itself the commodity; it is the promise of the commodity—"the promise of something bigger that is still to follow" that yields the big return and turns literature "into a financial instrument to generate speculative value" (157). Where, the novel asks implicitly, does this leave the role of the author?

In Chapter 2, I proposed a paranoid chronotope emerging in the transition between and partial doubling of discipline and control. I observed how the more long-term and tangible spaces and identities of discipline are increasingly overwritten by the fluid and adaptable modalities of control, and suggested, not least via my reading of *Your Fathers*, that the tension between these modes of power generates paranoia. Eggers brought out ways in which the novel itself as a form is entangled with a disciplinary chronotope and how it threatens to come undone in the face of control. Lerner's novel, too, points toward ways in which these layers are related to the literary but also points more specifically to the subject position and identity constructed not just in but also by literary writing under neoliberalism. We have noted Ben's constant search for a syncing of layers of reality, and even of the self and how ultimately it seems that they cannot be synced. In this sense, his paranoia lies not in imagining a different, more coherent layer of reality, as we saw in the more classic paranoid novels discussed in the Introduction, but rather in a reluctance to admit to his radically reduced ability to construct such a layer beyond a fluctuating and fluid neoliberal logic.

Mobilizing the Paranoid Chronotope to Write

Toward the second half of *10:04* we see that Ben attempts to escape—or is it engage—this unstable chronotope to write. The tension between authorial autonomy and neoliberal spatiotemporalities, the coordination of everything by money, becomes, as we have seen, acutely apparent in the restaurant where Ben dines with his editor. It is this rhythm and pattern, this prosody of money, that Ben tries to escape in his subsequent writer's residency in Marfa, Texas. "Marfa" resonates with the name of the physical condition doctors think Ben might have: "Marfan syndrome," a genetic condition that disturbs the connective tissue of the body. Lerner introduces the possibility of Ben having this syndrome, which affects the body's capacity to hold the cells, tissue, and organs together, in the beginning of the novel, immediately after the first recounting of Ben's dinner with the editor. In this instance, the unsettled connectivity of the syndrome is coupled with Ben's sense of spatiotemporal dislocation. Since diagnosis of Marfan usually occurs in childhood, the hospital wing in which he is evaluated is a pediatric ward and his body struggles to fit into an environment and furniture designed for children. Here, his body parts come to "possess a terrible neurological autonomy not only spatial but temporal," his future "collapses in upon [him]" as he is "older and younger than everyone in the room" (7). This syndrome, then, or perhaps Ben's perception of it, exacerbates his sense of being out of sync with the world around him. As this potential Marfan sufferer relocates to Marfa, however, he seems to affirm and physically reenact this sense of being spatiotemporally out of sync with the world, an act that proves productive for his writing. The Marfa episode is given its own section, which begins with the words "I felt like a ghost ..." (163) and Ben immediately allows himself to become temporally out of sync or, as he puts it, finds himself "falling out of time" (166). He spends his days "turning in around sunrise, waking a couple of hours before sunset" (169), and working "on the wrong thing" (170).

The house in Marfa becomes another chronotopic threshold, a liminal space, a space of crisis but also of opportunity. Ben's stay entails not just a geographical dislocation but also an individual and existential one. In it, the immobilization and indecisiveness of the threshold is gradually overcome, the breaking point ultimately generating a new stage. The chronotope of the threshold is a place of falls and resurrections, of renewals and epiphanies, of "decisions that determine the whole life of a man" (Bakhtin 1981, 248). And this spatiotemporal shift that Ben more or less purposefully allows to befall him eventually eases him over the brink. In Marfa, he gives up the book he has promised to write—one "about literary fraudulence, about fabricating the past" (194). It seems potent that he abandons a literary project based on the idea of an author falsifying his archive and fabricating letters from dead authors (118). This is a fictional falsification that the fictional author supposedly does not do for the money but as a "response to his own mortality" and to "meditate on all the ways that time is monetized" (118). In other words, Ben gives up a literary project about the author losing his grip (at least in that particular sense). Giving up the project and "destroying the fabricated correspondences" make the archive more real to him and Ben more real to himself. It also provides him with a sense of agency and selfhood: "Abandoning the book about forging my archive left me feeling as though I actually possessed one" (212). Empowered by the unsettled temporality he actively adopts and thus takes charge of in Marfa, he decides on a project that "is neither fiction nor nonfiction" and that expands into "an actual presence, alive with multiple futures" (194).

Ben's giving up the idea of writing the book he has been contracted to write, then, is also giving up lingering in the past and its continuous reconstruction in favor of a present and future with several openings. Poignantly, Ben finds strength and direction in the way poetry allows him to let go of "the correspondence between text and world" (171). Letting go of distinctions and correspondences between text and world and between fiction and nonfiction, he finally discovers a sense of "present tense" in the intensity and "possibilities of feeling" in the reading. In other words, his spatiotemporal dislocation to and in Marfa enables him to finally cross the threshold from his continuous and frustrated struggle to find his place both in everyday life and as a literary author and arrive at what appears to be an affective coincidence of his own body and the present tense.

Ironically, Ben's inspiration toward coincidence and integration comes from what is arguably one of the most institutionalized white male American writers there is—Walt Whitman. The only book Ben has brought to Marfa is the Library of America edition of Walt Whitman's poetry and it is a sense of merging with Whitman that gives him the tools to negotiate the strangeness of his surroundings (170). But although he seems to virtually live with Whitman, falling asleep at night with the book on his lap, he describes his relation to Whitman as a struggle, a "being hard on his impossible dream" while also making "if not a pact, a kind of peace" (194). In lyrical form:

> I've been worse than unfair, although he was
> asking for it, is still asking for it, I can hear
> him asking for it through me when I speak,
> despite myself, to a people that isn't there,
> or think of art as leisure that is work
> in houses the undocumented build, repair.
> It's among the greatest poems and fails
> because it wants to become real and can
> only become prose, founding mistake
> of the book from which we've been expelled. (194)

The sense of coincidence and integration is also, as Alexandra Kingston-Reese notes, formally instantiated in the way the poem's fictional composition is mirrored in its actual composition. Like Ben, Lerner apparently wrote this during a residency in Marfa. He has suggested in an interview that "'the novel was, in part, formed' around this poem" (2019, 144). If so, and if Lerner's work is an implicit "defense of the literary arts," as Kingston-Reese argues (145), it is one that centers precisely on its failing. Because of course, and despite the fact that Ben seems finally to have located himself in the present tense through poetry, his poem actively returns to questions of temporality and to the disjunctive chronotopes of literature and life that have shaped the novel as a whole. The poetic form, just identified as an opening beyond a representative correlation between text and world, immediately collapses back into precisely that, adding a nostalgic yearning for a prelapsarian literary coincidence and community.

What ultimately coincides, ironically, is the disintegration of Ben's personal embodied chronotope and its integration with a literary chronotope in the very final lines of the novel. Here, he begins to "remember our walk in the third person, as if I'd seen it from the Manhattan Bridge, but, at the time of writing, as I lean against the chain-link fence intended to stop jumpers, I am looking back at the totaled city in the second person plural. I know it's hard to understand/I am with you, and I know how it is" (240). Both space and time seem to flicker—where exactly is he? When is he? Who is he? While there is reassurance in this direct address—as if the narrator and the reader can, if nothing else, share and comfort each other in the inability to understand—it also points to a letting go of the third-person literary narrator, the one that is at least potentially omniscient and able to enter the minds and feelings of different characters, and an insistence on an "I" who might not understand but who knows what that is like.

This "I" is complicated, however, by two more disjunctions. To begin with, the final lines: "I am with you, and I know how it is" are very close but not identical to Whitman's "I am with you, and know how it is," which is quoted and discussed in the Marfa section of the novel. In this section, Ben comments on how Whitman "wants to stand for everyone, because he wants to be less a historical person than a marker for democratic personhood" (168). Alison Gibbons argues that the final framing of Lerner's autofictional project in the novel's closing pages highlights "the imaginative projection of subjectivities in fiction and their relationality" (2018, 92). She suggests also that Lerner "participates in Whitman's 'I' and, by adding the second one, allows readers to participate in his own (93). I propose, however, that this insertion of an additional "I" also accentuates a difference and distance from the addressees at the same time as it establishes a stronger sense of authorship and subjecthood—not only "I am with you" but also "I know how it is." The way Lerner adds another "I," ending the novel with words by Whitman (but not quite) and the way he addresses the reader—a signal of sincerity—in Whitman's voice, results in an ambivalent erasure of himself while forcefully reinserting an authorial "I," one that might admit to not knowing and might be empathic but also evinces grand ambitions and aspirations to knowing and coinciding with a readership.

The second disjunction at the basis of these final lines underlines the entanglements between literary writing and unsettling temporalities and realities key to our present analysis. Ben, says Daniel Katz, refers to lines in Whitman that were edited out of the Library of America edition that he explicitly tells us he is reading. In this way, the novel actually "ends with a line which was retrospectively made to fade out from the future it imagines" (2017, 329). Katz sees how the novel, in including lines that have been edited out from an edition that thereby does not exist, "creates a textual world like that suggested in the epigraph on the novel's threshold, about the world to come: 'Everything will be as it is now, just a little different'" (329). And as we have observed, what is different is not only the edition of Whitman but also the authorial position that the narrator not only recovers but also insists on and strengthens. Despite the fact that Ben has pondered quite carefully Whitman's strategic exclusion of an "I" from his book because it would make him "an empirical person rather than constituting a pronoun in which the readers of the future could participate" (168), he ultimately insists on this knowing "I" for himself. Ben, it seems, has overcome the chronotope of the threshold upon which he has been vacillating throughout the novel, and has arrived at a full-blown paranoid chronotope, including the grandeur symptomatic of the final stages of paranoia, as we saw earlier, as well as the paradigmatic white male American author as discussed in this section. Read in the light of Ben's explicit awareness of Whitman's attempt to "empty himself out" and "to be nobody in particular in order to be a democratic everyman" (168), the reassertion of this knowing "I" appears as a recuperation and insistence on both an authorial identity and a certain readership—one whose conceptions and perceptions of the world to a large extent will coincide with his own—"I know how it is."

Section 3: Critique

Introduction

The labor to discover and develop more genuine and caring modes of engagement with the world is something that the efforts associated with New Sincerity and postcritique have in common. These exertions are also reasonably parallel in time, as they became points of discussion in literary scholarship at the very end of the twentieth century and continuing in the first decades of the twenty-first. It is illuminating, if not unsurprising, to note the relatively simultaneous desire to move away from the cynicism and irony of postmodern culture and move beyond the suspicion and critique connected with its critical analyses. That said, there is a fatigue actually voiced by John Barth in his 1967 short story

"The Literature of Exhaustion." And even classic postmodern authors such as DeLillo and Pynchon, says Doyle, deviate in their later fiction from "high postmodernism" to "offer a more hopeful vision of community within a system of global capitalism and moral relativism" (259). Perhaps, also, it would take more reparative readings of postmodernism to recognize that the problem is not postmodern cultural expression or theory but rather the neoliberal culture in relation to which they emerged and reacted and by which they tend to be subsumed. Such reparative readings of postmodernism would in turn require a reparative reading of critique, one that retains its broader definitions and applications rather than apprehensively confining it to a contracted convention. However, postcritique seems too anxious about the institutional status of literary criticism itself to make space for such broader perspectives. In this final section of the chapter and the book, I employ the paranoid chronotope to show how postcritique relies on a delimitation of critique that does not consider the messy and conflictual conditions of the public sphere of which critique is an intrinsic part but rather assigns it a unitary and malicious purpose in order to reject it.

The Paranoid Chronotope of Postcritique

Critique, as I have stated throughout this book, emerges from the Kantian project as an eternal work-in-progress response to questions of what we can know about the world and how we should act in it. What is true, valid, and justified must be settled within the limited and necessarily failing bounds of our human capacity to determine these very things. Crucially, Kant also raises the question of the conditions under which true, valid, and justified claims can be made. In other words, in a secular world how do we establish the best possible spaces for critique? The centrality of these spaces has been a primary concern of theories and practices of critique ever since. These theories and practices have in common a recurring insistence on this best possible space as a public one that includes a plurality of views. For Arendt, as we saw in Chapter 1, these spaces are essential to the very possibility of appearance of world and self and of the action that such appearance enables. For Habermas, as we also saw in that chapter, the public sphere provides a necessary means of knowing and validating any political system. If it is possible to articulate one key definition of critique on a general level, then, it may be that critique encompasses interpretations of the world in spaces where these interpretations may be subjected to each other.

From the complex and evolving understanding of critique, it is nonetheless possible to discern some basic spatiotemporal components. We can even discuss it in terms of an abstract but generic and fairly continuous chronotope. Such a chronotope emerges from the dynamics between individual and world in the chronotope of the public sphere described in Chapter 1. As we saw there, it builds on a set of assumptions: first, that individuals must strive to comprehend dimensions of reality and society that are greater than themselves; second, that it is their duty not only to try to understand but also to interrogate and thereby critique and/or give legitimacy to these larger dimensions; and, third, that individuals are required to ascertain and perpetuate such spaces.

It is helpful to examine the conception of and relations between subject and world by means of the chronotope because it pays more concrete attention to the actual spatiotemporal conditions of critique over time and in its various forms. Like Kant, Bakhtin recognized that all perception is shaped by space and time, but as we began to see in earlier chapters, and as Holquist emphasizes, Bakhtin also made "a radical commitment to the historical particularity of any act of perception as it is actually experienced by living persons from their unique place in existence" (2002, 145). Taking Kant's emphasis on the essential role of space and time in perception, representation, and, ultimately, cognition into a literary context, space and time become key forms of cognition not only on a transcendental plane but also on a more immediate experiential plane. This is ultimately what enabled Bakhtin to study, via the chronotope, how categories of space and time correspond with artistic cognition under literary conditions (1981, 85n.). Bakhtin's conception of the chronotope was specifically developed in a literary context: it is in literature that time "thickens" and "takes on flesh" and that space "become[s] charged and responsive." It is in literature that we can ultimately explore the ways in which space and time are inseparable and fused "into one carefully thought-out, concrete whole" (84).

The chronotopic configurations of critique—understood here as dimensions that are too vast to grasp but that individuals nonetheless attempt to grasp, as well as the spaces for their grasping—have developed enormously not only since Kant but also since Arendt and Habermas. Indeed, the changes have been so fast and vast that they too have been hard to grasp. As we have seen, power—moving from national disciplinary models to global control mechanisms and turning individuals into "dividuals"; truth—whose function seems to have been radically transformed; and digitized public relations—by which platforms are multiplied but also fragmented and subject to algorithmic commercialization and radicalization, expand exponentially but also complicate the conditions of coming together, of sharing and thus making a world, as Arendt might put it. The logic of neoliberalism, maintaining participation and responsibility on the individual level, further complicates the sense of commonality and communality among individuals as crucial to the making of society. In this context, coproduction takes the form rather of a political strategy according to which individuals are encouraged to take responsibility via their own actions rather than joint effort. The public sphere thus becomes a competition of views, values, and identities rather than an essential dimension of the coproduction of society. In short, enormous pressure is put on the chronotopic configuration and conditions of critique.

In a specifically American context, and as we began to see in the previous chapter, the spatiotemporal conditions of critique have in part been differently configured than those conditions in the European tradition. On the one hand, we could, like Francois Cusset, see "subversive counterreadings" as "a quintessentially American tradition that started with the Founding Fathers and their reinterpretation of the Bible" (xvii). From this perspective, critique may be seen as an element of American history from its conception. Indeed, it makes critique co-productive and even co-constitutive of society, as an activity that would eventually be the making of the nation. Such a perspective also clearly signals an American history of suspicious hermeneutics considerably longer than that shaped by the Ricoeurian or French Theory influence in the late twentieth century. From this perspective, America as a nation may be recognized as in itself securing a space of critique on a more general and fundamental level, away from the conservative oppressiveness of Europe at the time. One may also see, like Eagleton, how the contemporary attention to critique may be traced back to American Puritanism: "The high moral or political tone, the air of spiritual superiority, the wariness of the aesthetic, the suspicion of outward appearances as deceitful, the search for an inner truth that's hard to come by, the anxious scanning for symptoms of impurity, which is also to be found in the cult of political correctness: none of this of course is peculiarly American," according to Eagleton, "but it is probably no accident that it has flourished so prodigally there" (n.p.). In this view, then, critique is intimately associated with America historically, socially, and politically.

On the other hand, and as we have seen, critique as articulated in contemporary debates on postcritique tends to rely on a much shorter spatiotemporal trajectory that relies largely on a post-Ricourian, and even post-Theory context. My earlier discussions of the American conception of critique showed how, at least in Anker and Felski's conceptualization, it is in effect a genre with distinct—but historically and politically determined—chronotopic dimensions. Bakhtin's original conception of the chronotope elucidates ways in which the same motif is configured quite differently depending on the chronotopic conditions of distinct genres. In postcritique, occasional mentions function as acknowledgments of a larger historical and geographical context. For example, Elizabeth S. Anker and Rita Felski recognize critique as "being closely linked to the diverse traditions of Kantianism, Marxist thought, the Frankfurt school, and post-1968 French theory" and as encompassing "a lengthy history of debate about governance, freedom, conflict, and the relations between the individual and the state" (13). Yet the focus of these debates is very much framed by American, post-seventies academia. In fact, critique as it emerges from current discourses on postcritique has a consistency and a spatiotemporal logic of its own. Let us review it here to remind ourselves of earlier accounts in this book and to make the chronotopic conditions it sets for itself more visible.

Critique as what postcritique tends to critique is primarily linked to a period reaching from around the seventies to the present. While it relies largely on French theories from this period and a couple of decades before, it is chiefly restricted to the reception and rearticulation of these theories in an American context. More than that, it is essentially confined to an academic context and principally—although not exclusively—materializing via English and comparative literature departments, It is here that various new modes of reading have surfaced in recent decades. And it is here that critique is frequently referred to as important in legitimizing the profession. Latour's references to the "French marshals," Felski's equation of critique with the hermeneutics of suspicion, and Best and Marcus's association of it with symptomatic reading all contribute to effectively confining critique as something that might have links to a longer history and a broader geographical context only in a second or third degree. Felski's explicit project, for example, is not the admittedly impossible one of presenting a general history of critique but is rather one that focuses on "the rhetoric of literary and cultural studies over the last four decades, with an emphasis on developments in the United States" (3).

Articulating the limits of critique in and as its appointment to literary studies in America in this narrow sense is not itself a problem—on the contrary, in some ways it is necessary and useful to delimit the field, not least when dealing with a concept so sprawling and elusive as critique. Critique and its applications not only span centuries, contexts, and disciplines; they are shaped by self-reflection—interrogating previous truths or mechanisms in any given field necessarily includes the constant evaluation and revaluation of the conditions for critique in the first place. However, and while Felski critically points to American literary studies' promotion of a limited understanding of critique, by virtue of her own purposeful limitation, she also effectively promulgates such conception. Indeed, this particular critique of critique, according to Eric Hayot, gains much of its rhetorical as well as hermeneutic force by "narrating the nature of an entire thirty-year span *as* a single period, and thus ... seeing a number of smaller movements that we might have thought of previously as opposed as elements in the same larger pattern." By seeing "the Theory era (or the era of critique) as a single thing," postcritique in fact follows the very pattern it hopes to escape. Groomed by the Theory years in American academia, which were characterized by a succession of schools, authors, modes, and stars, articulations of the current crisis in critique follow quite devotedly in this same temporal pattern. In this sense, postcritique not only reproduces the historical pattern that it aims to supersede; it becomes little more than "*critique under another name.*" The only thing these articulations do differently is envision Theory in its entirety as a period to be replaced by new theory (287).

On the one hand, we might be skeptical of the temporal delimitations, of the "historical presentness," of the current crisis in critique. For instance, Hayot is decidedly critical of a limited temporal conception that allows Latour to revaluate philosophical method based on the eight years of the Bush regime (2017, 290). While agreeing that it is time to move beyond Theory, he finds highly problematic the justification of theories about moving beyond Theory with such narrow measures. We must, as Hayot maintains, include broader historical structures when conceptualizing the contemporary moment, especially if we intend to declare that we need to, or have already, moved beyond critique. We need to situate the question in another, broader context that not least makes evident the peril to which conservative politics and neoliberal capital have exposed higher education (290). On the other hand, one may find it useful to assemble the various elements of the Theory era into a single phenomenon. Hayot points to the value of this in its "recognition of the multiple scales at which history takes place" (289). I am not so sure, however, that this recognition has been allowed much ground. Rather than taking into account the multiple scales of history, and as I have been showing throughout the critique sections, postcritique discourse considerably scales down and delimits the history of Theory and critique. Hayot, however, confirms this delimitation when he agrees with Felski that the "intellectual demands of the Theory era" can be "defined as the product of a hermeneutics of suspicious reading" (289). At this point, his characterization of Theory, which he earlier acknowledged worked in various disciplines such as gender and race studies, shrinks to fit the frame conceptualized in discourses on postcritique.

Indeed, once we reach the postcritique debates of the twenty-first century, the differences between distinctive French theories as well as the dissimilarities within the theoretical formation of Theory in America seem to have faded. It is precisely when postcritique narrates critique or Theory as a single period and identifies it as a pattern that engulfs singularities or even oppositions within itself that it acquires its contours and force. In other words, postcritique organizes itself around an oppositional mode. Thereby, Hayot maintains, it fails to imagine something different and new, it fails to "let go of the Theory era *enough*" (289). In the final essay in Anker and Felski's book on critique and postcritique, Hayot summarizes the current status of critique as it has presented itself here: "What we know is that something has been lost, that literary criticism, today, floats adrift on an open, darkling sea, which the sailors search desperately for new compasses" (279). But what has been lost exactly?

All of my analyses point to the possibility that it is not the political import of critique itself so much as the forms making it possible—the spacetimes, the vessels, the public sphere—that are disintegrating or at least changing so fast that we are struggling to keep up. Arguably, it is exactly the emaciation of the public sphere as well as the university as a critical space under neoliberalism that makes it possible for Latour to suggest that critique may have contributed to the frightful state of affairs in the new millennium. Latour asks: Have we "behaved like mad scientists who have let the virus of critique out of the confines of their laboratories and cannot do anything now to limit its deleterious effects; it mutates now, gnawing everything up, even the vessels in which it is contained?" (2004, 230). The metaphor of the vessel is noteworthy. Because what is this vessel? If not the public sphere as such, is it not at least a space in which critical thinking is made possible?

Throughout this book, we have seen ways in which the public sphere is eroding in American and Western society. This problem is never directly addressed in Latour's essay. He suggests that conspiracy theorizing is a sign that critique has escaped university laboratories. He also proposes that the roles have been reversed when he is seen as naive by his neighbor in a small French village for believing that terrorists attacked America on September 11, 2001, and points to the "whole industry" denying the moon landing (2004, 228). "What is the real difference," he asks, "between conspiracists and a popularized, that is, a teachable version of social critique inspired by a too quick reading of, let's say, a sociologist as eminent at Pierre Bourdieu?" (228). There may be a slightly facetious element to this question—or at least he admits to being "mean"—but the fact remains that Latour centers his entire argument on the idea that critique has escaped its academic confines and gone out to tear the world to pieces. There is, if you will, a leak in the vessel of critique. My answer to Latour's question is twofold. First, there is a real difference, or at least there used to be, and this pertains precisely to the notion as well as the spaces of critique. Second, we need to understand paranoia as it has developed as a general cultural demise during the last few decades to understand the similarity—and distinction—between the conspiracy theories Latour refers to and the academic critique he critiques.

To begin, there is the question of the difference Latour searches for between critique (as Theory in his case) and his neighbor's skepticism. Some answers, I hope, have already been provided here on the logics of the new public sphere. As we have seen, Latour's question implicitly speaks to prevalent anxieties and confusions in society regarding the nature of the public sphere and the increasingly pervasive role of conspiracy theories in it. As Didier Fassin and Bernard E. Harcourt note, social scientists—and literary scholars and theorists in general—are distraught and confounded by conspiracy theories that "mimic" critical thinking and by the reconfiguration of traditional critical channels in the public sphere due to the aggressive expansion of social media (2017, 1). Related to this is the "critiquiness" identified by Castiglia and discussed in Chapter 1: "the *sound* of critique without the ethical positioning" (214). Critiquiness is a performance of a certain disposition that is characterized by mistrust and indignation, by a lack of generosity and self-criticism. It comes with a preset expectation of the world and the text that prevents articulating clear ideals or alternatives and thus also precludes ethical positioning and new political possibilities (214). Critiquiness, as emphasized in Chapter 3, is also similar to "truthiness," or the production of something that sounds true to those already in agreement without having to resort to logic or fact (214). What critiquiness and truthiness have in common, apart from sounding like what they are not, is the projection and assertion of an already determined opinion or perspective.

While Castiglia himself is hesitant about the labels largely in circulation in contemporary debates on critique and postcritique, such as "suspicious" and "paranoid," he suggests that they are indicative in that they point to this same disposition, not to the nature of critique itself so much as the reinforcement of the disposition of critiquiness.

When Felski argues that critique, in spite of what she admits is its "eclectic array of philosophical tenets, political ideologies, and modes of interpretation," nonetheless has a "prevailing disposition" and that this disposition is, precisely, critiquiness (187), she speaks directly to the sense in which we struggle to keep critical thinking separate from its various deformed derivatives in conspiracy theories and paranoia in contemporary society. In fact, the crucial distinction that Castiglia labors to make—that might retrieve critique from critiquiness and other warped varieties such as conspiracy theory and general suspiciousness, and reinforce the role of critique in the public sphere—collapses when Felski regards critique and critiquiness as intimately conjoined. In this way, the "hardening of disagreement into a given repertoire of argumentative moves and interpretative methods" that Felski insists on (187) effectively conceives of a "vessel" inclusive of all levels and kinds of critique, critiquiness, suspicion, conspiracy, and paranoia.

While moderating Latour's near iconic contribution to the debates, Castiglia suggests that it is not critique but critiquiness that has run out of steam (226). This suggestion is useful because it suggests how literary criticism may to some extent have gotten stuck in a certain mode, or mood, as Felski would have it, and that postcritical discussions are, more than anything, an attempt to move beyond mood or mode. However, and as I have shown in this book, critiquiness may have run out of steam in academia but it has exploded in society at large. Via configurations of the public sphere, neoliberal logics, and new conservative forces, critiquiness has become normalized both in general debate in the new public sphere and in more specific and politically deliberate situations. Much as truthiness has clearly become a major player in contemporary politics, this is also, and perhaps even equally, true of critiquiness. Critiquiness has come to serve as a companion tool to truthiness: the eagerness to accept truthiness as long as it fits with one's views is matched only by critiquiness geared toward positions that do not fit. It is undoubtedly a neat concoction; one that allows us to more or less purposefully feel good about already existing convictions while mistrusting anything that goes beyond them. It is also a heady concoction, one that is quite influential in the increasingly polarized climate in the West. Arguably, it is *this* development, rather than the history of academic critique, that has led to a deplorable state of affairs.

In the very opening of my Introduction, I suggested that the modern West is haunted by a paranoia that has emerged with the sense that we ourselves are not what we seem, that others are not what they seem, that reality is not quite what it seems, and that this duality or even disjunction between perceived and true selves, others, and reality is the result of a malicious hiding or manipulation of more or less identifiable forces. In American culture, as I discussed in subsequent chapters, this is frequently evinced by a phenomenal reluctance to see society and the economy as shaping the conditions of thought and action. This reluctance is overshadowed, however, by an underlying awareness that society and the economy are doing precisely that. Postcritique, too, as I tried to show in the critique sections, is haunted by such a specter. The continued denial of market and capital forces in the shaping of the interdependence of critique and the public sphere creates the equivalent of a paranoid chronotope. As I have proposed, a paranoid chronotope appears when two spatiotemporal logics—one more commonly accepted reality and another less visible but supposedly truer reality—rub against each other. As we have seen, not least in the various novel readings, this occurs via nervous attempts to consolidate an insight that the social, cultural, economic, and political affect the subject with a hard-wearing conception of the subject as a free and autonomous agent.

I suggest that postcritique also constitutes such a nervous expression of a realization only half realized. The historicization of critique in America that I have provided points to a critique with clear links to the various philosophical and political projects from which it has evolved more generally. But it also elucidates a critique that has struggled to find a place—or has been reluctant to situate itself—in relation to the public sphere. As we have seen, most versions of postcritique are articulated as a response to societal logics. Still, and most commonly, the culprit has been identified as critique itself. Latour worries about critique being co-opted by climate change deniers. Best and Marcus worry about society not hiding its power structures. Anker and Felski worry about critique contributing to the undermining of the humanities. The latter worry ultimately seems to underlie them all. Theory's overbearing attitude, Latour argues, is the reason that "the humanities have lost the hearts of their fellow citizens, that they had to retreat year after year, entrenching themselves always further in the narrow barracks left to them by more and more stingy deans" (239). Similarly,

Anker and Felski contend that critique has an "adversarial stance" that has piqued the general public and failed to lead to "a more prominent public voice for literary critics." In its place, they want "more compelling accounts of why the humanities matter." Heather Love articulates this relation quite explicitly: "In the face of the defunding of the humanities, critics have been rethinking the epistemological and ethical grounds of the field and proposing new and often unfamiliar approaches" (2017, 364).

To the extent that scholars want to engage with questions of critique and its relation to society, it seems necessary to properly take into account the conditions that society enables for critique in the first place. These conditions can be articulated in terms of the public sphere—a key condition for critique as it has been theorized in earlier critical traditions. And as we have seen, this is the public sphere in terms of the possible modes of engagement of citizens in public debates as well as in terms of public education and universities as places for engaging with, teaching, and perpetuating critical thinking in society. Public spheres, as I have shown, are profoundly affected and transformed by social, technological, economic, and political developments. Therefore, I argue that it is necessary for debates on critique to consider its relation to market forces, global capital, and neoliberalism as well as attacks on free thinking coming from conservative and nationalist forces.

Unfortunately, current configurations of postcritique tend not only to disregard but to effectively disable such engagement. Because its central targets are the hermeneutics of suspicion, Theory, and symptomatic reading—with a central argument against engaging with what is beyond or "below" the text—an engagement with the economic and sociopolitical conditions of critique speaks directly against this very ambition. Instead, the argument is forced into an ambivalent recognition and simultaneous disavowal of critique's own conditions of possibility. Like Thomas in *Your Fathers*, like Jeremy in *I Am No One*, and like Ben in *10:04*, critique is caught up at the threshold, ambivalently recognizing the forces and the crises beyond it but hesitating to take the leap. Instead, it remains stuck in the "biographical" and more delimited duration of its specific American historical evolution that prevents it from taking on the larger context and implications of the crisis that has befallen it.

In connection with Cusset's conception of French Theory as disaligned with the political and economic, which I discussed in Chapter 2, this state of affairs is an unsurprising continuation of the same tendency. If we follow his description of the fate of Theory in American academia, this ambivalence can be traced back to what he calls its decontextualization and domestication in an American context. In his description, Theory has always been slightly out of sync with the American public. Indeed, what he describes may itself be seen as chronotopic disjunctions between the broad and politically informed theoretical engagement in France in the sixties and seventies and Theory as practiced in academic departments in the late twentieth century as well as between this Theory and the realities of American society, economic, and politics in the twenty-first. In this sense, the lack of attention to problems in the present may be ultimately related to a lack of a longer history and the conditions of critique. Narrowly focused on "critique" as in literary studies in America, the bigger picture is missing. Recognizing threats to the university and humanistic inquiry, Anker and Felski want to preempt critique of this kind. They realize that they might be understood as defeatist and unprepared join the opposition (what they call "gadflies and oppositional figures" [18]). Yet they insist that critique does not have the tools to respond to the threats of larger political frameworks. Furthermore, they suggest that it lacks the vocabulary for defending the humanities under siege (19), primarily because of its "adversarial stance," which is unlikely to be persuasive. They therefore question "some scholars' insistence on the big picture: namely, the increasingly pervasive influence of neoliberalism and economic rationality in recent decades" (18).

The paranoid chronotope of postcritique emerges precisely in such half-recognitions and simultaneous disavowals of the current economic and sociopolitical situation. It materializes also from the increasingly unsustainable denial of the messy political reality of which the exercise of critique is inevitably a part. As we have seen throughout this book, paranoia can be a means of creating order in a messy world. In the Introduction, I noted how psychiatric and psychoanalytical definitions of paranoia, such as Krafft-Ebing's in the nineteenth century and Freud's in the twentieth, as well as political definitions from Hofstadter to Jameson, in different ways underline its repudiation of mess. Mess, chance, accident, and unoverviewable conditions are effectively remedied by paranoid constructions of coherence, systematicity, and meaning. Perhaps we also need to see postcritique as such a paranoid response. It creates an illusion of stability, coherence, and progression in a discipline, in a university, and in a world where all that is solid seems to have melted into air. Thus, postcritique finds itself with no need to ask, as does Hayot, what "kinds of theories of criticism ... we develop if we imagine ourselves in a longer or shorter *durée*?" (290). It also does not need to consider critique as carrying what Russ Castronovo, via

Benjamin, calls a "*weak* Messianic power," that is less firmly rooted in a specific earthbound course of action or direction and more an "ever-present possibility" of "the spaces and times where politics might emerge" (2017, 246). Instead, and by constructing a particular, and particularly spatiotemporally delimited sense of critique as well as postcritique, critique itself becomes identifiable and stabilized in an apparent but ultimately false opposition to what surrounds it.

Caught up in such a paranoid chronotope, postcritique not only disables engagement with the larger and more fluid and complicated political conditions of critique. Inadvertently, it also comes to incorporate and encourage an insistence on productivity, reinvention, and immediate relevance that these larger political frameworks perpetuate. From this perspective, new ways of reading—not individually but as a trend—begin to look suspiciously similar to neoliberal practices of innovation, resilience, individual responsibility, and positive thinking. In such a framework, postcritique's recurring attention to affect, mood, and feeling suddenly also begin to feel uncomfortably attuned to neoliberal individualism. Read in this way, postcritique as a phenomenon is itself proof that the radical configurations of economic and political strategies and the precarious status of the public sphere today do indeed require us to talk about a crisis in critique. But the crucial question is where to locate the crisis as well as the critique. As long as it remains at this threshold, as I have tried to show throughout this book, postcritique may be seen as perpetuating and perhaps also aggravating a paranoid chronotope of American society and culture more generally as it does and does not engage with its political present.

ACKNOWLEDGMENTS

The idea for this project emerged and soon appeared as almost a necessity as I was finishing an earlier book that centered on how political resistance and critique have become fashionable themes in mainstream culture. The longer I worked on that project, the more uncertain I felt about my own position vis-à-vis the cultural and political processes I was trying to understand and describe. Was recognizing such co-option of critique a symptom of being overly suspicious? Was identifying allegories speaking to larger systems being paranoid? And why was I questioning my own critical position in the first place?

On the one hand, the questioning of one's own position, knowledge, and capacity for interpretation is a recurrent, healthy, and quite important dimension of scholarly research in general and critique in particular. On the other hand, I believe my uncertainties are linked specifically to a contemporary moment in which it has become acutely difficult to locate oneself and one's position in relation to whatever material one attempts to understand or interrogate. Thus, I am, like everyone else, deeply entangled in the processes I am trying to describe.

It is hard to diagnose the present. There have been times when I have felt that I might get lost forever in this project, not only because it has been a work in progress across years during which almost every day has offered new and more extreme examples of what I am trying to theorize but also because, when diving deep into the dark and murky waters of paranoia, it is sometimes hard to find stable ground or even a small lifebuoy to keep one floating.

For these reasons, I am immensely grateful for the colleagues, friends, and family that in different ways have helped me navigate the surfaces and depths and stay (more or less) sane. The book has laboriously taken form over the course of several years and has benefited enormously from numerous invaluable conversations. I discussed paranoia with Gregory Flaxman on the streets of New Orleans and he knew I would be working on paranoia almost before I did so myself (which is very suspicious no doubt …), I wondered, co-writing an essay with Charlie Blake, if we have always been paranoid. I talked about the public sphere and the liberal subject with Bruce Robbins over jetlagged coffees, I had a lengthy email exchange with Nancy Armstrong about the history of the novel, and I tested out the concept of the paranoid chronotope on Gregg Lambert and Jeff Nealon in a bar in Seattle. Charlie was also an invaluable help—as always—in reading and responding to drafts throughout, Jeff provided very useful feedback on chapters toward the end, as did Ulf Olsson, whose response was brutal and productive.

I have presented papers and given talks related to the project and received very valuable input at symposia and conferences in many different places. I am grateful for the invitations that facilitated many of these stimulating encounters, including those from Simone Bignall, Dag Blanck, Ron Broglio, Jeffrey Di Leo, Ellen Mortensen, Manoj NY, Jesper Olsson, Danielle Sands, Jan Aart Scholte, and Dimitris Vardoulakis. I presented the project proposal in progress to my now former colleagues at the Department of English at Stockholm University and received very helpful comments from them, not least Stefan Helgesson, who drew my attention to Patrick Flanery's work. My new colleagues, at the Department of Culture and Aesthetics at Stockholm, provided input and encouragement once the project was in place.

Toward the end of the writing, the two readers selected by SUP offered tremendously generous reports on the full manuscript. The critical and perceptive suggestions and the encouragement they provided contributed immensely toward finishing the project as well as surfacing from it. And what a nice place to surface! Stanford's Erica Wetter maintained belief in the project even when I failed to fully account for it. I want to extend a large thanks to her and to the rest of the team at the press, especially Faith Wilson Stein and Sunna Juhn.

When work serves to both drive you mad and keep you sane, you are very lucky to have family, even if they may not always feel as lucky to have you when you are in that state. Julia and Logan, I guess, are rather immune to it all by now. Tomas has been exceptionally patient and loving. A lifeline for sure.

Some sections of the book were previously published in different fragments and forms. The reading of Dave Eggers's novel in Chapter 2 appeared in a slightly different version as "Control and the Novel: Dave Eggers and Disciplinary Form" in 2020 in *Modern Fiction Studies* (Copyright © 2020 Purdue University). My argument about postcritique appeared in bits and pieces in 2020 in *Symplokē* as "The Paranoid Style in Postcritique" and as part of "Has

Postcritique Run Out of Steam?" first as a paper delivered at an MLA session in Seattle in January 2020 and then in published form in 2020 as "Postcritique and the Leakiness of Spheres." "Paranoia, Conspiracy, and White Male Identity Politics," which built on other sections of the book, appeared in *Symplokē* in 2021. A fragment of the postcritique analysis appeared in Swedish in 2020 as "Kris, Kritik, Teori: Postkritik och den nya offentligheten" in the Norwegian journal *Norsk Litteraturvitenskapelig Tidsskrift*.

Several of the key strands of the present book—the history of paranoia in theories of the subject, postcritique, and the entanglements of the history of the novel and disciplinary society—were initially developed together with Charlie Blake in "We've been Paranoid Too Long to Stop Now" in the 2019 book *New Directions in Philosophy and Literature* published by Edinburgh, which I co-edited with Ridvan Askin and David Rudrum. Features pertaining to discussions of the elusiveness of neoliberal power, the liberal subject, truth, and expertise share some similarities with my chapter "A Governmentality Perspective on Polycentric Governing" in Frank Gadinger and Jan Aart Scholte's *Polycentrism: How Governing Works Today*, which will be published in by Oxford University Press in 2022.

A generous research grant from the Swedish Research Council for the project "Paranoia and Post-Truth Politics: Negotiating Selves and Systems in U.S. Literature after 1950" secured the time to do the research and writing.

For Tomas

REFERENCES

Ahmed, Sara. 2014. *The Cultural Politics of Emotion*. 2nd. ed. Edinburgh: Edinburgh University Press [2004].

American Psychiatric Association. 2013. *Diagnostic and Statistical Manual of Mental Disorders*. (5th ed.). https://doi.org/10.1176/appi.books.9780890425596

Anker, Elizabeth S., and Rita Felski, eds. 2017. *Critique and Postcritique*. Durham: Duke University Press.

Apter, Emily S. 2006. "On Oneworldedness: Or Paranoia as a World System." *American Literary History* 18 (2): 365–389.

Arendt, Hannah. 1998. *The Human Condition*. Chicago: University of Chicago Press [1958].

Armstrong, Nancy. 2011. "The Future in and of the Novel." *Novel: A Forum on Fiction* 44 (1): 8–10.

———. 2005. *How Novels Think: The Limits of British Individualism from 1719–1900*. New York: Columbia University Press.

Ashton, Jennifer. 2017. "Totaling the Damage: Neoliberal and Revolutionary Ambition in Recent American Poetry." In *Neoliberalism and Contemporary Literary Culture*, edited by Mitchum Huehls and Rachel Greenwald Smith. 122–139. Baltimore: Johns Hopkins University Press.

Austen, Jane. 2009. *Pride and Prejudice*. New York: Penguin Group [1813].

Auster, Paul. 2006. *Travels in the Scriptorium*. London: Faber and Faber.

———. 1987. *The New York Trilogy*. London: Faber and Faber.

Bakhtin, Mikhail M. 1986. "The Bildungsroman and its Significance in the History of Realism (Toward a Historic Typology of the Novel)." In *Speech Genres and Other Late Essays*, edited by Caryl Emerson and Michael Holquist, translated by Vern W. McGee. 10–59. Austin: University of Texas Press.

———. 1981. *The Dialogic Imagination: Four Essays*, edited by Michael Holquist, translated by Caryl Emerson and Michael Holquist. Austin: University of Texas Press [1975].

Bates, Laura. 2020. *Men Who Hate Women: From Incels to Pickup Artists, the Truth about Extreme Misogyny and How It Affects Us All*. London: Simon & Schuster.

Bemong, Nele, and Pieter Borghart. 2010. "Bakhtin's Theory of the Literary Chronotope: Reflections, Applications, Perspectives." In *Bakhtin's Theory of the Literary*

Chronotope: Reflections, Applications, Perspectives, edited by Nele Bemong, Pieter Borghart, Michel De Dobbeleer, Kristoffel Demoen, Koen De Temmerman and Bart Keunen. 3–16. Ghent, Belgium: Academia Press.

Benhabib, Seyla. 1997. "The Embattled Public Sphere: Hannah Arendt, Juergen Habermas and Beyond." *Theoria: A Journal of Social and Political Theory* 90: 1–24.

Ben-Merre, David. 2011. "Wish Fulfillment, Detection, and the Production of Knowledge in *Bleak House*." *Novel: A Forum on Fiction* 44 (1): 47–66.

Benn Michaels, Walter. 2011. "Model Minorities and the Minority Model—the Neoliberal Novel." *Cambridge Histories Online*. Cambridge, UK: Cambridge University Press.

Best, Stephen, and Sharon Marcus. 2009. "Surface Reading: An Introduction." *Representations* 108 (1): 1–21.

Bewes, Timothy. 2010. "Reading with the Grain: A New World in Literary Criticism." *differences* 21 (3): 1–33.

Blake, Charlie. 2020. "Critique." *Oxford Research Encyclopedia of Literature*. Oxford, UK: Oxford University Press.

Bowles, Nellie. 2018. "Jordan Peterson: Custodian of Patriarchy." *New York Times*. https://www.nytimes.com/2018/05/18/style/jordan-peterson-12-rules-for-life.html. Accessed October 15, 2020.

Bridle, James. 2018. *New Dark Age: Technology and the End of the Future*. London: Verso.

Brock, David, Ari Rabin-Havt, and Media Matters for America. 2012. *The Fox Effect: How Roger Ailes Turned a Network into a Propaganda Machine*. New York: Anchor Books.

Brown, Wendy. 2019. *In the Ruins of Neoliberalism: The Rise of Antidemocratic Politics in the West*. New York: Columbia University Press.

———. 2015. *Undoing the Demos: Neoliberalism's Stealth Revolution*. New York: Zone Books.

Buechler, Steven M. 1995. "New Social Movement Theories." *Sociological Quarterly* 36 (3): 441–464.

Burroughs, William. 1962. *The Ticket That Exploded*. London: Fourth Estate.

Castells, Manuel. 2008. "The New Public Sphere: Global Civil Society, Communication Networks, and Global Governance." *Annals of the American Academy of Political and Social Science* 616: 78–93.

Castiglia, Christopher. 2017. "Hope for Critique?" In *Critique and Postcritique*, edited by Elizabeth S. Anker and Rita Felski. 211–229. Durham, NC: Duke University Press.

Castronovo, Russ. 2017. "What Are the Politics of Critique? The Function of Criticism at a Different Time." In *Critique and Postcritique*, edited by Rita Felski and Elizabeth S. Anker. 230–251. Durham, NC: Duke University Press.

Chen, Adrian. 2016. "The Real Paranoia-Inducing Purpose of Russian Hacks." *New Yorker*. https://www.newyorker.com/news/news-desk/the-real-paranoia-inducing-purpose-of-russian-hacks. Accessed June 20, 2019.

Collington, Tara. 2010. "The Chronotope and the Study of Literary Adaptation: The Case of *Robinson Crusoe*. In *Bakhtin's Theory of the Literary Chronotope: Reflections,*

Applications, Perspectives, edited by Nele Bemong, Pieter Borghart, Michel De Dobbeleer, Kristoffel Demoen, Koen De Temmerman and Bart Keunen. 179–210. Ghent, Belgium: Academia Press.

Cusset, François. 2008. *French Theory: How Foucault, Derrida, Deleuze & Co. Transformed the Intellectual Life of the United States*, translated by Jeff Fort. Minneapolis: University of Minnesota Press.

Davies, William. 2018. *Nervous States: How Feeling Took Over the World*. London: Jonathan Cape.

Dean, Jodi. 1996. *Solidarity of Strangers: Feminism after Identity Politics*. Berkeley: University of California Press.

De Boever, Arne. 2018. *Finance Fictions: Realism and Psychosis in a Time of Economic Crisis*. New York: Fordham University Press.

Defoe, Daniel. 2001. *Robinson Crusoe*. William Taylor [1719].

DeKoven, Marianne. 2004. *Utopia Limited: The Sixties and the Emergence of the Postmodern*. Durham, NC: Duke University Press.

Deleuze, Gilles. 1992a. "Postscript on the Societies of Control." *October* 59: 3–7.

———. 1992b. "What Is a Dispositif?" In *Michel Foucault: Philosopher*, translated by Timothy J. Armstrong. Hempstead, UK: Harvester Wheatsheaf.

———. 1985a. "Foucault/01." Lecture delivered at the University of Paris, Vincennes-St. Denis October 22, 1985. In *The Deleuze Seminars*, transcribed by Annabelle Dufourcq, translated by Mary Beth Mader. deleuze.cla.purdue.edu. Accessed September 6, 2021.

———. 1985b. "Foucault/02." Lecture delivered at the University of Paris, Vincennes-St. Denis October 29, 1985. In *The Deleuze Seminars*, transcribed by Annabelle Dufourcq, translated by Mary Beth Mader. deleuze.cla.purdue.edu.

Deleuze, Gilles, and Félix Guattari. 1983. *Anti-Oedipus: Capitalism and Schizophrenia I*, translated by Robert Hurley, Mark Seem, and Helen R. Lane. Minneapolis: University of Minnesota Press.

DeLillo, Don. 2010. *Point Omega*. London: Picador.

———. 2003. *Cosmopolis*. London: Picador.

———. 2001. *The Body Artist*. Basingstoke, UK: Picador.

———. 1992. *Mao II*. London: Vintage Books.

———. 1989. *The Names*. New York: Vintage Books [1982].

Dewey, John. 2012. *The Public and Its Problems: An Essay in Political Inquiry*. State College, PA: Pennsylvania State University Press [1927].

Dick, Philip K. 1954. "Adjustment Team." *Orbit Science Fiction* (Sept–Oct): n.p.

———. 2003. *Time Out of Joint*. London: Gollancz [1959].

———. 2001. *Valis*. London: Orion Publishing Group [1981].

Di Leo, Jeffrey R., and Peter Hitchcock. 2016. "Introduction: Before the Beginning, After the End: Toward the New Public Intellectual." In *The New Public Intellectual: Politics, Theory, and the Public Sphere*, edited by Jeffrey R. Di Leo and Peter Hitchcock. ix–xxix. Houndmills, UK: Palgrave Macmillan.

Docx, Edward. 2014. "Dave Eggers's Accomplished Hostage Drama." Review of *Your Fathers, Where Are They? And the Prophets, Do They Live Forever? Guardian*. https://www.theguardian.com/books/2014/jul/20/your-fathers-where-they-prophets-do-live-forever-review-dave-eggers-accomplished-hostage-drama, accessed December 5, 2021.

Doyle, Jon. 2018. "The Changing Face of Post-Postmodernism Fiction: Irony, Sincerity, and Populism." *Critique: Studies in Contemporary Fiction* 59 (3): 259-270.

Eagleton, Terry. 2017. "Not Just Anybody." *London Review of Books* 39 (1): 35-37.

Eggers, Dave. 2013. *The Circle*. London: Penguin Books.

———. 2014. *Your Fathers, Where Are They? And the Prophets, Do They Live Forever?* London: Penguin Books.

Ellison, Ralph. 2001. *Invisible Man*. London: Penguin [1952].

Esquirol, Jean Étienne Dominique. 1945. *Mental Maladies: A Treatise on Insanity*, translated by E. K. Hunt. Philadelphia: Lea and Blanchard [1938].

Farrell, John. 2006. *Paranoia and Modernity: Cervantes to Rousseau*. Ithaca, NY: Cornell University Press.

Fassin, Didier. 2017. "How Is Critique?" In *A Time For Critique*, edited by Didier Fassin and Bernard E. Harcourt, 13-35. New York: Columbia University Press.

Fassin, Didier, and Bernard E. Harcourt. 2017. "Introduction." In *A Time for Critique*, edited by Didier Fassin and Bernard E. Harcourt, 1-10. New York: Columbia University Press.

Felski, Rita. 2015. *The Limits of Critique*. Chicago: University of Chicago Press.

Finney, Jack. 1954. *Invasion of the Body Snatchers*. New York: Touchstone.

Flanery, Patrick. 2016. *I Am No One*. London: Atlantic Books.

———. 2013. *Fallen Land*. London: Atlantic Books.

Foster Wallace, David. 2011. *The Pale King*. London: Little, Brown and Company.

———. (1999) *Brief Interviews with Hideous Men*. Boston: Little, Brown and Company.

———. 1996. *Infinite Jest*. London: Little, Brown and Company.

———. 1993. "E Unibus Pluram: Television and U.S. Fiction. *Review of Contemporary Fiction* 13 (2): 151-194.

Foucault, Michel. 2008. *The Birth of Biopolitics. Lectures at the Collège de France 1978-1979*, edited by Michael Senellart, translated by Graham Burchell. New York: Palgrave.

———. 2007. *Security, Territory, Population. Lectures at the Collège de France 1977-1978*, edited by Jacques Lagrange, translated by Graham Burchell. New York: Palgrave.

———. 2006. *Psychiatric Power. Lectures at the Collège de France 1973-74*, edited by Jacques Lagrange, translated by Graham Burchell. New York: Palgrave.

———. 2000. "Truth and Power." In *Power: The Essential Works of Michel Foucault 1954-1984*, edited by J. D. Faubion, translated by C. Lazzeri. New York: New Press.

———. 1977. *Discipline and Punish: The Birth of the Prison*, translated by Alan Sheridan. London: Penguin Books.

Frankenheimer, John, dir. 1962. *The Manchurian Candidate*. Beverley Hills, CA: United Artists.

Fraser, Nancy. 2003. "From Discipline to Flexibilization? Rereading Foucault in the Shadow of Globalization." *Constellations* 10 (2): 160-171.

———. 1990. "Rethinking the Public Sphere: A Contribution to the Critique of Actually Existing Democracy." *Social Text* 25/26: 56–80.
Freud, Sigmund. 2013. *Psycho-Analytic Notes on an Autobiographical Account of a Case of Paranoia (Dementia Paranoides)*. Redditch, UK: Read Books [1903].
Frye, Northrop. 1957. *Anatomy of Criticism: Four Essays*. Princeton, NJ: Princeton University Press.
Gallop, Jane. 2004. "Introduction." In *Polemic: Critical or Uncritical*, edited by Jane Gallop, 1–12. New York: Routledge.
Gibbons, Alison. 2018. "Autonarration, I, and Odd Address in Ben Lerner's Autofictional Novel *10:04*." In *Pronouns in Literature: Positions and Perspectives in Language*, edited by Alison Gibbons and Andrea Macrae, 75–96. London: Palgrave Macmillan.
Gibson William. 2020. *Agency*. Berkley, CA: Random House.
———. 2003. *Pattern Recognition*. New York: G. P. Putnam's Sons.
———. 1995. *Neuromancer*. London: HarperCollins [1984].
Ging, Debbie, and Eugenia Siapera. 2018. "Special Issue on Online Misogyny." *Feminist Media Studies* 18 (4): 515–524.
Giroux, Henry A. 2016. "Writing the Public Good Back into Education: Reclaiming the Role of the Public Intellectual." In *The New Public Intellectual: Politics, Theory, and the Public Sphere*, edited by Jeffrey R. Di Leo and Peter Hitchcock, 3–28. Houndmills, UK: Palgrave Macmillan.
Goodlad, Lauren M. E. 2003. "Beyond the Panopticon: Victorian Britain and the Critical Imagination." *PMLA* 118 (3): 539–556.
Gordon, Douglas. 1993. *24 Hour Psycho*, art installation.
Habermas Jürgen. 1991. *The Structural Transformation of the Public Sphere: An Inquiry into a Category of Bourgeois Society*, translated by Thomas Burger with the assistance of Frederich Lawrence. Cambridge, MA: MIT Press [1962].
Hale, Dorothy. 1998. *Social Formalism: The Novel in Theory from Henry James to the Present*. Stanford, CA: Stanford University Press.
Harcourt, Bernard E. 2015. *Exposed: Desire and Disobedience in the Digital Age*. Cambridge, MA: Harvard University Press.
Hardt, Michael, and Antonio Negri. 2000. *Empire*. Cambridge MA: Harvard University Press.
Harper, David J. 1994. "Histories of Suspicion in a Time of Conspiracy: A Reflection on Aubrey Lewis's History of Paranoia." *History of the Human Sciences* 7 (3): 89–109.
Harsin, Jayson. 2015. "Regimes of Posttruth, Postpolitics, and Attention Economies." *Communication, Culture & Critique* 8: 327–333.
Hayes-Brady, Clare. 2016. *The Unspeakable Failures of David Foster Wallace: Language, Identity, and Resistance*. New York: Bloomsbury Academic.
Hayot, Eric. 2017. "Then and Now." In *Critique and Postcritique*, edited by Rita Felski and Elizabeth S. Anker, 279–295. Durham, NC: Duke University Press.
Hermansson, Patrik, David Lawrence, Joe Mulhall, and Simon Murdoch. 2020. *The International Alt-Right: Fascism for the 21st Century?* London: Routledge.
Hobbes, Thomas. 2018. *Leviathan*. Minneapolis: First Avenue Editions [1651].

Hofstadter, Richard. 2008. *The Paranoid Style in American Politics and Other Essays*. New York: Vintage Books [1952].

Hollywood, Amy. 2004. "Reading as Self-Annihilation." In *Polemic: Critical or Uncritical*, edited by Jane Gallop, 39–63. New York: Routledge.

Holquist, Michael. 2010. "The Fugue of Chronotope." In *Bakhtin's Theory of the Literary Chronotope: Reflections, Applications, Perspectives*, edited by Nele Bemong, Pieter Borghart, Michel De Dobbeleer, Kristoffel Demoen, Koen De Temmerman and Bart Keunen, 19–33. Ghent, Belgium: Academia Press.

———. 2002. *Dialogism: Bakhtin and His World*, 2nd ed. London: Routledge.

Horning, Rob. 2012. "Agents without Agency," *New Inquiry*. https://thenewinquiry.com/agents-without-agency/. Accessed September 28, 2021.

Huehls, Mitchum, and Rachel Greenwald Smith. 2017. "Four Phases of Neoliberalism and Literature: An Introduction." In *Neoliberalism and Contemporary Literary Culture*, edited by Mitchum Huehls and Rachel Greenwald Smith, 1–20. Baltimore: Johns Hopkins University Press.

Jackson, Edward, and Joel Nicholson-Roberts. 2017. "White Guys: Questioning *Infinite Jest*'s New Sincerity." *Orbit: A Journal of American Literature*, 5 (1): 1–28.

Jameson, Fredric. 1992. *The Geopolitical Aesthetic: Cinema and Space in the World System*. Bloomington: Indiana University Press.

———. 1991. *Postmodernism, Or, The Cultural Logic of Late Capitalism*. Durham, NC: Duke University Press.

———. 1981. *The Political Unconscious: Narrative as a Socially Symbolic Act*. London: Routledge.

Johnson, Jessica. 2018. "The Self-Radicalization of White Men: 'Fake News' and the Affective Networking of Paranoia." *Communication Culture & Critique* 11: 100–115.

Johnston, Hank, Enrique Laraña, and Joseph R. Gusfield. 1994. "Identities, Grievances, and New Social Movements." In *New Social Movements: From Ideology to Identity*, edited by Hank Johnston, Enrique Laraña, and Joseph R. Gusfield, 3–35. Philadelphia: Temple University Press.

Kabaservice, Geoffrey. 2017. "The Great Performance of Our Failing President." *New York Times*. https://www.nytimes.com/2017/06/09/opinion/great-performance-of-donald-trump-our-failing-president.html?searchResultPosition=1. Accessed March 27, 2020.

Kafka, Franz. 2015. *The Trial*, translated by David Wyllie. Createspace Independent Publishing Platform edition (Virginia Beach, VA: Createspace) [1925].

Katz, Daniel. 2017. "'I Did Not Walk All the Way Here from Prose': Ben Lerner's Virtual Poetics." *Textual Practice* 312: 315–337.

Kelly, Adam. 2017. "David Foster Wallace and New Sincerity Aesthetics: A Reply to Edward Jackson and Joel Nicholson-Roberts." *Orbit: A Journal of American Literature* 5 (2): 4: 1–32.

———. 2016. "The New Sincerity." In *Postmodern/Postwar and After: Rethinking American Literature*, edited by J. Gladstone, A. Hoberek, and D. Worden, 197–208. Ames: University of Iowa Press.

———. 2010. "David Foster Wallace and the New Sincerity in American Fiction." In *Consider David Foster Wallace: Critical Essays*, edited by David Hering, 131–146. Los Angeles: Sideshow Media Group Press.

Kelly, Casey Ryan. 2020. *Apocalypse Man: The Death Drive and the Rhetoric of White Masculine Victimhood*. Columbus: Ohio State University Press.

Kennedy, Liam. 1996. "Alien Nation: White Male Paranoia and Imperial Culture in the United States." *Journal of American Studies* 30: 87–100.

Keunen, Bart. 2010. "The Chronotopic Imagination in Literature and Film: Bakhtin, Bergson and Deleuze on Forms of Time." In *Bakhtin's Theory of the Literary Chronotope: Reflections, Applications, Perspectives*, edited by Nele Bemong, Pieter Borghart, Michel De Dobbeleer, Kristoffel Demoen, Koen De Temmerman and Bart Keunen, 35–55. Ghent, Belgium: Academia Press.

Kimmel, Michael. 2017. *Angry White Men: American Masculinity at the End of an Era*. New York: Bold Type Books [2013].

Kingston-Reese, Alexandra. 2019. *Contemporary Novelists and the Aesthetics of Twenty-First Century American Life*. Ames: University of Iowa Press.

Klay, Phil. 2014. "Troubled Inquisitor: Dave Eggers's 'Your Fathers, Where Are They? And the Prophets, Do They Live Forever?'" *New York Times*. https://www.nytimes.com/2014/06/29/books/review/dave-eggerss-your-fathers-where-are-they-and-the-prophets-do-they-live-forever.html, accessed December 5, 2021.

Knight, Peter. 2000. *Conspiracy Culture: From the Kennedy Assassination to the X-Files*. London: Routledge.

Kosofsky Sedgwick, Eve. 2002. "*Touching Feeling: Affect, Pedagogy, Performativity*. Durham, NC: Duke University Press.

Lambert, Gregg. 2001. *Report on the Academy (Re: The New Conflict of the Faculties)*. Aurora, CO: Davies Group.

Latour, Bruno. 2004. "Why Has Critique Run out of Steam? From Matters of Fact to Matters of Concern." *Critical Inquiry* 30: 225–248.

Lemke, Thomas. 2012. *Foucault, Governmentality, and Critique*. Boulder, CO: Paradigm Publishers.

Lerner, Ben. 2019. *The Topeka School*. London: Granta.

——— 2014. *10:04*. London: Granta.

Lewis, Aubrey. 1970. "Paranoia and Paranoid: A Historical Perspective." *Psychological Medicine* 1: 2–12.

Love, Heather. 2017. "Critique Is Ordinary." *PMLA* 132 (2): 364–370.

Lukács, György. 2005. "The Ideology of Modernism." In *The Novel: An Anthology of Criticism and Theory 1900–2000*, edited by Dorothy J. Hale. Malden MA: Blackwell.

Lynskey, Dorian. 2018. "How Dangerous Is Jordan B. Peterson, the Rightwing Professor Who 'Hit a Hornets' Nest?" *Guardian*. https://www.theguardian.com/science/2018/feb/07/how-dangerous-is-jordan-b-peterson-the-rightwing-professor-who-hit-a-hornets-nest. Accessed November 13, 2019.

Macpherson, C.B. 1962. *The Political Theory of Possessive Individualism: Hobbes to Locke*. Oxford, UK: Oxford University Press.

Marclay, Christian (2010) *The Clock*. Video projection.
Marwick, Alice E., and Robyn Caplan. 2018. "Drinking Male Tears: Language, the Manosphere, and Network Harassment." *Feminist Media Studies* 18 (4): 543–559.
Mayer, Jane. 2009. *The Dark Side: The Inside Story of How the War on Terror Turned into a War on American Ideals*. New York: Anchor Books.
Mazzoni, Guido. 2017. *Theory of the Novel*, translated by Zakiya Hanafi. Cambridge, MA: Harvard University Press.
McClennen, Sophia A. 2016. "The Public Sphere Can Be Fun: Political Pedagogy in Neoliberal Times." In *The New Public Intellectual: Politics, Theory, and the Public Sphere*, edited by Jeffrey R. Di Leo and Peter Hitchcock, 29–43. Houndmills, UK: Palgrave Macmillan.
McLaughlin, Robert L. 2004. "Post-Postmodern Discontent: Contemporary Fiction and the Social World." *Symplokē*, 12 (1/2): 53–68.
Melley, Timothy. 2021. "The Melodramatic Mode in American Politics, and Other Varieties of Narrative Suspicion." *Symplokē*, 29 (1–2).
———. 2012. *The Covert Sphere: Secrecy, Fiction, and the National Security State*. Ithaca, NY: Cornell University Press.
———. 2000. *Empire of Conspiracy: The Culture of Paranoia in Postwar America*. Ithaca, NY: Cornell University Press.
Michelsen, Nicholas, and Pablo de Orellana. 2019. "Discourses of Resilience in the US Alt-Right." *Resilience* 7 (3): 271–287.
Miller, D. A. 1988. *The Novel and the Police*. Berkley: University of California Press.
Miller, Laura. 1996. "David Foster Wallace." *Salon*. https://www.salon.com/1996/03/09/wallace_5/. Accessed Sept 17, 2020.
Mills, Jon. 2019. "Lacan on Paranoiac Knowledge." In *Lacan on Psychosis: From Theory to Praxis*, edited by Jon Mills and David L. Downing, 10–46. London: Routledge.
Milne, Drew. 2003. "Introduction: Criticism and/or Critique." In *Modern Critical Thought: An Anthology of Theorists Writing on Theorists*, edited by Drew Milne, 1–22. Malden, MA: Blackwell.
Mirowski, Philip, and Edward Nik-Khah. 2017. *The Knowledge We have Lost in Information: The History of Information in Modern Economics*. New York: Oxford University Press.
Morris, Pam. 2004. *Imagining Inclusive Society in Nineteenth-Century Novels: The Code of Sincerity in the Public Sphere*. Baltimore: Johns Hopkins University Press.
Murphy, Jessica. 2016. "Toronto Professor Jordan Peterson Takes on Gender-Neutral Pronouns." *BBC News Toronto*. https://www.bbc.com/news/world-us-canada-37875695. Accessed November 13, 2019.
Nagle, Angela. 2017. *Kill All Normies: Online Culture Wars from 4chan and Tumblr to Trump and the Alt-Right*. Winchester, UK: Zero Books.
Nealon, Jeffrey T. 2008. *Foucault beyond Foucault: Power and Its Intensifications Since 1984*. Stanford: Stanford University Press.
Neiwert, David. 2017. *Alt-America: The Rise of the Radical Right in the Age of Trump*. London: Verso.

New York Times. 2014. "My Twisted World: The Story of Elliot Rodger." https://www.nytimes.com/interactive/2014/05/25/us/shooting-document.html. Accessed April 23, 2020.

Noble, Safiya Umoja. 2018. *Algorithms of Oppression: How Search Engines Reinforce Racism*. New York: New York University Press.

Noys, Benjamin. 2011. "The Discreet Charm of Bruno Latour, Or, the Critique of 'Anti-Critique.'" Paper presented at the University of Nottingham, December 8, 2011.

Obeidallah, Dean. (2020) "'Trump's 'Stand Back and Stand By' Moment Was More Than a Dog Whistle. *Think: Opinion, Analysis, Essays*. September 30. https://www.nbcnews.com/think/opinion/trump-s-proud-boys-stand-back-stand-debate-moment-was-ncna1241570. Accessed September 27, 2021.

O'Dell, Jacqueline. 2019. "One More Time with Feeling: Repetition, Contingency, and Sincerity in Ben Lerner's *10:04*." *Critique: Studies in Contemporary Fiction* 60 (4): 447–461.

O'Donnell, Patrick. 2000. *Latent Destinies: Cultural Paranoia and Contemporary U.S. Narrative*. Durham, NC: Duke University Press.

Oxford English Dictionaries Online. 2017. "Word of the Year 2016." https://languages.oup.com/word-of-the-year/2016/. Accessed January 11, 2020.

Pakula, Alan J., dir. *All the President's Men*. 1976. Burbank, CA: Warner Brothers.

Parisi, Luciana. 2013. *Contagious Architecture: Computation, Aesthetics, and Space*. London: MIT Press.

Pease, Donald, E. 2009. *The New American Exceptionalism*. Minneapolis: University of Minnesota Press.

Peterson, Jordan B. (n.d.) "The Gender Scandal: Part One (Scandinavia) and Part Two (Canada). https://www.jordanbpeterson.com/political-correctness/the-gender-scandal-part-one-scandinavia-and-part-two-canada/. Accessed Nov 13, 2019.

Pynchon, Thomas. 2013 *Bleeding Edge*. London: Vintage Books.

———. 2009. *The Crying of Lot 49*. London: Vintage Books [1966].

Readings, Bill. 1996. *The University in Ruins*. Cambridge, MA: Harvard University Press.

Revelli, Marco. 2019. *The New Populism: Democracy Stares into the Abyss*. London and New York: Verso.

Review of Reviews. 1892. "Are you a Paranoiac? Or the Latest Nickname for Cranks." In *Science in the Nineteenth-Century Periodical* 6: (56): n.p. https://www.sciper.org/browse/RR1-6.html.

Ricoeur, Paul. 1970. *Freud and Philosophy: An Essay on Interpretation*, translated by Denis Savage. New Haven, CT: Yale University Press.

Robbins, Bruce. 1993. "Introduction: The Public as Phantom." In *The Phantom Public Sphere*, edited by Bruce Robbins, Minneapolis: University of Minnesota Press.

Roberts-Mahoney, Heather, Alexander J. Means, and Mark J. Garrison. 2016. "Netflixing Human Capital Development: Personalized Learning Technology and the Corporatization of K-12 Education." *Journal of Education Policy* 31(4): 405–420.

Robertson, Ritchie. 2004. *Kafka: A Very Short Introduction*. Oxford, UK: Oxford University Press.

Rose, Nicholas. 1990. "Psychology as 'Social' Science," In *Deconstructing Social Psychology*, edited by I. Parker and J. Shotter, 103–116. London: Routledge.

Roth, Philip. 1998. *American Pastoral*. London: Vintage Books [1997].

Sacks, Sam. 2017. "They Could Be Heroes: Today's Biggest Novelists Are Throwbacks to a Simpler Time." *New Republic*. https://newrepublic.com/article/140954/nostalgic-fiction-booming-eggers-chabon-lethem Accessed September 3, 2020.

Saltman, Kenneth J. 2018. *The Swindle of Innovative Educational Finance*. Minneapolis: University of Minnesota Press.

Santner, Eric L. 1997. *My Own Private Germany: Daniel Paul Schreber's Secret History of Modernity*. Princeton, NJ: Princeton University Press.

Smethurst, Paul. 2000. *The Postmodern Chronotope: Reading Space and Time in Contemporary Fiction*. Amsterdam: Rodopi.

Sobieraj, Sarah, and Jeffrey M. Berry. 2011. "From Incivility to Outrage: Political Discourse in Blogs, Talk Radio, and Cable News." *Political Communication* 28 (1): 19–41.

Spivak, Gayatri Chakravorty, and Jane Gallop. 2004. "'What Is 'Enlightenment?'" In *Polemic: Critical or Uncritical*, edited by Jane Gallop, 179–200. New York: Routledge.

Sunstein, Cass R. 2007. *Republic.com 2.0*. Princeton, NJ: Princeton University Press.

Tambling, Jeremy. 1995. *Dickens, Violence and the Modern State: Dreams of the Scaffold*. Houndmills, UK: MacMillan.

Tolentino, Jia. 2018. "The Rage of the Incels," *The NewYorker*. https://www.newyorker.com/culture/cultural-comment/the-rage-of-the-incels. Accessed April 22 2020.

Trotter, David. 2001. *Paranoid Modernism: Literary Experiment, Psychosis, and the Professionalization of English Society*. Oxford, UK: Oxford University Press.

Trump, Donald J. (@PresidentTrump). 2020. "Lamestream Media is totally CORRUPT, the Enemy of the People!" Twitter, May 3, 2020. https://www.thetrumparchive.com. Accessed June 22, 2021.

———. 2019. "Lamestream media, which is the Enemy of the People." Twitter, November 7, 2019. https://www.thetrumparchive.com. Accessed June 22, 2021.

———. "The Failing @nytimes, &, ratings challenged @CNN, will do anything possible to see our Country fail! . . . truly The Enemy of the People!" Twitter, June 9, 2019. https://www.thetrumparchive.com. Accessed June 22, 2021.

Tufekci, Zeynep. 2018. "YouTube, the Great Radicalizer." *New York Times*. https://www.nytimes.com/2018/03/10/opinion/sunday/youtube-politics-radical.html. Accessed June 20, 2019.

von Krafft-Ebing, Richard. 1905. *Textbook of Insanity*, authorized and translated from the last German edition by Charles Gilbert Chaddock. Philadelphia: F. A. Davis Company [1870].

Wachowski, Lana and Lily, dir. 1999. *The Matrix*. Burbank, CA: Warner Bros

Warner, Michael. 2005. *Publics and Counterpublics*. New York: Zone Books.

———. 2004. "Uncritical Reading." In *Polemic: Critical or Uncritical*, edited by Jane Gallop, 13–38. New York: Routledge.

Watt, Ian. 2001. *The Rise of the Novel: Studies in Defoe, Richardson and Fielding*. Berkley: University of California Press.

Whitehead, Colson. 2017. *The Intuitionist*. London: Fleet [1999].
Williams, Iain. 2015. "(New) Sincerity in David Foster Wallace's 'Octet.'" *Critique: Studies in Contemporary Fiction*. 56 (3): 299–314.
Williams, John A. 1971. *The Man Who Cried I Am*. Harmondsworth, UK: Penguin Books [1967].
Zemeckis, Robert, dir. 1985. *Back to the Future*. Universal City, CA: Universal Pictures.

INDEX

affective economy: Sara Ahmed, 162–63; networks, 165–66; post-truth, 103
agency panic, 28, 188; gender, 32; liberal subject, 29, 57, 149, 188; paranoia, 56–57; power, 69, 85
algorithms: algorithmic grooming, 116; algorithmic radicalization, 106–7, 117; control, 55, 65, 69, 150–51; filtering, 42, 70, 112, 114–16; post-truth society, 105
allegory: critique, 95; the novel, 71; paranoid chronotope, 15–16, 136, 140; postmodernity, 92
alt-right: conspiracy theory, 110–11; identity politics, 158; manosphere, 33–34, 163; networks, 165; political correctness, 110, 174; post-truth, 109–11; resilience, 111, 166
attention economy, 114, 119, 171
authority: authorship, 181, 189, 196, 201, 202; conspiracy, 123–24, 126; expertise, 10, 113, 142–43; individual, 73, 120; white male identity, 160, 169, 196
authorship: authority; 181, 189, 196, 201, 202; white male, 31–32, 155, 177–78, 181–82; 196, 200–1; neoliberalism, 180, 203–5; paranoia, 19–20, 177–78, 186–209

Bakhtin, Mikhail, 12–13, 16–17, 21–22, 23, 47–48, 71, 80, 83, 127, 201–2, 211
Brown, Wendy: homo politicus, 38; neoliberalism, 58, 66–68, 69–70, 105, 119–23, 157–8, 160–1; post-truth, 121–2; the university, 149

capitalism: globalization, 31, 147, 193; disciplinary society, 61; just-in-time capitalism, 64; late capitalism, 29, 40, 92, 197; neoliberalism, 66–67, 149, 189, 198; the novel, 75; the public sphere, 39–40, 100; schizophrenia, 182–83, 190
chronotope, 12–13, 16–17, 22–23, 25, 47–48, 125, 135, 201–2; control, 57–58, 62–65; critique, 211–13; discipline, 58–62, 68–70, 75–76, 80–81, 204–205; generic, 17, 71; the novel, 18, 71, 75–76, 80, 85; the public sphere, 36–37, 102, 211–2, 220; threshold, 15, 83–84, 136, 191, 192–93, 206, 209
class: Walter Benn Michaels, 156; Nancy Fraser, 41; Marco Revelli, 161
climate change, 183, 192–93, 198; conspiracy, 30, 109, 111, 170
conspiracy theory: alt-right, 3, 74, 109–11, 165; climate change, 30, 111, 170; communism, 55; critique, 215–17; gender ideology, 175–76; knowledge, 123–24, 126, 144; liberal mind control, 111, 166, 174; manosphere, 163–65, 169, 176; McCarthyism, 30; misandry, 163–64, 167; oneworldedness, 46–47, 190; Jordan B. Peterson, 174–75; political correctness, 110–111, 174–75; power, 56–57, 74; racism, 175; truth, 106, 109–12, 124; Trump, 30, 165, 170–72

control: agency panic, 29, 56–58, 69, 188; algorithms, 65, 66, 69, 150; chronotope, 57–58, 62–66, 70, 205; computation, 65, 70; conspiracy, 3, 56, 124, 126, 165; control society, 26, 54, 56, 70, 101, 118, 134, 154; Gilles Deleuze; 63, 65–66, 134; dispositif, 64, 70, 83
covert sphere, 42–44, 124, 135–36
critique, 49–53, 86–97, 142–52, 209–21: Hannah Arendt, 38–39; chronotope, 211–13, 214, 219, 221; Jürgen Habermas, 39, 210; hermeneutics of suspicion, 50, 88, 93–94, 212–13; Immanuel Kant, 36, 38, 87–88, 100, 106, 210; public sphere, 36, 38–41, 86–87, 91, 99–101, 216–19, 215; Theory, 51, 97–101, 152, 212–16, 218–20. *See also* postcritique
critiquiness, 45–46, 49, 216–17

Deleuze, Gilles: control, 63, 65–66; difference, 182; discipline, 59–62, 82, 134; dispositif, 61–62; with Félix Guattari on schizophrenia, 182–83, 190; on Franz Kafka, 134
discipline: chronotope, 57–62, 65, 68–70, 72, 75–76, 80–81; Gilles Deleuze, 59–62, 82, 134; dispositif, 62, 75, 81–83; Fordism, 26, 60–61, 63, 69; Michel Foucault, 10, 58–61, 84; identity, 25–6, 70, 76, 79, 81, 205; the novel, 68–69, 72, 75–76, 82, 85, 189; the subject, 58–62, 68–69, 76, 84–86, 101; the university, 148
dispositif, 61–62, 64, 70, 75, 81–85, 118

education: conspiracy, 123–24, 175; critical pedagogy, 152; knowledge, 123, 149–51; neoliberalism, 149–52; public sphere, 146, 152, 219; training, 51, 149
Eggers, Dave: *The Circle*, 23; *Your Fathers, Where Are They? And the Prophets, Do They Live Forever?* 75–86
expertise: in *I Am No One*, 130–31; knowledge, 143–44, 151; paranoia, 10, 103; posttruth, 104, 109, 121–22; public sphere, 103–4, 109, 113–14, 119, 121–22, 142–44; the university, 148

fake news, 106, 109–11, 121, 165, 170–71
Felski, Rita, 50, 86, 90, 93–96, 213–14, 217; Anker and Felski, 95–96, 213, 218–19, 220
filtering: algorithms, 112, 114–16; "daily me," 115; filter bubbles, 42, 116, 119
Flanery, Patrick: *Fallen Land*, 13; *I Am No One*, 125–42
Foucault, Michel: discipline, 58–61, 84; dispositif, 61–62; knowledge–power, 95, 118; liberalism, 59, 73–74; the novel, 73, 75–76; power, 57–63; psychiatric power, 10; security, 63; truth, 103–4, 117–18
Fox News, 108–9, 161, 166, 171
freedom: American, 29, 46, 69, 73–74; of expression, 115, 174; liberalism, 59, 73, 120; security, 48–49; subject, 38, 46, 56, 67, 100; neoliberalism, 68, 74, 121; paranoia, 5, 14, 46, 111–12

gender: agency panic, 32; gender ideology, 175–76; identity politics, 155–62, 197; manosphere, 163–65; misandry, 163–64, 167; misogyny, 34, 163–64, 176; neoliberalism, 67, 158, 161; Jordan B. Peterson, 174–75. *See also* masculinity
hermeneutics of suspicion, 88–90, 212; postcritique, 50, 93–94, 96, 215; Paul Ricoeur, 88–89
Hofstadter, Richard, 11, 22, 29–30, 56, 173
humanities, the, 147; neoliberalism, 145–46, 149; postcritique, 49–51, 96–97, 98; 218–19

identitarianism, 49, 110, 119, 153, 160
identity politics, 155–62, 197
incel, 33, 164, 175–77
information: knowledge, 113, 144–45; overflow, 113–14; paranoia, 4, 20, 21; public sphere, 42, 106, 110, 119, 142; technology, 66, 114–16
irony, 178, 186–89, 191, 194–95

Jameson, Fredric: allegory, 16; cognitive mapping, 11, 31; conspiracy, 11, 16; symptomatic reading, 92–93
judgment: René Descartes, 27–28;

Immanuel Kant, 47–48, 87–88, 106; public sphere, 48, 102–3, 124; subject of, 38, 47–48, 72, 103, 105, 125–26

Kant, Immanuel: the chronotope, 12, 47–48, 125, 211; critique, 36, 38, 41, 50, 51, 87–88, 210; judgment, 47–48, 87–88, 106; public sphere, 38, 41–42, 48, 100, 106, 210
knowledge: conspiracy, 123–34; education, 123, 146, 149–51; expertise, 10, 114, 142–46, 151; Michel Foucault, 83–84, 95, 118; Immanuel Kant, 47, 87–88, 106; François Lyotard, 113; paranoia, 8, 10, 27; public sphere, 36, 37, 123–24; subject of, 123–24; University, 146, 149, 151–52

Lerner, Ben: New Sincerity, 178–80, 187–89; *The Topeka School*, 179–80; *10:04*, 180–209
liberal subject, 15, 27–35, 41, 146–47; agency panic, 28, 32, 56–57; America, 15, 29–31, 38, 69, 70; René Descartes, 27–28; masculinity, 31–32, 33, 74, 76, 180, 190, 199; neoliberalism, 4, 26, 31, 66–68; the novel, 72–73, 101, 189–90; paranoia, 5–6, 67, 74; possessive individualism, 28, 37, 38, 67, 189–90; the public sphere, 35, 38–39, 102–3, 147

manosphere, 33, 163–64, 167–69, 176–77
masculinity: alt right, 33–34, 110, 163; authority, 160, 196; authorship, 19–20, 31–32, 133, 155, 177–81, 190–2, 196–97, 201, 209; identity politics, 160–2; identitarianism, 110, 160–1; incel, 33, 164, 175–77; manosphere; 33, 163–4, 167–9; 176–7; misandry, 2, 163–4, 167; misogyny, 163–64, 176; nostalgia, 78, 172–73, 175, 193; Jordan B. Peterson, 174–76; white male subject, 31–32, 33, 68, 76, 162–63, 180, 181, 190, 192–93. *See also* gender
morality: identity politics, 159–60; liberalism, 37, 67; neoliberalism, 119–21, 161; the novel, 71–72, 73, 189

neoliberalism, 26, 69–70, 157–58, 160–61; education, 149–52; flexibilization, 63; literature, 178, 180–1, 183, 189, 194; measurements, 105, 122–23; morality, 119–21, 161; postcritique, 51–53, 179, 215, 219, 221; subject, 4, 66–68; university, 52, 145–49
networks: Actor-Network Theory, 164–66; manosphere, 163–64, 169; paranoia, 31, 47, 141, 171
New Sincerity, 178–80, 187–88, 191–92, 193–97
novel, the: Nancy Armstrong, 72–73, 81–82, 84, 85–86, 189; Mikhail Bakhtin, 17, 71, 80; discipline, 68–9, 72, 75–76, 80–82, 84, 134, 189; Dorothy Hale, 81; liberal subject, 72–74, 84–85, 101, 189–90; Guido Mazzoni, 18, 71–72; D.A. Miller, 75, 82, 86; Jeremy Tambling, 75; Ian Watt, 75.
nostalgia, 10, 26, 78, 172–73, 175, 193–96

online culture: Breitbart, 34, 109, 165, 166, 171; "daily me," 115; Google, 114, 116; Infowars, 34, 109, 165, 166, 169, 171; Internet, 100, 114, 116, 161, 163; Internet Research Agency, 106; manosphere; 33, 163–64, 167–69, 176–77; Reddit, 116, 164, 175; self-confirming groups, 116–7; social media, 109, 110, 117, 121, 144, 165, 171, 195, 216; trolls, 49, 106, 121, 163, 164, 175; YouTube, 117, 174; 4chan/8chan, 109, 116, 164, 165

paranoia: agency panic, 28–29, 56–57, 198; chance, 11, 22, 78–79, 128, 141, 220; climate change, 30, 109, 111, cognitive mapping, 11, 31; Cold War, 11, 25, 26, 44–46, 74, 154; Communism, 25, 44, 45, 55, 56; contingency, 12; James Cowles Pritchard, 7; René Descartes, 27–28; J.E.D. Esquirol, 7; Sigmund Freud, 8, 89; Johann Christian August Heinroth, 6; immigration, 30, 44, 111, 112, 124, 160, 162, 163, 170, 176; Melanie Klein, 9; knowledge, 8, 10, 27, 123–24, 126, 143–45; Richard von Krafft-Ebing, 7,

paranoia (*continued*)
11; Jacques Lacan, 8–9, 167; language, 5, 14, 18–19, 57, 88; Patrick O'Donnell, 29, 31, 187, 196, 197; McCarthyism, 4, 11, 30; Timothy Melley, 11, 18, 28–29, 32, 33, 42–44, 56–57, 74, 173, 177, 188; modernity, 10, 143–44; oneworldedness, 31, 46–47, 190; polarization, 4, 50, 107, 109, 114, 124–25, 153, 159, 165; Daniel Paul Schreber, 8, 11; Ludwig Snell, 6; David Trotter, 3, 6, 10, 11, 143–44; trust, 3, 112–13, 118–20, 121, 170–71, 178; writing, 19–20, 179

paranoid fiction: Kathy Acker, 32; Paul Auster, 19, 22, 190, 191; William Burroughs, 18, 29, 177; Don DeLillo, 13, 17, 18, 19, 20, 21, 22, 27, 190, 191, 195, 199, 210; Philip K. Dick, 1, 4, 13, 17, 20–1, 22, 24–25, 46, 138; Joan Didion, 32; Ralph Ellison, 32–33; Jack Finney, 23, 46; William Gibson, 13, 17, 20, 21; Diane Johnson, 32; *The Matrix*, 137, 138, 167, 168; Jordan Peele, 33; Marge Piercy, 32; Thomas Pynchon, 13, 17, 20, 21, 195, 210; Philip Roth, 172, 194; John. A. Williams, 33

paranoid style in American Politics, 11, 29, 55, 56, 173

populism, 109, 161–62, 195

postcritique: Elizabeth S. Anker and Rita Felski, 95–96, 152, 213, 218–19, 220; Stephen Best and Sharon Marcus, 91–93, 213; Timothy Bewes, 93; Christopher Castiglia, 216–17; Russ Castronovo, 220–21; Rita Felski, 50, 86, 90, 93–96, 213–14, 217; Jane Gallop, 90–1; generous reading, 93; Eric Hayot, 114–15; hermeneutics of suspicion, 50, 90, 91, 93–94, 96, 213, 215; Bruno Latour, 50, 98, 213, 215–18; Heather Love, 219; neoliberalism, 51–52, 179, 214, 215, 219, 221; public sphere, 51–53, 86, 91, 99–101, 152, 215–21; Eve Kosofsky Sedgwick, 90, 93; reparative reading, 93, 179, 210; surface reading, 93; symptomatic reading, 50, 92–93, 95, 213; Theory, 51, 97–101, 152, 212–16, 218–20;

uncritical reading, 90–91; Michael Warner, 90. *See also* critique

postmodernism, 11, 14, 18, 81, 178, 182, 193–95, 209–10; allegory, 16, 92–93; irony, 179, 187–88, 194; postmodernity, 10, 16, 68, 178

post-truth, 45, 104–5, 118–19; expertise, 104, 109, 121–22; neoliberalism, 105, 121–23; skepticism, 110–13, 119; suspension of belief, 109, 153; symbolic truth, 109–10, 112, 122, 124, 153

public sphere, the, 4–5, 35–42, 51–53, 100–3, 106–7, 112–14, 119–25; 142, 159, 170–1, 173–74, 212, 215–16; Hannah Arendt, 38–39, 42, 102, 210, 212; Seyla Benhabib, 41, 153–34; Manuel Castells, 39; covert sphere; 42–49; critique; 36, 38–41, 86–7, 91, 99–101, 216–19, 215; John Dewey, 41; Nancy Fraser, 40–41; Jürgen Habermas, 39–40, 42, 102, 107, 210; Immanuel Kant, 38, 41–42, 48, 100, 106, 210; Walter Lippman, 41; Bruce Robbins, 39–40; the University, 52, 101, 145–48, 151–52, 175, 215

racism, 109, 116, 156, 160, 162, 166, 175
radicalization, 112–13, 117, 124, 164–65
resilience, 111–12, 166, 174

schizophrenia, 10, 182–83, 190
security, 42–46, 49, 56, 121; Foucault, 58, 60, 63–64, 69–70, 73–74
skepticism, 44–45, 110, 111, 112–13, 119, 178, 195
sovereignty: individual, 38, 41, 66; society, 58–59, 85; state, 64
surveillance, 42, 46, 48–49, 56, 64–65, 70, 75, 129–31, 134, 138
suspicion: America, 74, 157–58, 170, 212; the covert sphere, 44–46; justified suspicion, 35; the liberal subject, 28, 37, 74; masters of suspicion, 89; paranoia, 3, 7, 30

terrorism, 13, 17, 19, 33, 45, 47, 121, 124, 130–1, 136, 162–63, 165, 190, 216

theory, 51, 97–101, 152, 212–16, 218–20
truth: allegory, 15–16; conspiracy, 105–6, 109–12, 124; critique, 5, 36, 51, 87–89, 142, 214; hermeneutics of suspicion, 88–89; metrics, 105, 122–24; post-truth, 45, 104–5, 109–10, 119; public sphere, 36, 102–3, 106, 112, 119–25; resilience to, 111–12; symbolic truth, 109–10, 112, 122, 124, 153; truthiness, 104, 216; truth regimes, 59, 104, 117–19, 159; as viewpoint, 120–22; as weaponized, 121–2, 145
Trump, Donald: conspiracy theory, 30, 165, 169–72; fake news, 109, 170–1; nationalism, 112, 170; nostalgia, 193, 196; paranoid style, 173; political correctness, 174, 193; post-truth, 104, 109, 112; radicalization, 117

university: Wendy Brown, 149; excellence, 147–48; Gregg Lambert, 148; post-historical university, 147–48; as public sphere; 36, 49, 52, 101, 145–48, 151–52, 175, 215; Bill Readings, 146–48; theory, 98–100, 215

weaponization, 121–22, 145, 171
white supremacy, 68, 116, 121, 153, 163, 164, 170

Made in United States
North Haven, CT
26 June 2023